Parliaments in Transition

Parliaments in Transition

The New Legislative Politics in the Former USSR and Eastern Europe

EDITED BY

Thomas F. Remington

Westview Press

BOULDER • SAN FRANCISCO • OXFORD

Copyright © 1994 by Westview Press, Inc.

Published in 1994 in the United States of America by Westview Press Inc., 5500 Central Avenue, Boulder, Colorado 80301-2877, and in the United Kingdom by Westview Press, 36 Lonsdale Road, Summertown, Oxford OX2 7EW

A CIP catalog record for this book is available from the Library of Congress.
ISBN 0-8133-8814-7

Printed and bound in the United States of America

The paper used in this publication meets the requirements
of the American National Standard for Permanence of Paper
for Printed Library Materials Z39.48-1984.

10   9   8   7   6   5   4   3   2   1

Contents

Acknowledgments

The idea for this book was conceived at a conference held at Emory University in April 1993, which brought together specialists in legislative politics and in the politics of Eastern Europe and the former Soviet Union who shared an interest in the emergent legislatures of the former communist sphere. The revised papers presented in this book provide the first cross-national assessment of the development of parliamentary politics in the region.

A great deal of effort went into the organization of the conference and the preparation of the book, which I gratefully wish to acknowledge here. The conference was sponsored by a Title VI grant from the US Department of Education and by the Emory University Graduate School of Arts and Sciences. I would particularly like to thank Vice President George H. Jones and Associate Vice President Eleanor C. Main for their interest in and support of the project. The conference was sponsored by Emory's Center for Soviet, Post-Soviet, and East European Studies, whose Director, Professor Juliette R. Stapanian-Apkarian, enthusiastically backed the project from the beginning. The Center's Educational Program Coordinator, Robbie King, and Program Assistant, Mary Jo Duncanson, smoothly handled myriad organizational details. Theresa Sabonis-Chafee, a graduate student in the political science department, oversaw the planning and management of the conference with skill and finesse. In addition, other graduate students in political science, Susan Davis, Moshe Haspel, Kathleen Montgomery, Sarah Oates, Svetlana Savranskaya, and Mark Whitehouse, generously assisted with the logistics of the conference itself. I would also like to thank Rebecca Ritke at Westview Press for her encouragement and advice on the book. Finally, for the preparation of the book itself I am deeply indebted to Kathleen Montgomery, whose excellent research and editorial assistance benefitted the book substantially.

Thomas F. Remington

The Post-Soviet States.

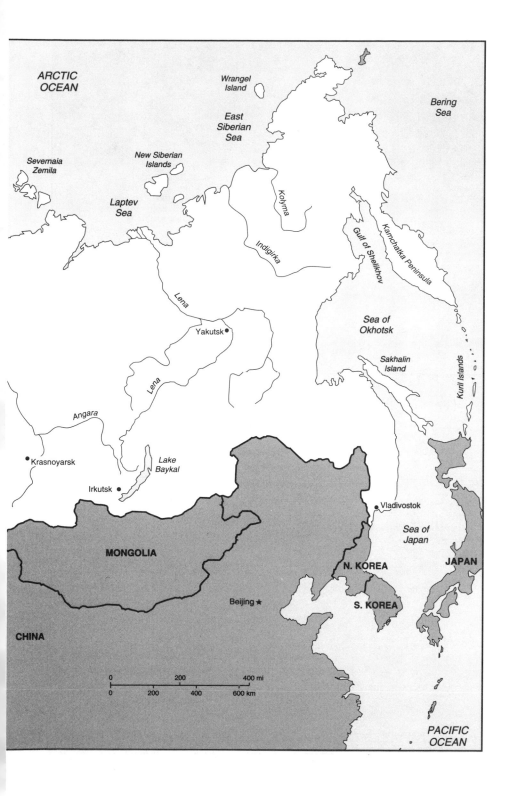

East-Central Europe.

1

Introduction: Parliamentary Elections and the Transition from Communism

Thomas F. Remington

While the communist regimes in the Soviet Union and Eastern Europe were established by violence—revolution, civil war, occupation and terror—their transformation into democratic systems began with a series of parliamentary elections. In some instances, elections served to precipitate a deeper crisis that overwhelmed a country's embryonic representative institutions. In others, they contributed to the stabilization of a democratic order. In this introduction and the chapters that follow, we will examine several of the parliaments that were formed by the first wave of elections following the transition. Who were the members of these parliaments? What united them and what divided them? What features of their demographic composition, institutional structure, historical evolution and political alignments give us insight into the process by which democracies emerge from authoritarian regimes?

Founding Elections

In several cases, the elections of 1989-1990 served as popular referenda on ending communist rule. In the Polish election of June 1989, which was the first and most dramatic of the products of roundtable agreements on new elections in the region, the "electoral success of Solidarnosc depended profoundly on mobilizing the broad base of animosity toward the government. . . antiregime feelings are virtually inseparable from pro-Solidarnosc attitudes." (Heyns and Bialecki 1991:356, 365). In Hungary, although there was no single popular front to mobilize the anti-regime vote in the March 1990 elections, the former communists (running as the Socialist Party) received fewer than

11% of the votes, and the hard-line communist faction and Social-Democrats each received fewer than 4%. The outcome led observers to conclude that the first round of elections "was much more a referendum on the transition towards a multi-party democracy than a vote on specific policy issues." (Körösenyi 1991:65). The Czechoslovak elections of June 1990 resembled a plebiscite in that the broad popular support for the Civic Forum and Public against Violence movements overwhelmed the other parties running (Wightman 1991:110). The East German election of March 1990 was similar to the Polish, Hungarian and Czechoslovak cases, although the election was even more a referendum on unification with the Federal Republic than on the transition to democracy. The Christian Democrats, closely linked to the CDU/CSU in West Germany, formed an electoral alliance that won nearly half the vote on a platform of early unification by merger into the Federal Republic. They then formed a government which promptly proceeded to carry out unification.

The "pacted" transitions of Central Europe differ from the USSR pattern, where the 1989 and 1990 elections were subject to much more control by central and local authorities. Mikhail Gorbachev tied his perestroika program to a far-reaching but still limited political reform that would open the soviets to freer electoral competition, while leaving the CPSU as the "leading force" of Soviet society (Chiesa 1993; White 1991; Kiernan 1993; Urban 1990). His strategy failed, not so much because the elections created an uncontrollable momentum of popular demands for liberal democracy, as because they upset the balance between central controls and local autonomy that maintained the union of national republics. Caught between popular nationalism and weakening central power, republic-level rulers either joined with indigenous nationalist movements or turned to their own personal political machines in order to coopt or suppress them. The desperate attempt in August 1991 by the old forces of central power—bureaucracy, army, security agencies and communist party—to seize control and save the union collapsed ignominiously. Although Gorbachev failed in his effort to craft a neo-Leninist political architecture that would accommodate the new energies released by his reforms, he left behind a partly liberalized institutional framework which each successor republic has adapted to its own circumstances. As a result, the paths of political change in the newly independent states have become increasingly differentiated.

The first stage of Gorbachev's reform plan for a new system of soviet power took the form of elections in March 1989 to a new USSR legislature. In the design both of the legislature and the rules governing the nominations and elections, the new system built in a number of mechanisms to prevent the elections from turning into a runaway popular rejection of the regime. On the other hand, Gorbachev evidently hoped to use the democratized legislative system as a counterweight to the conservative party and state bureaucracies that were blocking his reform program. Whatever Gorbachev's expectations, because of the limited opening that the reform allowed for free electoral campaigning, the 1989 elections in several regions did take the form of referenda on communist rule. As Giulietto Chiesa observes, "Where a real struggle occurred, the *apparat* lost almost universally" (1993:35). The popular fronts of the three Baltic states swept the races in their republics and defeated a number of leading officials (Chiesa 1993:37; Urban 1990:113; Kiernan and Aistrup 1991; Hough 1989). In fact the pattern of political development in the Baltic Republics in 1989 and 1990 resembles that of Central Europe far more than it does other republics of the Soviet Union, in that intelligentsia-led popular fronts formed to challenge the communist incumbents in the initial elections, won sweeping victories, and then split apart into a number of competing political parties. But in a number of cities in Russia and Ukraine as well, organized independent political movements ran successful campaigns to elect anti-establishment candidates or defeat prominent representatives of the ruling elite. In Leningrad, Kiev, Lvov, Minsk, Alma-Ata, Frunze, Dushanbe, and Kishinev, party first secretaries lost their races (Chiesa 1993:36). In Russia, they also lost in all of the mining and heavy-industry cities of the Urals and Siberia (Hough 1989:14).[1] One of the most significant victories was that of Boris Yeltsin, running in a Moscow-wide district on a strongly democratic and populist platform, who received almost 90% of the vote.

In keeping with Gorbachev's plan, elections to the Supreme Soviets of the constituent republics were held the following year, in 1990, along with elections to all lower-level soviets (Slider 1990; Montgomery and Remington, forthcoming; Helf and Hahn 1992; Embree 1991). Once again, these became referenda on communist rule in regions where challengers were strong enough and organized enough to get candidates nominated and registered and mount public campaigns. In the Russian Republic, a coalition of reform-minded candidates formed a movement called "Democratic Russia" which opposed communist party power and privileges. Its candidates won a number of races in cities and industrial regions. Close to 40% of the RSFSR deputies elected in 1990 aligned themselves with the democratic cause.

On the other hand, although many of the USSR races in 1989 and 1990 bore a resemblance to the East European elections, in most of the Soviet republics, political parties as such did not participate in the elections and have not dominated parliamentary politics. This difference continues to distinguish most of the former Soviet republics from virtually all of the Eastern European cases.[2] Although broad coalitions and labels (such as "Popular Front" or "Democratic Russia") in many areas served to give programmatic cues about the candidates to Soviet voters, most candidates were not chosen or supported by party organizations, and seats were awarded to candidates who won majorities in single-member constituencies rather than by a system of proportional representation. The fact that 86% of the elected deputies of the Russian republic were communist party members at the time of election is not in itself a strong indication of their actual policy leanings or party ties; but the fact that two thirds still registered as communists at the Fifth Congress's second session, in October 1991—*two months after the August coup*—tells us a good deal more. The majoritarian electoral system, the continuing strength of the old political establishment in many localities, and the absence of historic parties capable of reviving inhibited the formation of new parties in response to the electoral opening in the USSR. Another factor is sometimes cited as well: the antipathy of most voters to the very idea of organized political parties, based on their experience with the monopolistic, bureaucratized communist party. Whatever the reasons, party identification in Russia remains extremely low. A national survey conducted in spring 1993 found that 83% of respondents declared they would never join a political party (Oates 1993). From the standpoint of comparative theory, therefore, it will be interesting to observe the effects of changes in the electoral laws in the post-USSR republics. If Russia and other republics adopt systems of proportional representation for their next elections, how great will be the impetus to party development?

The Balkan cases (Romania, Bulgaria, Albania, and the former Yugoslavia) constitute an intermediate band between the Central European and Soviet elections with respect to the strength of parties and the extent of contestation in their founding elections. Liberal elements of the ruling communist parties took control of their parties and gave them a reform orientation; the renamed communist parties then swept the elections but allowed other parties greater opportunities for participation than in the past. Romania's regime broke down in December 1989 because of a conspiracy within the ruling elite rather than a negotiated agreement with a popular opposition group. The ascendant dissident section of the ruling communists formed an electoral alliance called the National Salvation Front to compete in the national elections of May 1990, winning two thirds of the votes. A direct popular election for the president was held simultaneously and the NSF candidate for president, Ion Iliescu, took 85% of the vote.

In Bulgaria, the former communists, running as the Socialist party, took nearly half the popular vote, which translated into a clear majority of parliamentary seats, in the June 1990 elections, and in Albania, the April 1991 elections brought the ex-communists two thirds of the popular vote as well as of the seats in parliament. Romania held a second set of parliamentary and presidential elections in September 1992 with somewhat different results than in 1990. The ruling NSF had split, and opposition parties had gained in popular support. As a result, the rump NSF fell from two thirds of the seats in each chamber of parliament to around ten percent, the new NSF splinter wing won over a quarter of the seats in each chamber, and a wide array of opposition groups won the rest (Shafir 1992). Their presidential candidate, Iliescu, won a large popular majority although somewhat lower than in 1990.

Yugoslavia should be seen as a collection of republic-level cases, since there were no Yugoslav-wide parliamentary elections.[3] In the two western republics, Slovenia and Croatia, parliamentary elections in April 1990 brought new, non-communist governments to power which began to press for independence from Yugoslavia, while the Serbian republic held elections in December 1990 that gave the renamed communists a majority much as in the other Balkan cases. In all three republics, as in the Soviet Union, the elections of 1990 gave parties a strong incentive to bid for power on programs of ethnic nationalism and to oppose concessions to the other republics that would preserve the unity of the federal state. Civil war followed the independence acts of Slovenia, Croatia, and Bosnia-Herzegovina.

Party Systems and Social Cleavages

Because of their importance in demonstrating popular endorsement of the passage from communist to democratic rule, the Central European parliamentary elections of 1989 and 1990 have been regarded as "founding elections" (Bogdanor 1990:288; White 1990:286). That is, they gave the stamp of democratic consent to parliamentary arrangements which were made, typically, through a negotiated agreement between elements of the ruling elite and leaders of the organized opposition. The plebiscitarian character of the election, the inchoate nature of political divisions among the electorate, and the success of the opposition movement in winning seats legitimate the new parliamentary arena in which political life in the future will be concentrated (Bogdanor 1990:290). In theory, as Bogdanor notes, it is possible for a founding election to "freeze in" the initial dominance of a particular party or coalition, as was the case in post-war Italy and Japan. More common is a lengthy period of reconstruction of cleavage lines and party identities following the initial election. One reason for this is the loss of social bearings and attachments that resulted from the *Gleichschaltung* of society under communism, a process George Schöpflin compares to desertification (1991:235). Therefore the second and third rounds of elections in many cases also serve as founding elections, as Krzysztof Jasiewiecz observes (1993:133). The plebiscite-like quality of the first elections and the fluidity of political cleavages mean that a stable party system develops only after multiple elections. In the immediate post-communist environment, for example, voters are often attracted to candidates for their personal qualities or their reputations as outsiders. In later elections, the same factor may explain the preference of voters for former party bureaucrats or enterprise managers on the grounds that these individuals have proven credentials as competent administrators. Voters are not necessarily firmly attached to parties, nor are party labels useful guides to judging how politicians will decide policy issues. As Herbert Kitschelt observes, during the early period, actors are still determining where their interests lie, and how best to secure them (1992:9).

If voter preferences are fluid and volatile, so are those of many of the first generation of elected officials. In Russia, for instance, parliamentary deputies such as Vladimir Isakov and Mikhail Chelnokov, who began their parliamentary careers identified strongly with the democratic camp, made radical shifts to the conservative, pro-communist side; Ruslan Khasbulatov, whom Yeltsin had made his own first deputy chairman of the Supreme Soviet, later led the congress in the campaign to impeach Yeltsin. In Georgia, Zviad Gamsakhurdia was elected, together with the coalition of parliamentary candidates he headed, on a program combining an anti-communist democratic program with a strong anti-Soviet nationalist appeal, only to turn to authoritarian methods of rule and denunciations of his political opponents as "agents of the Kremlin." Similar conversions to authoritarian nationalism by politicians who ran originally on platforms of anti-communist populism are common throughout the region, and demonstrate that support for liberal democratic values had considerably shallower roots than the popular impulse to turn out the old rulers. Since many of the new parties are poorly suited to channeling the ambitions of the new generation of politicians, candidates are likely to seek support by emphasizing personal rather than partisan appeals, sometimes by proposing extremist or demagogic solutions to the country's problems. Many of the new deputies themselves seem often to have been unprepared for their roles as advocates of constituency interests, as Timothy Colton's chapter to this volume indicates. Colton hypothesizes that *legislative* professionalization will require the emergence of *political* professionalism.

Social cleavages and their political expression reflect the impact of communist rule and it is unclear whether and when they might come to resemble those of Western Europe. In most of the region, intellectuals from outside the political establishment supplied the first generation of leadership for the opposition movements that successfully challenged the communist regimes. As Gerhard Loewenberg's chapter in this volume shows, it was the new parties in Hungary that changed the social composition of the political elite, bringing into parliament a group of professionals, intellectuals and local notables whose election was favored by strength of the catch-all Democratic Forum in single-member districts. In a number of countries, industrial workers voted for the radical free-market parties as the surest way to defeat communist hegemony, while the collectivized peasantry turned out loyally in support of the communists. In a number of countries, however, the first wave of deputies found themselves edged out as a second generation of professional politicians took their places in succeeding elections or as crises returned durable figures from the previous regime to power. Parliamentary elections in Lithuania in October-November 1992 brought back the former Lithuanian communist party leader, Algirdas Brazauskas, whose party, the Lithuanian Democratic Labor Party, won an absolute majority of the seats running on a platform of moderation and competence. With the return of Gaidar Aliev to power in Azerbaijan (where parliament elected him chairman) in June 1993, eleven of the fifteen former Soviet republics were headed by erstwhile members of the CPSU Politburo.[4] In the Polish elections of September 1993, parties that arose out of the former ruling communist party and its popular front allies won a majority of the seats in parliament.

Andras Körösenyi's delineation of the three kinds of parties that competed in Hungary's 1990 races—historic, new, and communist successors (1991: 56–7)—provides a useful way to classify the types of political cleavages likely to determine the strength and political positions of the parties that emerge in the 1990s. Some parties will organize around religious, class, ethnic, regional, or other identities of the pre-communist past, while others will express new interests and values in response to the remodeling of society that occurred under communism. These include liberal anti-communist parties that appeal to populist resentment of the power and privileges of the nomenklatura while simultaneously defending the interests of the rising new entrepreneurial class, as well as the groups which try to preserve the old nomenklatura's strategic position by promoting a technocratic, pragmatic program. It is reasonable to foresee that the party systems which will emerge will neither fully replicate those of the pre-communist period nor freeze the political alignments of the moment when the old regime fell, but will combine elements of each with the interests generated by the post-communist development of society. Signposts of future alignments may include the weakness of working-class socialist parties, the entrenchment of former communist elites in rural constituencies, and the new popularity of parties appealing for stability, centrism, managerial competence and national consensus.

The fluidity of social identities and political attachments in the post-communist societies helps to explain why Juan Linz and Alfred Stepan's "sequencing" theory does not work well in the case of multi-ethnic polities of the former communist world, although, as David Olson observes in his chapter in this book, their argument may apply to the case of Czechoslovakia (Linz and Stepan 1992). Linz and Stepan point out that transitions from authoritarianism typically pose challenges to the integrity of the state by allowing challengers to appeal to regional or ethnic separatism. This problem, they argue, is affected by the order in which founding elections are held. Reasoning from the Spanish case, where three important union-wide elections were held over the period 1975-77, they claim that the Spanish parliament and government gained strength from the participation of groups in these elections; had regional elections been held first, parties in the Basque country and in Catalonia would likely have campaigned for the independence cause and Spanish unity would have been imperiled. Instead, the elections strengthened the Spanish state and Spanish identity. By the same token, they claim, the sequence of elections in the USSR and Yugoslavia was precisely that which was most likely to accelerate the disintegration of each state along ethnic-regional lines. In the case of Yugoslavia, this is because all-union elections were never held,[5] and republic-level elections in the spring of 1990 reinforced the independence movements in Slovenia and Croatia. As for the Soviet Union, they believe that the 1989 elections were too tightly controlled by the communist party to stimulate union-wide party political activity; they argue that since the 1990 republican elections were more important and more open, they were more likely to mobilize nationalist groups. Of course they recognize that the effects on society of communist rule—the "flattening out" of civil society—stand in contrast to the consequences of Francoist authoritarianism (Linz and Stepan 1992: 132) but they hold that politicians are capable of tailoring their appeals to whatever will be the most reliable path to power. Therefore if the union-level elections of 1989 had been freer, they conclude, candidates would have constructed their platforms around cleavages that would have worked to strengthen the integration of the union rather than weaken it.

The available evidence, however, does not support this argument. Where the 1989 USSR elections did allow for the free mobilization of voters, political movements almost invariably everywhere campaigned for national-territorial sovereignty. Most members of the delegations from the Baltic republics showed less interest in strengthening democratic tendencies at the union level than in preparing for independence for the Baltic states. The elections the next year altered the opportunity structure, but not the objectives, of nationalist forces in the republics. The analogy of Spain to the three communist ethno-federations is problematic because Spain lacked any national territory equivalent to Russia in the USSR or Serbia in Yugoslavia: that is, a country *dominant* in territory and population whose leaders and populace demanded to increase its autonomy and weight within the federation. Indeed, neither Yugoslavia nor the USSR had a national identity coterminous with the state, in stark contrast to Spain, and neither "Yugoslavia" nor "the Union of Soviet Socialist Republics" had any national identity or history other than that given it by the communist regime. In Czechoslovakia, Slovak demands for autonomy reached a point where the leadership of the Czech Republic was unwilling to pay the price of preserving the union. These are quite different cases from the peripheral ethnic regional separatism in Spain (or other West European countries). Were Catalonia and the Basque country to break away from Spain, a Spanish nation and territory would still exist, whereas the success of the national independence movements in Yugoslavia, Czechoslovakia and the USSR meant the disappearance of the state itself.[6]

Therefore, in both the Soviet Union and Yugoslavia, it was the core nation that ultimately broke the union by demanding a renegotiation of the terms of its participation in it. In the case of Yugoslavia, Milosevic's "Greater Serbia" policies of the late 1980s (his heavy-handed assertion of Serb control in Kosovo and Vojvodina, for instance) repulsed pro-union elements in Slovenia and Croatia. In the Soviet case, the democratic movement in Russia, much as in other republics, opposed the stultifying centralism of union-level political and economic bureaucracies: both democrats and conservatives wanted to claim more power for Russia. Although most members of both the democratic and nationalist movements in Russia wanted to preserve some sort of union, they agreed on a demand for Russian sovereignty and the precedence of Russian law over federal law. This demand in turn was realized in the Declaration on Sovereignty adopted shortly after the opening of the First Russian Congress of People's Deputies in May-June 1990. Freer USSR elections in 1989, therefore, would probably have accelerated the pace of the country's dissolution because of the weakness of horizontal ties linking segments of society across republics. It is another matter whether nationalist leaders misjudge their ability to steer the popular forces they activate— clearly they often act as if the movements they create will remain under their control. Still, the forces of integration in the USSR depended too heavily on the communist political and economic structures built up under Stalin, and too little on an authentic national identity, to have permitted Gorbachev simultaneously to democratize and preserve the union. The Soviet and Yugoslav cases seem only to confirm the prescience of Robert Dahl's observation that "the price of polyarchy may be a breakup of the country. And the price of territorial unity may be a hegemonic regime" (1971:121).

Crisis and Stabilization

Some of the new parliaments of the former communist sphere have withstood the strains of transition more successfully than others. Boris Yeltsin's dissolution of the Russian legislature on September 21, 1993, followed by the violent uprising of its defenders, underlines the difference between systems where parliaments have been arenas for contests between opposing parties, and those where they have become power centers challenging the executive for ultimate control over policy. Under what conditions do political actors accept the rules of parliamentary competition as a given, and seek to win control for their party or coalition over parliament, and when do they attempt to change the rules and alter the system?

The system-defining rules of parliamentary democracy are of different orders: the operation of a set of rules at a higher level is a condition for the operation of lower-level rules (Pridham 1990:226). At the regime level, a set of unwritten ("meta-") rules determines whether parliament makes laws that matter, or whether instead it is a rubber-stamp façade, and whether a political opposition is permitted to compete for control of government. Change at this level takes more than constitutional revision since constitutions may bear little relation to the operative rules of the game. The disintegration of communist regimes in Central Europe in 1989 resulted from the confluence of large-scale popular opposition to the regime, severe internal divisions among the ruling elite, and a hands-off policy in Moscow. Under these unique conditions, where the entire balance between force and consent in maintaining public order had been upset, the old elites sought to resolve the crisis by agreeing to new elections for a democratized parliament.[7] This of course was not the sequence of events in the Soviet Union, where the Gorbachev leadership hoped to democratize the soviets as a counterweight to other structures of power, rather than to surrender control to a new government. Within a few years the soviets then became vehicles for conservative opposition to reform.

The rules at an intermediate level of generality govern the parliament's relationship to other political structures, such as the executive branch, territorial governments, and political parties. They specify the mixture of presidential or parliamentary power, proportional or plurality electoral mechanisms, centralism and devolution. Change of the rules at this level may require a less extraordinary or dangerous conjuncture than does regime change, but still may be the consequence of a serious constitutional crisis because of the intensity of the struggle between the forces benefitting from the existing order and those locked into a permanent disadvantage by it. This is because those players who share a common interest in retaining the existing rules are usually stronger, or better organized, than the outsiders who want to alter them. Indeed, one of the best indications of the importance of the institutionalization of rules at this level is their persistence once the period of constitutional crisis is past. Dieter Nohlen has found that "fundamental changes [in electoral systems] are rare and arise only in extraordinary historical situations" (Nohlen 1984:218) and Arend Lijphart has argued more generally that the structural characteristics of democratic systems tend to be highly stable over time (1992a; 1984:222). How firmly the rules at this level have been locked into place in the former communist world will be examined below.

At the most immediate level the rules determine the operation of the parliamentary institution itself and are enshrined in the standing orders of the chambers as well as in precedent and tacit understandings. They define the powers of institutions such as the speaker and the committees, and the procedures for forming the agenda and enacting legislation. These are more readily changed than those defining the type of regime or its constitution, although unusual circumstances may still be required to produce the majorities (or qualified majorities) needed to change them. For example, Steven Smith's book *Call to Order* demonstrates how stubbornly the two houses of the U. S. Congress have resisted alteration of the rules governing majority/ minority rights because of the difficulty of forming a majority coalition that puts itself at a disadvantage by altering the rules to the advantage of minorities (Smith 1989). By the same token, vagueness and ambiguity in the rules, and a habit of bending them by the law-makers themselves, can undermine the institution's influence and weaken it in its relations with other structures (Foster 1993).

When they are accepted by the actors, however, the rules at any given level tend to have staying power. Consolidation or institutionalization means that these arrangements replicate themselves over time, as they are adopted, adjusted and utilized by new players who come onto the political scene. Since the rules at a more general level determine how those at more specific levels are changed, we expect regime-level arrangements to change less often than constitutions, and constitutions less often than parliamentary procedure. All else being equal, time should therefore favor consolidation, which we understand as the persistence over time of any given set of institutional arrangements forming the system. The consolidation of a newly democratic parliament is the consequence of the investment of the players' resources in winning majorities under existing rules rather than gaining enough power to overturn the rules themselves. Playing by the rules may perhaps have a socializing, habituating effect on the players, but is ultimately explained as the product of players' calculations about the balance of gains and costs in trying to change them.[8]

Let us compare the degree to which the East European and post-Soviet parliaments are consolidated, then, at the intermediate, constitutional level of their institutional arrangements. We will examine two important issues: type of electoral system and balance of presidential-parliamentary power. In both cases, there is a continuum of possible arrangements, with a wide range of variants in place in the region, as Table 1.1 demonstrates. In many, constitutions and electoral laws have continued to evolve since the initial round of elections. In Russia and several other former Soviet republics, severe political crises have erupted over basic constitutional arrangements.

Electoral Systems

Generally speaking, the element of proportional representation in Eastern Europe's electoral systems has expanded with time, although some continue to use hybrid forms that mix proportionalism with single-member district plurality or majority voting (Jasiewicz:140-145). Most of the former Soviet republics, by contrast, have retained the older majoritarian model of single member districts. Where they occurred, the round-table talks between the elites of the old regime

TABLE 1.1 Constitutional and Electoral Systems in Eastern Europe and Former Soviet States

Country	Constitutional Type[1]	Electoral System[2]	Legislative Elections
Albania	parliamentary	hybrid PR (4%)[3]	March-April 1991; March 1992
Armenia	semi-presidential[4]	majoritarian	May 1990
Azerbaijan	presidential[5]	majoritarian	Sept./October 1990
Belarus	parliamentary	majoritarian	March 1990
Bulgaria	parliamentary[6]	PR (4%)	June 1990; Oct. 1991
Croatia	semi-presidential[7]	hybrid PR (3%)	April-May 1990 August 1992
Czechoslovakia	parliamentary	PR (5%)*	June 1990; June 1992
Czech Republic	parliamentary	PR (5%)*	June 1992
East Germany	parliamentary	hybrid PR (5%)	March 1990; Dec. 1990
Estonia	semi-presidential[8]	PR	Mar. 1990; Sept. 1992
Georgia	presidential[9]	PR	October 1990 October 1992
Hungary	parliamentary	hybrid PR[10]	March-April 1990
Kazakhstan	presidential	majoritarian	March 1990
Kirgizstan	presidential[11]	majoritarian	February 1990
Latvia	parliamentary	PR (4%)	March 1990; June 1993
Lithuania	semi-presidential[12]	hybrid PR (4%)[13]	Feb./March 1990; Oct./November 1992
Moldova	semi-presidential	majoritarian	Feb.-March 1990
Poland	semi-presidential	1. PR (seats reserved)[14] 2. PR (no threshold)[15] 3. PR (5% threshold)[16]	June 1989 October 1991 September 1993
Romania	semi-presidential	PR (3%)[17]	May 1990; Sept. 1992
Russia	presidential[18]	majoritarian	March 1990
Slovakia	parliamentary	PR (5%)*	June 1992

(continues)

TABLE 1.1 (*continued*)

Country:	Constitutional Type[1]	Electoral System[2]	Legislative Elections
Slovenia	parliamentary	PR[19]	April 1990; Dec. 1992
Tajikistan	parliamentary[20]	majoritarian	March 1990
Turkmenistan	presidential[21]	majoritarian	January 1990
Ukraine	semi-presidential	majoritarian	March 1990
Uzbekistan	presidential	majoritarian	February 1990
Federal Republic of Yugoslavia	semi-presidential	PR (5%)[22]	May 1992; Dec. 1992

*Coalitions must clear higher thresholds than parties.

Sources:

1. James McGregor, "How Electoral Laws Shape Eastern Europe's Parliaments," *RFE/RL Research Report* 2:4 (22 January 1993), pp. 11-18.

2. James P. McGregor, "Fragmentation and Capacity in Central and East European Parliaments," paper presented to 1993 annual meeting of American Political Science Association, Washington, DC, September 1993.

3. British Broadcasting Corporation (BBC), Summary of World Broadcasts (SWB), various issues.

Notes:

1. According to the most recent constitutional changes. Most former Soviet republics adopted presidencies in 1990-91 after the 1990 parliamentary elections. Note that throughout the region, the actual power of presidents vis-a-vis assemblies may exceed their constitutional powers.

2. Threshold levels for allocating seats indicated in parentheses.

3. Threshold applied to those seats allocated to seats reserved for proportional party representation; such seats comprise around 30% of total.

4. The president is directly elected and has specific legislative powers, e.g. in foreign policy. The delineation of powers between the president and assembly is in dispute, however.

5. The constitutional powers of president and assembly are in dispute.

6. Bulgaria's president is directly elected, but the office has very little formal power.

7. The president's actual political power considerably exceeds his limited formal powers.

8. The president is now directly elected, but the formal powers of the office are strictly limited. As the president has pressed for greater powers, particularly in foreign policy, he has come into conflict with the parliament.

9. Following the civil war that resulted from President Gamsakhurdia's rule, Eduard Shevardnadze urged that the post of chairman of the assembly become a popularly elected post. Shevardnadze ran unopposed and won. Although a member of the parliament, he has broad legislative powers and the position was declared chief of state. Shevardnadze became president in all but name. In September 1993, he forced the parliament to suspend itself by threatening to resign.

10. Hungary applies a 4% threshold to the seats allocated to parties running on regional and national lists but not to the single-member district seats, which comprise 46% of the total.

(*continues*)

TABLE 1.1 *(continued)*

11. In February 1992, the president claimed full power over the executive branch.

12. A referendum held at the time of the October 1992 elections approved a new constitution providing for a directly elected president. The president appoints the prime minister, who names a cabinet with parliamentary approval.

13. Threshold requirement does not apply to parties representing ethnic minorities.

14. 65% of the seats in the lower chamber and none in the upper were reserved for the communist party and its satellite parties.

15. The 1991 electoral law provided for a 5% threshold for representation for those seats, 15% of the total in the lower house, that were set aside for national party lists. The rest of the seats were awarded without thresholds to representation.

16. The 1993 electoral law provides a 5% threshold for parties and an 8% threshold for coalitions. Parties representing ethnic minorities are exempt from the threshold requirement.

17. Threshold raised for coalitions; level depends on number of parties in coalition.

18. Powers of president in dispute; much-amended current constitution combines traditional soviet system (where all power in the state is exercised by soviets) with strong, directly elected presidency possessing power to issue laws by decree. On September 21, 1993, President Yeltsin declared the parliament dissolved, nullified the powers of deputies, and called for new elections to parliament, to be followed by early presidential elections.

19. A 3% threshold is used to allocate seats to parties for a set of national seats.

20. In late 1992, in the midst of civil war, the Tajik parliament seized back state power and declared its chairman to be head of state. A much-weakened presidency still exists.

21. The constitution adopted in May 1992 made the president both chief of state and head of government.

22. Threshold lowered to 1% for parties representing ethnic minorities.

and the organized forces of opposition produced agreements about the rules for parliamentary representation depending on the calculations on each side's part about what sort of electoral and constitutional system was likely to favor it. The communist side held out for various forms of protection against the possibility of electoral defeat. In Poland, the regime accepted an agreement under which all seats in a new upper house would be openly contested while a majority of seats in the lower chamber were reserved for the ruling party coalition. Similarly, in the USSR, where there were no round-table talks, Gorbachev's plan provided that one third of the seats in the new Congress of People's Deputies would be reserved for representatives of officially recognized public organizations.

Typically, communist parties calculated in the beginning that they would be better off under winner-take-all arrangements, on the grounds that they were better organized than the opposition and that they still held certain advantages in mobilizing the voters (Jasiewicz 1993: 141). In Hungary, as Arend Lijphart has shown, the communists overestimated their chances of winning under majoritarian rules, and pressed to reduce the share of seats elected proportionally; they were saved from the full effect of their misjudgement by the opposition's desire to increase the number of PR seats (Liphart 1992a). Consequently, in later rounds, communists in Eastern Europe in some cases opted for elements of PR to defend their weakened positions. Throughout the East European and former Soviet region, the electoral and constitutional systems adopted at the time of transition brought about significant changes in the balance of political forces in the country, rather than freezing into place the relative positions of the major actors. As a result, the rules have continued to evolve rather than to stabilize and push the political struggle to more immediate levels of rule-making.

In a recent article, James McGregor compared the electoral systems of seven East European countries to analyze the effect of the electoral rules on two important aspects of representation—how fragmented the resulting spectrum of parties in parliament is, and how close to full proportionality between votes and seats each system came (McGregor 1992). He examined several aspects of the electoral laws that are relevant to their effect on outcomes: ballot structure, the number of seats per district, the existence of vote thresholds, the use of compensatory seats, and the formulas for awarding seats. He found that the Hungarian and Albanian cases show the greatest impact of electoral law on representation in the region, whereas in Poland, contrary to the common wisdom, the electoral law used for the October 1991 election had little effect on parliamentary fragmentation. This interpretation is debatable, however. Polish politicians have tinkered extensively with the electoral rules in order to achieve the desired balance between representation and stability. Indeed, Poland is the only country in the region to have held three national parliamentary elections between 1989 and 1993. Each election was held under a different electoral system, illustrating the opportunities and limits of political engineering through electoral laws.

Poland's 1989 election was the first of the "roundtable" parliamentary elections. The details of the agreement between Solidarity and the government have been recounted often and do not bear repeating here. Basically, the pact provided for a bicameral assembly in which 65% of the seats in the lower chamber were to be reserved for the communists and their popular front allies, and all of the seats in the upper house would be open to free competition. In the June election the government suffered a huge defeat in every openly contested race, and could scarcely win the seats that had been reserved for the ruling party and its satellites because of the rule that winning candidates had to have a majority of votes cast. The landslide meant that, contrary to both sides' initial expectations, Solidarity had to take the responsibility for forming a government. The parliament resulting from these elections was far more democratic than its counterparts in any other communist system, but far less so than the parliaments elected that year and the next in other Central European countries, where the outgoing rulers were too weak to shelter reserved seats from open contests. Major political forces considered themselves unrepresented, while the two actors that produced the April 1989 agreement, Solidarity and the communists, both splintered into smaller, rival fractions. The "contract" parliament, as the Poles came to call it, finally, and with some reluctance, adopted a new electoral law to govern the next elections, which were held in October 1991 (Zubek 1993; Millard 1992; Vinton 1993).

The outcome of the drafting process reflects the usual fears of small parties about the effects of single-member-district, majoritarian electoral systems. The small and fractious parties could readily agree on the desirability of proportionalism. Moreover, although politicians could agree abstractly that it was desirable to keep fringe parties out of parliament, each lowering of the proposed percentage threshold for representation encouraged yet more groups to press to lower the barrier further. Ultimately, the authors of the law dropped any threshold to representation in the 37 multi-member electoral districts whatever.[9] A similar momentum built up behind the principle that free television time should be granted equally to every party, even those which ran candidates in only one district. The extreme proportionalism of the system resulted in a highly fragmented lower chamber, where 29 parties gained seats, only two of them with more than 10% of the seats, and eleven with only one seat each.

Immediately after the no-confidence vote in May 1993, the Polish parliament passed a new electoral law which raised the hurdles for representation in the future parliament although it eased the effect of the changes for those parties that had at least 15 seats in the outgoing parliament. Whereas under the previous law, there were no percentage thresholds to gaining seats in the district races, now parties had to receive at least 5% of the vote nationwide and electoral blocs 8%. Moreover, the average magnitude of electoral districts (i.e. the number of seats per constituency) was reduced by increasing the number from 37 to 52, which was to reduce proportionalism further. The new law encouraged parties to band together into coalitions before the election and eliminated micro-parties from parliament altogether.[10] The election, held in September 1993, suggests that these changes in the electoral rules did have some impact on the degree of fragmentation of the parliamentary party system: the number of parties winning seats in the lower house of parliament fell from 29 to six.

The former USSR republics have moved at varying tempos to modify the basically majoritarian electoral system inherited from the communist past and amended by Gorbachev's electoral reforms.[11] Alterations have concerned five issues: whether districts should be expanded from single to multiple seats; whether party lists and proportionalism should be used rather than majority or plurality rules; how the supervisory electoral commissions are to be formed; how nominations are to be made; and whether seats are to be reserved for representatives of particular public organizations.

Among the Soviet parliaments, Georgia and Estonia were the only ones to have used proportionalism in their initial (1990) elections,[12] but mixed systems combining single-member-district and proportional, party-list systems are gaining in appeal in other republics. For instance, Lithuania adopted a half-and-half system for its 1992 election and Yeltsin decreed such a law into effect when he dissolved parliament in September 1993. Likewise, of the republics, only Kazakhstan used the rule of reserving seats for representatives of public organizations which the USSR electoral law adopted in 1988 incorporated.[13] A much less obvious violation of the norm of equal representation was built into the electoral law of the USSR, Russia and other republics by retaining the traditional practice of nominating candidates from "labor collectives" (Chiesa 1993:21). Under this provision, local authorities could assemble the workforce at their place of work and seek their approval for a nomination, while to nominate a candidate from a place of residence one had to gather at least 300 signatures on a petition to hold a nominating meeting, obtain the consent of the local electoral commission and soviet to hold the meeting, and ensure that at least 300 voters were at the meeting. These rules reflect the longstanding use by the Soviet regime of the enterprise as the basic organizational unit for political mobilization as well as the persistence of corporatist and patrimonial elements in the structure of Soviet society. In practice, of course, they militated against nominations except through labor collectives, and, as Alexander Sobyanin notes in his contribution to this book, this tended to bias the nominations and hence the composition of the deputy corps toward candidates who enjoyed good relations with party, state, and economic officialdom.

Yet another feature of the electoral laws of 1989 and 1990 that remained unchanged from the communist past was the composition of the electoral commissions overseeing the elections: many of the local commissions comprised the same communist officials who had been supervising soviet elections for decades, and there was no way that democratic activists could appeal their right to supervise the 1989 and 1990 elections.

These and other features of the electoral law became subject to intense debate in Russia.[14] By 1993 many sections of the political elite had come to accept that some mixture of proportional and majoritarian representation was desirable for the next parliamentary elections. The arguments over alternative versions of the new law revealed how much uncertainty surrounded the calculations of the advantages and disadvantages different political groups would face under various alternatives. One flank of the liberal-democratic movement strongly advocated a highly proportional system in order to force candidates to identify themselves with parties; they reasoned that the unpopularity of communists with the voters would give the democrats an advantage under a system of party lists. Other leaders of the democratic wing countered that democrats were not especially popular themselves, and voters might very well not support a list of candidates that they thought was proposed by a handful of Moscow party activists. They advocated relying more on single-member-districts, reducing the number of seats in the new parliament that were elected by national party lists to a small share, such as 15 or 20%, and seeking to form local electoral alliances with entepreneurs and managers. This difference of opinion within the democratic camp reflected uncertainty over the best strategy for the democratic movement generally—whether the democrats should move to the center of the spectrum and seek a more pragmatic, pro-business orientation, or continue to fight the legacy of the communist system and run against the nomenklatura.

Groups with low name recognition and weak organizational bases tended to fear that a proportional system would leave them unable to compete so they preferred a majoritarian system. They recognized, however, that if the threshold to representation were low enough, they might nonetheless succeed in winning more seats through party lists than in single member district races, so they were willing to accept a hybrid model, where half the seats in the future parliament would be proportionally elected by a national party list contest, and the other half by winner-take-all races in single member districts. They also voiced a view that was commonly cited as an argument against a strictly majoritarian system: that it would bias the resulting parliament in favor of deputies concerned with strictly local, regional, or ethnic interests. A proportional system, on the other hand, would have the tendency of encouraging parties to seek support throughout the country and would therefore counteract disintegrating forces.

Finally, the communists were also uncertain where their advantage lay, since they expected a voter backlash against the democratic wave of 1990 and the problems of economic reform, and hoped for an electoral bonus; on the other hand, several regional elections in 1993 demonstrated that voters tended to prefer candidates presenting themselves as competent, non-partisan pragmatists. Therefore the communists believed that at least half and perhaps more of the seats in the future parliament should be filled through majoritarian elections in single-member constituencies. Each group, therefore, sought to maximize the possible gains and minimize the risks of each model by hedging its bets and accepting an electoral system in which half the seats would be majoritarian and half proportional. Such was the draft law sent to the Supreme Soviet for consideration in July which reflected an agreement of the main tendencies in parliament. This version, in turn, was decreed by Yeltsin as the basis of the elections he called for December 1993.

Thus, many of the countries of the region have modified their electoral systems since their earlier elections, often in conjunction with adoption of a new constitution or attempts to resolve a political crisis.

Presidential-Parliamentary Relations

Conflict between presidents and parliaments has also been prevalent. Virtually all the former communist states have instituted some form of presidency (only Belarus has preserved the old model of a collective presidency in the form of a presidium of a Supreme Soviet headed by a chairman). And none of the countries of the former communist world has restored a monarchy, although in a few cases, heirs to the throne are ready and willing should the call come. All the rest elect a president to serve as chief of state. But the systems vary considerably in the relative powers of president and parliament, and in many the relationship between them continues to evolve. Generally speaking, in Eastern Europe, parliaments predominate; in the former Soviet republics, strong presidents have emerged.

Poland's constitution gives the president significant powers to name the head of government, but the government must hold the confidence of parliament. In Hungary, the president is elected by parliament and has no executive powers. In Romania, the president is popularly elected and oversees the government. Several countries have what Shugart and Carey would call "premier-presidential" systems in which the executive power is divided between president and parliament (Shugart and Carey 1992). Lithuania resolved the issue by putting a new draft constitution to the voters in the first round of parliamentary elections in fall 1992; the constitution created a semi-presidential or "premier-presidential" model. In Russia a bitter deadlock between president and legislature developed over the president's executive powers; Yeltsin broke it by decreeing the dissolution of the congress and Supreme Soviet and demanding new elections for a new single-tier, bicameral parliament.

For years scholars have debated the relative merits and weaknesses associated with presidential as opposed to parliamentary systems as models for young democracies.[15] The consensus in the past was that the cause of stability in fragile democratic systems was best served by institutional arrangements that reward representativeness over effectiveness; therefore parliamentarism, and electoral systems facilitating a sense of inclusion by all organized sections of the population through proportionalism, were thought more likely to survive than systems that allow the electoral victors to win all the stakes, as is the case with presidencies and majoritarian legislatures. The crises in Russia, Georgia, Ukraine, and several other former Soviet republics seem to support this view. But recently several writers have made strong claims for presidentialism or for institutional arrangements that allow for stable combinations of the more attractive features of presidential and parliamentary government. For example, Scott Mainwaring finds that it is not the coexistence of a president and a representative legislature in itself that creates dangerous crises, but the presence of multiple parties in parliament, since it is both difficult and unrewarding to cobble together majorities to pass the president's bills. But presidentialism in a two-party system, he finds, discourages extremism and creates incentives for the president's party in the legislature to build majorities for the president's program (1993). Shugart and Carey take a different tack and distinguish between presidential systems where the president has extensive legislative powers and frequently collides with the legislative branch, and dual-executive systems where the president oversees the executive branch but the government depends upon the confidence of the legislature and must therefore seek accommodation with it (1992). In the coming years, the former Soviet republics and Eastern Europe will present us with a large record of pertinent evidence on this issue.

Indeed, all sides in the debate can find confirmation of their positions. In Poland, the confrontation between the governing party coalition and the opposition over economic policy reached a head in the no-confidence vote of May 28, 1993. The government headed by Hanna Suchocka lost by one vote. Despite the constitution's requirement that a no-confidence vote be constructive, no alternative premier was named. President Walesa responded by refusing to accept the government's resignation, and instead dissolved parliament, exercising his power to do so under circumstances not anticipated by the constitution. He acted here as "arbiter," a characteristic role for presidents in a semi-presidential system, in order to break the impasse that had developed in parliament due to the weakness of the governing majority (Shugart and Carey 1992:48-9). The result of the crisis was parliament's prompt approval of a new election law which, although relaxing the extreme proportionalism of the current system, also built certain guarantees into the new law for the parties currently in parliament: all parties with at least 15 deputies in the old Sejm are spared the requirement of collecting 3000 signatures in each of 26 districts in order to run candidates (Vinton 1993:11).

In Russia's case, a debilitating constitutional crisis over the respective powers of president and parliament is an outgrowth of questions unresolved in the Soviet period. Gorbachev's attempt to infuse democratic practice into soviet structures was a logical impossibility, since the theory of the soviets as institutional embodiment of state power had never been more than a tactic for seizing power and legitimating Bolshevik party rule (Anweiler 1974:158-161). The soviets in practice had never fused legislative and executive power since both had always lain elsewhere. Gorbachev's initial model would have to have been modified sooner or later to resolve the question of the relationship between executive and legislative power. The USSR legislature, and those of most of the republics, grafted a French or US-type presidency onto a structure that was neither soviet nor parliamentary. In those republics where the legislatures had assumed some powers, executive-legislative confrontation has followed. Russia presents a very striking example of a significant shift in the voting strength of the democratic and communist wings following the creation of the new presidency, Yeltsin's departure from the legislative branch to fill it, and the deepening rift between the two branches over their rightful powers to oversee the government at a time of momentous social and economic change. The chapters by Sobyanin and by Remington, Smith, Kiewiet, and Haspel discuss the changing political balance in the Russian parliament in greater detail. The violent aftermath of the confrontation between president and parliament casts doubt on the prospects for democratic consolidation in Russia.

In sum, many of the countries of the region have continued to modify the rules of the electoral and constitutional game without calling into question the commitment of political elites to working through the rules to do so. In others the frustration of one side or another with the current system has vitiated the hopes raised by the democratic breakthroughs of 1989 and brought about the collapse of the fragile democratic institutions which became prominent during the transition from communist party rule. Parliamentary elections, it seems, can achieve a peaceful transition to democracy in systems where the old ruling elites are willing to share or surrender power and challengers are sufficiently organized, powerful and self-disciplined to assume responsibility for government. In the chapters that follow, we report on the first generation of parliaments to assume power after communist rule. By analyzing their experience, we hope to offer some insight into the prospects for a democratic outcome of the transition.

Notes

1. Jerry Hough warns, however, against exaggerating the extent of the anti-CPSU vote. He points out that of the 191 party secretaries of republics and regions who ran, 153 won (1989:14).

2. The exceptions are the Baltic Republics, where the popular fronts behaved as parties in nominating their own candidates, and Georgia, which held its republican elections in October 1990 under a mixed proportional and majoritarian electoral system in which 29 parties were registered, and formed six electoral blocs.

3. Yugoslav elections were held in 1992, but by then, Slovenia and Croatia had seceded, so the legal entity corresponding to Yugoslavia was a rump state dominated by Serbia.

4. The only that were not were Estonia, Latvia, Moldova, and Kirgizstan.

5. See note 4 above.

6. Calling the rump state of Serbia and Montenegro "Yugoslavia" only confirms the point.

7. The "extrication game" has been thoroughly analyzed in works on democratic transition by O'Donnell and Schmitter (1986); Przeworski (1991); di Palma (1990b); Karl and Schmitter (1991) and others, and applied to the Soviet and East European cases by Ekiert (1991); Hasegawa (1992); Remington (1990, 1992); and Bova (1991), among others.

8. Habituation is discussed as a phase in the democratization process outlined by Dankwart Rustow in his classic article on transitions to democracy. As he explains it, habituation involves learning on the part of major contenders that practices of accommodation and compromise are advantageous, or more so than stalemate and unregulated conflict (Rustow 1970:358-9). As some writers using the rational choice approach acknowledge, explanatory theories resting on assumptions of rational calculation are far more successful in modeling elite behavior than mass-level behavior (Tsebelis 1990:32-8). Indeed, as Herbert Kitschelt observes, the knowledge of actor identities and goals, and of rules, that is required for rational calculation is still often missing in the East European context. See Kitschelt (1992:9).

9. A threshold level of 5% applied to a small number of seats apportioned by voting for national party lists. 85% of the races for the lower house, the Sejm, were free of electoral thresholds in districts whose numbers of seats ranged from seven to seventeen.

10. Louisa Vinton compares the 1991 Sejm election results with the distribution of seats that would have occurred had the thresholds to representation in new 1993 election law been in force in 1991. She finds that some 18 small parties and groups that gained seats in the 1991 lower house would not have been represented, but only 2 parties still would have commanded more than 10% of the seats each. She observes, therefore, that the results would still have brought about instability and confrontation (1993:9). This is arguing ex post, however. It is not unreasonable to suppose that the parties, facing serious uncertainty about their chances, would have formed larger electoral coalitions ex ante.

11. In 1987 Gorbachev instituted multi-seat districts for 5% of the seats to the USSR Supreme Soviet as a means of cautiously expanding the degree of contestation in soviet races: more candidates ran than there were seats to fill in these new districts. However, the limited nature of the experiment is suggested by the fact that even those candidates who failed to win seats would be given the status of "reserve" deputies.

Second, Gorbachev's 1988 reforms expanding the union legislature designated that one third of the mandates (750) in the new Congress of People's Deputies would be reserved for representatives of public organizations. The USSR Congress then subsequently amended its electoral law to drop this provision for future elections (though of course none were ever held, since the USSR itself ceased to exist after 1991) and most of the republics, in adopting their own new electoral laws, did not build in reserved seats for public organizations. As Timothy Colton notes in his chapter in this book, however, Kazakhstan did use reserved seats.

12. Estonia's system was effectively proportional in that it used multi-seat districts, but the candidates were not identified by party on the ballot. Georgia used party lists.

13. In the USSR elections of 1989, this feature of the system led to the anomaly that an individual voter who was a member of a trade union, a professional association, certain amateur societies, and the communist party, might have the opportunity to cast a ballot in each of these organizations for a slate of deputies from that organization. The same voter, like all others, would also have two additional ballots to cast for deputies from his or her territorial district and national-territorial district. Therefore some individuals cast a half dozen or more votes, others only two.

14. The following discussion is based upon a series of interviews conducted in Moscow with politicians and political advisors in May and June 1993.

15. A valuable collection of some of the classic contributions to this discussion is Lijphart (1992b). A comparison of the ability of presidential and parliamentary systems to enact policy is a volume edited by Weaver and Rockman (1993).

References

Anweiler, Oskar. 1974. *The Soviets: The Russian Workers, Peasants, and Soldiers Councils, 1905–1921* trans. Ruth Hein. New York: Pantheon.

Bogdanor, Vernon. 1990. "Founding Elections and Regime Change." *Electoral Studies* 9: 288–294.

Bova, Russell. 1991. "Political Dynamics of the Post-Communist Transition," *World Politics* 44: 113–138.

Chiesa, Giulietto with Douglas Taylor Northrop. 1993. *Transition to Democracy: Political Change in the Soviet Union, 1987–1991*. Hanover and London: Dartmouth College; University Press of New England.

Dahl, Robert A. 1971. *Polyarchy: Participation and Opposition*. New Haven: Yale University Press.

di Palma, Giuseppe. 1990a. "Parliaments, Consolidation, Institutionalization: A Minimalist View," in Ulrike Liebert and Maurizio Cotta, eds., *Parliament and Democratic Consolidation in Southern Europe: Greece, Italy, Portugal, Spain, and Turkey*. Pp. 31–51. London: Pinter.

Ekiert, Grzegorz. 1991. "Democratization Processes in East Central Europe: A Theoretical Reconsidation," *British Journal of Political Science* 21: 285–314.

――――. 1990b. *To Craft Democracies: An Essay on Democratic Transitions*. Berkeley: University of California Press.

Embree, Gregory J. 1991. "RSFSR Election Results and Roll Call Votes," *Soviet Studies* 43: 1065–84.

Foster, Frances H. 1993. "Procedure as a Guarantee of Democracy: The Legacy of the Perestroika Parliament," *Vanderbilt Journal of Transnational Law* 26:1–109.

Hasegawa, Tsuyoshi. 1992. "The Connection between Political and Economic Reform in Communist Regimes," in Gilbert Rozman with Seizaburo Sato and Gerald Segal, eds., *Dismantling Communism: Common Causes and Regional Variations*. Pp. 59–117. Washington, DC, and Baltimore: Woodrow Wilson Center Press and Johns Hopkins University Press.

Helf, Gavin and Jeffrey W. Hahn. 1992. "Old Dogs and New Tricks: Party Elites in the Russian Regional Elections of 1990," *Slavic Review* 51: 511–530.

Heyns, Barbara and Ireneusz Bialecki. 1991. "Solidarnosc: Reluctant Vanguard or Makeshift Coalition?"*American Political Science Review* 85:3 51–370.

Hough, Jerry F. 1989. "The Politics of Successful Economic Reform," *Soviet Economy* 5: 3–46.

Jasiewiecz, Krzysztof. 1993. "Structures of Representation," in Stephen White, Judy Batt and Paul G. Lewis, eds., *Developments in East European Politics*. Pp. 124–146. Durham: Duke University Press.

Karl, Terry Lynn and Philippe C. Schmitter. 1991. "Modes of Transition in Latin America, Southern and Eastern Europe," *International Social Science Journal* 43: 269–284.

Kiernan, Brendan. 1993. *The End of Soviet Politics: Elections, Legislatures and the Demise of the Communist Party*. Boulder: Westview.

Kiernan, Brendan and Joseph Aistrup. 1991. "The 1989 Elections to the Congress of People's Deputies in Moscow," *Soviet Studies* 43: 1049–64.

Kitschelt, Herbert. 1992. "The Formation of Party Systems in East Central Europe," *Politics and Society* 20: 7–50.

Kolosov, V. A., N. V. Petrov, and L. V. Smirnyagin, eds. 1990. *Vesna 89: Geografiia i anatomiia parlamentskikh vyborov.* Moscow: Progress.

Körösenyi, Andras. 1991. "Revival of the Past or New Beginning? The Nature of Post-Communist Politics." *Political Quarterly* 62: 52–74.

Lijphart, Arend. 1984. *Democracies: Patterns of Majoritarian and Consensus Government in Twenty-One Countries.* New Haven: Yale University Press.

————. 1992a. "Democratization and Constitutional Choices in Czechoslovakia, Hungary and Poland, 1989–91," *Journal of Theoretical Politics* 4:207–223.

————, ed., 1992b. *Parliamentary versus Presidential Government* Oxford: Oxford University Press.

Linz, Juan J. and Alfred Stepan. 1992. "Political Identities and Electoral Sequences: Spain, the Soviet Union, and Yugoslavia," *Daedalus* 121: 123–137.

Mainwaring, Scott. 1993. "Presidentialism, Multipartism, and Democracy," *Comparative Political Studies* 26: 198–228.

McGregor, James. 1993. "How Electoral Laws Shape Eastern Europe's Parliaments," *RFE/RL Research Report* 2:4 (22 January), pp. 11–18.

Millard, Frances. 1992. "The Polish Parliamentary Elections of October 1991," *Soviet Studies* 44: 837–855.

Montgomery, Kathleen and Thomas F. Remington. (forthcoming), "Regime Transition and the 1990 Republican Elections," *Journal of Communist Studies.*

Nohlen, Dieter. 1984. "Changes and Choices in Electoral Systems," in Arend Lijphart and Bernard Grofman, eds., *Choosing an Electoral System: Issues and Alternatives.* Pp. 217–224. New York: Praeger.

Oates, Sarah. 1993. "Elected Officials, Political Groups, and Voting in Russia," *RFE/RL Research Report,* 2:33 (20 August), pp. 62–64.

O'Donnell, Guillermo and Philippe C. Schmitter. 1986. *Transitions from Authoritarian Rule: Tentative Conclusions about Uncertain Democracies* Baltimore: Johns Hopkins University Press.

Pridham, Geoffrey. 1990. "Parliaments in the Consolidation of Democracy: A Comparative Assessment of Southern European Experiences," in Ulrike Liebert and Maurizio Cotta, eds., *Parliament and Democratic Consolidation in Southern Europe: Greece, Italy, Portugal, Spain, and Turkey.* Pp. 225–248. London: Pinter.

Przeworski, Adam. 1991. *Democracy and the Market: Political and Economic Reforms in Eastern Europe and Latin America.* Cambridge: Cambridge University Press.

Remington, Thomas F. 1990. "Regime Transition in Communist Systems: The Soviet Case," *Soviet Economy* 6: 160–90.

————. 1992. "Reform, Revolution, and Regime Transition in the Soviet Union," in Gilbert Rozman with Seizaburo Sato and Gerald Segal, eds., *Dismantling Communism: Common Causes and Regional Variations.* Pp. 121–151. Washington, DC, and Baltimore: Woodrow Wilson Center Press and Johns Hopkins University Press.

Rustow, Dankwart A. 1970. "Transitions to Democracy." *Comparative Politics* 2: 337–64.

Schöpflin, George. 1991. "Post-Communism: Constructing New Democracies in Central Europe." *International Affairs* 67: 235–50.

Shafir, Michael. 1992. "Romania's Elections: More Change than Meets the Eye," RFE/RL *Research Report*, 1:44 (6 November), pp. 1–8.

Shugart, Matthew Soberg and John M. Carey. 1992. *Presidents and Assemblies: Constitutional Design and Electoral Dynamics.* Cambridge: Cambridge University Press.

Slider, Darrell. 1990. "The Soviet Union," *Electoral Studies* 9: 295–302.

Smith, Steven S. 1989. *Call to Order: Floor Politics in the House and Senate.* Washington, D.C.: Brookings Institution.

Tsebelis, George. 1990. *Nested Games.* Berkeley: University of California Press.

Urban, Michael E. 1990. *More Power to the Soviets: The Democratic Revolution in the USSR.* Aldershot, England and Brookfield, Vermont: Edward Elgar.

Vinton, Louisa. 1993. "Poland's New Election Law: Fewer Parties, Same Impasse?" *RFE/RL Research Report* 2:28 (9 July), pp. 7–17.

Weaver, R. Kent and Bert A. Rockman, eds. 1993. *Do Institutions Matter? Government Capabilities in the United States and Abroad* (Washington, D.C.: Brookings Institution).

White, Stephen. 1990. "Democratizing Eastern Europe: The Elections of 1990." *Electoral Studies* 9:277–287.

———. 1991. *Gorbachev and After* (Cambridge: Cambridge University Press).

Wightman, Gordon. 1991. "The Collapse of Communist Rule in Czechoslovakia and the June 1990 Parliamentary Elections," *Parliamentary Affairs* 44: 94–113.

Zubek, Voytek. 1993. "The Fragmentation of Poland's Political Party System," *Communist and Post-Communist Studies* 26: 47–71.

2

The New Political Leadership of Central Europe: The Example of the New Hungarian National Assembly

Gerhard Loewenberg

Three years after the appearance of parliamentary regimes based on competitive elections in Central Europe, the continuities and discontinuities between these regimes and their communist and pre-communist predecessors are of enormous concern to all observers. To what extent does the *nomenklatura* of the Communist regime continue to govern? Did communism merely freeze the pre-existing social and ethnic divisions in these societies, so that the demise of communism leads to a return of pre-communist alignments and conflicts? Or, did communism fundamentally transform these societies, destroying the old alignments and making room for a distinctively new political pattern? And if there is a new pattern, can its outline be discerned?

Answers to these important, indeed fateful questions, can be approached by examining the political institutions that structure social conflict in central Europe, and the political leaders who have assumed positions in them. If we focus on the Czech Republic, Hungary, and Poland, we observe sharp discontinuities between the post-communist regimes and their predecessors. In all three countries, new institutions of government or significant adaptations of their predecessors are in place. New political parties have arisen, and new rules govern elections of political leaders and policy-making processes. In form these structures may resemble those that existed under the communist regime but in fact they are modelled on parliamentarism as it developed in Western Europe after the Second World War. In this sense they comprise a set of arrangements reflecting the bitter experiences of parliamentary democracy between the world wars. These arrangements, sometimes called "rationalized parliament-arism," were designed to stabilize parliamentary democracy by various electoral and constitutional mechanisms (Tanchev 1993). They have succeeded in Western Europe but have never before been tried in this part of the world. It misrepresents events to refer to a return to parliamentary government in Central Europe because parliamentary government had at best a very short, interrupted life there before 1949, and when it existed it took forms that failed in Western Europe as well.

An entirely new political leadership inhabits these institutions. The selection of political leaders through competitive elections has replaced the communist system of one-party recruitment in all of Central Europe. Some of the political parties competing in these elections are new formations. Others are revivals of earlier parties that competed before 1939 and briefly between 1945 and 1949. In two of these three countries a succession of elections occurred within a short span of time. Czechoslovakia had two competitive parliamentary elections and a presidential election before the division of the country into the Czech Republic and the Republic of Slovakia on January 1, 1993. A year after its first at least partly free parliamentary election in 1989, Poland had a presidential election and within the following three years it had two fully free parliamentary elections. Hungary alone had a single free parliamentary election, and a referendum that had the effect of rejecting the direct election of the president. Thereby its first competitively elected National Assembly was able to serve a full four-year term.

In all three countries parliaments have assumed a central importance in the system of government but in one of them, Hungary, a unicameral parliament, the National Assembly, is the only nationally elected institution. That Assembly therefore provides a particularly good focus for an examination of the recruitment and composition of the new political elites of Central Europe for in Hungary all but perhaps a half dozen significant political leaders sit in parliament. This chapter describes the membership of the Hungarian National Assembly elected in 1990, the contrasts between this membership and the membership of parliament under the communist regime, the process that brought these members to power, the groups in society that the new membership appears to represent, some of the relevant attributes and skills of these leaders, and the prospects they have of becoming a newly established elite.

The Composition of the National Assembly

One way of describing the sharp break between the new political leadership of Hungary and its forerunners is to note that of the 386 members of the National Assembly elected in two ballots in March and April 1990, only twenty-one had ever served in a previous parliament: over 95 percent of the membership is new. Sixteen of the new MPs served in the immediately preceding assembly, five had actually served in parliament in the late 1940s, and one had served in both. In this respect the break between the new Hungarian parliament and its communist predecessors was similar to the sharp break that occurred in Poland, where despite the compartmentalized election that was designed to reserve seats for the ruling party, only 6 percent of the members elected in 1989 were incumbents (Olson 1993:434). In Czechoslovakia only slightly over 1 percent of the members of the Federal Assembly elected in 1990 had served in its communist predecessor. All of the new parliaments throughout the region were therefore astonishingly lacking in members with any previous parliamentary experience but, as we shall see, the transition to a democratic parliament followed a distinctive sequence in Hungary.

While twenty-eight parties competed for seats in the Hungarian Assembly, various provisions of the electoral law that we will discuss below (including a four percent minimum required for the allocation of seats to county and national lists) had the result that only six parties were successful. Three of these were entirely new—the Hungarian Democratic Forum (MDF), the Alliance of Free Democrats (AFD), and the Young Democrats (FIDESZ)—and three had existed in the past— the Independent Smallholders Party, the Hungarian Socialist Party, and the Christian Democratic People's Party. The Assembly is therefore a parliament of newcomers and of political amateurs, almost by necessity, because candidates for parliament in 1990 believed that they had to demonstrate that they had not been implicated in the failed communist regime. Even among the thirty-three successful candidates of the Socialist Party, organized out of the reform wing of the Hungarian Socialist Workers' Party that had governed the country since 1949, only six had sat in the previous Assembly and that Assembly, in any case, still bore most of the marks of a trivial, Communist-style parliament, although it was beginning to show some independence; one of the Socialist MPs had also served between 1948 and 1953. Nearly forty-three years—almost two generations— separated the last freely elected Hungarian Parliament from the National Assembly elected in 1990. This Assembly is therefore a new structure, playing a new role, and composed of new political leaders recruited by new rules.

Standard demographic measures of the composition of the Assembly can be used to distinguish it from the composition of its immediate predecessors. By conventional categories of age, education, and occupation, it is not the product of a social revolution but of a restoration. Hibbing and Völgyes (1991) have shown that "the new elites appear to be products of an old elite," "heavily male," "much better educated than the population as a whole," "amazingly white collar," and "middle aged." In all of these respects the membership of the Assembly elected in 1990 can be seen as more "traditional" than the membership of the last Assembly elected under the Communist regime.

The Hungarian Socialist Workers' Party, like communist parties throughout Eastern Europe, had characteristically composed parliament so that it would appear representative of society in salient respects. Over one-third of the Assembly elected in 1985 consisted of "workers," over one-fifth were women, and while over 70 percent had post-secondary education, most of these held degrees in technological or agricultural fields and were industrial or agricultural managers. Fewer than 4 percent were lawyers. Over three-fourths were communist party members although forty to forty-five independent candidates succeeded in entering this last of the communist-dominated Hungarian parliaments (Heinrich 1986). Of course the real political elite in Hungary before 1989 consisted not of members of the National Assembly but of about 100 communist politicians belonging to the governing party's politburo and secretariat. This elite had an even more pronounced "working class" appearance than did the National Assembly that it recruited. The "educational deficit" exhibited by these leaders, their lack of adequate professional skills and their predominantly blue-collar industrial and agricultural backgrounds contributed significantly to the weakening of their hold on the economy, and explains their increasing reliance on non-party specialists (Tökés 1990:54-55). The ascent of a new elite of intellectuals in 1989 can be explained in part by the growing recognition even within the Hungarian Socialist Workers' Party that the old party elite could no longer govern.

It is true that the first freely elected parliament vastly overrepresents the best educated portion of the population. Over 90 percent of its members have had college or university education, predominantly in the social sciences, broadly defined. Nearly half hold doctorates. Eight are candidates for doctorates conferred by the prestigious Hungarian Academy of Science, six hold such doctorates, and one is a full member of the Academy. By educational background there are seventy-three lawyers, 19 percent of the membership, although only two-thirds of these are practicing law. But the Assembly includes only twenty-nine women, less than 8 percent of its total. In these respects the Assembly elected in 1990 resembles many of the parliaments of Western Europe, whose composition is similarly the product of multi-party systems that overrepresent some groups in society and underrepresent others. These party systems tend to be socially segmented, skewing the composition of parliament in favor of the particular social groups that are party-organized. Furthermore, the electoral system in each country determines—sometimes quite unpredictably—the translation of party and voter preferences into parliamentary seats.

To be sure, the composition of legislatures varies not only across parties but also over time and across nations. Throughout this century, however, European parliaments have generally contained large numbers of members drawn from white collar occupations and from the professions. They have, moreover, included a growing proportion of members who earn their livelihood from the political professions (Loewenberg and Patterson 1978:68-75). This is what the Hungarian Parliament lacks. Paradoxically, freely elected parliaments are always less "representative" of their societies by standard demographic categories than are parliaments deliberately composed by a dominant party eager to compensate for the failure to represent political diversity by careful attention to social diversity. The occupations held by members of the last communist-dominated and the first competitively elected parliaments at the time they entered the chamber exhibit the characteristic differences between assemblies so differently recruited, as seen in Table 2.1.

However, although traditional in some respects, the membership of the Hungarian National Assembly also exhibits the characteristics of a new elite. At forty-five its median age is young in comparative perspective. Not only do over 95 percent of its members lack all previous parliamentary experience, but nearly one-third regard themselves as having suffered various forms of political deprivation under the previous regime. Many of the new insiders were outsiders in the communist era; most of them were simply non-players.

This snapshot of the aggregate membership of the new Assembly hides sharp distinctions between members belonging to the old parties and those belonging to the new ones. That comparison reveals the effect on the composition of the National Assembly of the new movements that entered Hungarian politics in the three years leading up to the elections of 1990. While the social composition of

competitively elected parliaments always varies by party, indicating
the impact of party on the recruitment of MPs, the inter-party contrast
in the Hungarian National Assembly helps to specify the ways in
which this is a new parliamentary elite. For example, the members
belonging to the old parties—the Smallholders, Socialists, and
Christian Democrats—average fifty-five years of age, while those
belonging to the new parties, the Democratic Forum, the Free
Democrats, and the Young Democrats, are fully thirteen years younger
on the average. This is due only in small part to the twenty-one
members of the Federation of Young Democrats, a party that had
originally limited its membership to those thirty or under, raising it
then to thirty-five before lifting the age limit altogether in

TABLE 2.1   A Comparison of the Occupational Composition of the Hungarian
National Assemblies Elected in 1985 and 1990 (in percent membership)

Occupation	1985 (n=386)	1990 (n= 386)
Industrial managers, business	**15.5**	**8.0**
Workers, employees, skilled trades	**14.2**	3.4
Farm managers	**1.9**	3.1
Physicians, veterinarians	**7.7**	**9.8**
Foremen	**7.5**	0.3
Managers of the coop/service sector	4.9	—
Local government	4.6	—
Teachers	4.4	**8.3**
Local, regional/party secretaries	3.9	—
University teachers	—	**9.8**
Lawyers	0.7	**8.8**
Scientists, engineers, architects	2.8	**8.0**
Writers, editors	—	**5.7**
Government employees	2.1	3.4
University staff	—	3.1
Retired politicians	4.1	—
Interest groups	3.8	2.3
Clergy	2.0	2.1
Artists	1.8	1.6
Mass media personnel	1.5	1.0
Trade union	2.1	0.3
Party employees	2.6	—
Military	1.0	0.3
Police officers	0.2	—
None	—	2.3
Not given	0.7	**18.4**
Total	100.0	100.0

Entries of 5 percent or higher in boldface.

Source: Heinrich, 1986; Handbook of the National Assembly, 1990.

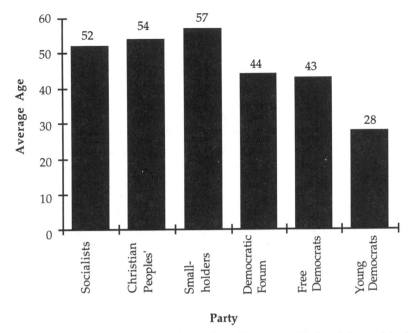

FIGURE 2.1 Average Age of Members of the Hungarian National Assembly, by Party

preparation for the election of 1994 (*The New York Times*, April 18, 1993). As Figure 2.1 demonstrates, the FIDESZ contingent of MPs elected in 1990 had an average age of twenty-eight at the time of their election.

The members of the new parties include a remarkable number of members of the free professions who are completing or have completed university education in law, the health sciences including medicine, and the humanities including history. By occupation they have disproportionately been university faculty members, physicians, dentists and pharmacists, engineers and architects, and research scientists.

What is remarkable is the extent to which these members are academic intellectuals including an astonishing number of historians, economists, sociologists, philosophers, writers, and actors and a surprisingly small number of individuals who can be regarded in any sense as political professionals. By contrast the members of the old parties are much more likely to have had their education in technical colleges if indeed they had gone beyond secondary school. By occupation they are drawn from agricultural or industrial management and from the political professions, including the labor unions and government service. Table 2.2 demonstrates that, since the new parties occupy three-fourths of the seats in the Assembly, it is their educational and occupational background that is the dominant note in the chamber.

That the Hungarian National Assembly is a parliament of intellectuals is most evident when one looks at the governmental leadership that has arisen from it. The Prime Minister and leader of the Democratic Forum, József Antall, is a historian of medicine. The President, a member of the Free Democrats, Arpád Göncz, is a novelist. The foreign minister, the minister of defense, and the speaker of the house are all professors of history (Kovacs 1990). The Minister of Industry and Trade is a professor of economics, the Minister of Urban Development is an architect, the Minister of Culture and Education is a University faculty member, two other cabinet members are engineers, and two are lawyers.

Thus while it is not exceptional in the European perspective that the Hungarian National Assembly is a highly educated parliament, it is exceptional that this is a parliament of academic intellectuals among whom few have had political occupations let alone parliamentary experience. How can one explain this distinguishing characteristic of its composition?

Determinants of Recruitment

Three aspects of the political environment leading to the 1990 election bear examination as determinants of parliamentary recruitment:

1. The stages by which the legitimacy of the communist regime eroded;
2. The political rules negotiated at the "round table";
3. The array of political parties that succeeded in nominating and electing candidates.

The economic reforms of the 1970s had led to the development of a middle class and had allowed some autonomy for those intellectual critics of the regime who avoided confrontational tactics. These groups gradually coalesced into politically oppositional groups as they became increasingly frustrated by the political limits maintained by the regime on civil liberties and on economic development. They were dissatisfied by the slow pace by which political restrictions were

TABLE 2.2 A Comparison of the Occupations of Members of the Old and New Parties (in percentages)

Current Occupation	Old Parties (n=98)	New Parties (n=288)
Lawyer	12	11
University faculty or research institution	11	24
School teacher	5	11
Clergy	0	3
Physician/dentist/ pharmacist	2	13
Engineer/architect	2	5
Journalist/editor	8	8
Skilled trades	8	2
Business	8	8
Agriculture	6	3
Veterinarian	5	2
Industrial manager	5	2
Government/civil service	14	1
Labor union	6	0
Social interest group	0	1
Other, none, not given	8	6
Total	100	100

being relaxed by the communist government even as that government moved increasingly to rely on non-party experts in economic policy making. Though change was slow it was persistent, moved by apprehension within government circles that in the absence of change there could be a repetition of the popular uprisings of 1956. As the inability of the Communist government to cope with the economic consequences of its policy of liberalization became increasingly evident in the 1980s, the erosion of the authority of the regime proceeded more rapidly though without manifest public participation. The withdrawal of support for the regime by the Soviet government under Gorbachev accelerated the process of erosion in 1987 and 1988.

This erosion set the stage in the spring of 1989 for negotiations between government and the opposition groups outside the communist-dominated parliament to arrange a peaceful transition from a one-party to a multi-party regime. The terms of the transition were influenced by the government's confidence that it could win a parliamentary majority in a free election and the opposition's confidence in its own electoral prospects. Both sides, in other words, preferred an uncertain electoral outcome to the growing crisis facing the existing regime. Neither dared to try to strengthen its negotiating position by appeals to the mass public, with the important exception of the referendum on holding an early presidential election which I will discuss below. The result was a non-public negotiation among elites to establish "the new rules of the political game and defining it as party politics" (Bruszt and Stark 1992: 47). The government guaranteed that parliament would enact the agreements that would be reached. Furthermore, it formally abandoned the communist party's *nomenklatura* authority for filling public jobs although in fact most of the incumbents in these positions remained in them (Tökes 1990: 55 - 61).

The framework for these extra-parliamentary negotiations became known as the "round table," a three-sided forum far more complex than its name implies. It consisted of fifty chief delegates representing the government, government controlled "social organizations," and the opposition groups—the whole staffed at times by 1000 experts. The round table was further organized into two main committees, twelve subcommittees, and two supplementary committees. It began to meet six days after the elections in Poland had led to a disastrous defeat for the communists who, however, held on to a majority of seats in parliament that had been reserved for them. Although the government tried in various ways to divide the opposition, the opposition groups realized the importance of reaching agreement among themselves and to that end organized their own informal "opposition round table" to deliberate in advance of the formal meetings with the government. Thus, in three months of negotiations, the way was prepared for the multi-party system that emerged in the winter of 1989-1990. And the habits developed in these sessions, notably the development of consensus among the leaders of the opposition groups, set the tone for much that followed (Bruszt 1990: 366-368).

The most important results of the roundtable negotiations for the composition of the National Assembly were agreement on a law guaranteeing freedom of association, a law on the organization of political parties, a law establishing a constitutional court, and an electoral law that served as gatekeeper to the new parliament. The electoral law was an interesting compromise. The communist government had favored maintaining the existing system of plurality voting in single-member constituencies with an added run-off second ballot, expecting that this would enable its candidates to sweep over a divided opposition. An alliance among the opposition groups supported proportional representation, the system that had been used in 1945 and 1947, combined with an equal number of seats to be contested in single-member constituencies (Kukorelli:140-142). A later compromise changed the balance between these two components of the system slightly in favor of proportional lists. Government and opposition were each anxious to reserve for themselves a privileged place in the coming political system. They were both therefore quite prepared to introduce a minimum requirement for the allocation of seats to candidates on regional and national lists. A similar restriction was later adopted in Czechoslovakia, where the minimum was set at 5 percent. In Poland, however, where competitive politics had been further developed when the first semi-free elections were held, no such restriction had been built in. The leaders of all groups in Hungary were also anxious to assure places in parliament for themselves, and so the system they proposed included not only regional lists of candidates but a national list that they could fully control, preserving a provision that had existed in the Hungarian electoral law since 1967.

The resulting Hungarian electoral system was based on the German model, familiar to Hungary's opposition political leaders who had had increasing contacts with German democrats throughout the 1980s. But the Hungarian variant departed from the German model by specifying that seats in Parliament would be allocated in a way that would be less proportional to the distribution of votes than the German system provides. In mixing single-member constituencies with regional and national lists from which seats would be assigned by proportional representation, the Hungarian system allowed parties to retain disproportionate numbers of seats won in the constituencies without greatly reducing their claim to a fully proportionate share of list seats. This gave a premium to parties with strong local appeal.

The gatekeeper function of the electoral law also consisted of regulations governing the nominating process, which had the result of reducing fifty-four registered parties to twenty-eight that actually put up candidates, among which only nineteen succeeded in putting up at least one county list and only twelve managed to nominate a national list. The gatekeeper function narrowed these twelve parties to six that were able to surmount the 4 percent minimum requirement for winning seats by proportional representation (Körösényi 1990; Racz 1991; Kukorelli 1991). The formula for translating votes into seats kept out of parliament six parties that among them had won 15 percent of the votes and therefore disproportionately favored the parties that were able to surmount the four percent threshold.

Furthermore, the mixed system ended up favoring the candidates of the Hungarian Democratic Forum to an unexpected extent because it was able to exploit its broad, "catch-all" appeal. This was particularly apparent in the two weeks between the two ballots that took place in the 176 single-member constituencies, when voters whose first choices did not make it to the run-off had to pick a second-best candidate (Hibbing and Patterson 1992). The Forum won 114 of these seats, 64 percent of the total, on the strength of 41 percent of the votes on the second ballot where plurality was sufficient to bring victory. Two weeks earlier, when a majority was required in a district, only five seats had been won, three of them by the Forum; it had won only 24 percent of the constituency vote on the first ballot. The increase in its vote share between the first and second ballot appears to have been due to its ability to attract voters whose first round choices had dropped out of the running, its ability, in other words, to be the second best alternative to many electors. In thirty-five constituencies a Democratic Forum candidate who had placed second or third on the first ballot actually won in the second round. Among all the other parties that feat was accomplished by only eight other candidates. These over-achieving candidates, who can be regarded as a surprising addition to the Democratic Forum contingent in Parliament, came disproportionately from Budapest and from a rural district in the eastern plains. They tended to be candidates born in the county in which they were campaigning, and by occupation were quite frequently school teachers—in short individuals with strong local roots.

All told the Forum alone ended up with more seats than it would have had under pure proportional representation, so that its candidate recruitment affected the composition of the Assembly unexpectedly and disproportionately. Also very significant was the fact that the electoral system, while denying to any party a majority of seats, limited the number of parties achieving representation in parliament to six. This created the condition for a three-party coalition government facing a multi-party opposition.

The recruitment of candidates was therefore structured by six political parties that passed through the gates defined by the electoral law. As it happened, the law affected them unpredictably and unequally. Among the parties that entered the Assembly only one can be associated with the pre-1990 communist ruling elite: the

Hungarian Socialist Party. In the two years leading up to the election, the governing Hungarian communist party had been decaying rapidly, its legitimacy ebbing in the eyes of the population, its leadership divided. A reform wing, using the name of the interwar socialist party, was the only organization related to the ruling party that won parliamentary seats; two other successor organizations failed to win any mandates. But two other parties that had antecedents in earlier regimes, in this case prior to 1947, succeeded in entering parliament. The old Independent Smallholders Party that had dominated the only fully free elections after the Second World War, those held in 1945, reappeared to advocate the validity of titles to land that existed prior to collectivization. The Christian Democratic People's Party was the second interwar party to reorganize itself successfully in the months leading up to the election. Its traditional appeal to Christian values resonated particularly in the rural areas. So there were three "nostalgic" parties that successfully participated in the recruitment of members of parliament, though none of them did particularly well in the elections. Among them they won only fourteen of the 176 seats in the single-member constituencies. With "compensation" mandates from the lists they elected ninety-eight MPs altogether, just about one-fourth of the total.

It was the three entirely new parties that altered the political landscape. Several political movements had been organized in 1987 and 1988 in opposition to the communist regime. They were based on the intellectual groupings that had enjoyed considerable autonomy in the last decade of communist rule. In the Hungarian setting where, as we have seen, the change of regime was negotiated among elites, these movements required no mass organizations to exercise influence. Among them the most effective were the Hungarian Democratic Forum and the Alliance of Free Democrats, distinguished from each other by the social and occupational backgrounds and intellectual directions of their followers rather than by programmatic differences. A youth organization originally affiliated with the Free Democrats formed its own party in the pre-election period as the Federation of Young Democrats. These three groups moved easily into the vacuum created by the decay of communism by becoming the principal negotiators at the "round table" that prepared the outline of a new regime, as we have noted. Thereupon they transformed themselves into political parties in the sense of recruiting parliamentary candidates and organizing campaigns. These three new parties and the three "nostalgic" parties therefore dominated the political recruitment process in the winter of 1989-90.

The transformation of oppositional movements into political

parties was limited so far as grass roots organization with defined membership was concerned; the incentive for transforming themselves into "mass parties" was not strong. The result was that the elections of 1990, while dominated by the parties, had a remarkably low voter turnout: 65 percent in the first round and 45 percent in the second. By contrast, the election in Czechoslovakia two months later had a 96 percent turnout.

All parties recruited a substantial number of candidates who had legal education. With seventy-three members, those trained in the law constituted the largest contingent in the Assembly. The candidates of the Democratic Forum were distinguished by the remarkable number of individuals with medical degrees and degrees in history and philosophy. By contrast, Table 2.3 shows that individuals with degrees in the social sciences were more numerous among the candidates of the Free Democrats and the Young Democrats.

National party leaders had great influence in the selection of candidates. The electoral law provided for nominations in the single-member constituencies by petition but the national parties managed to influence these local nominations considerably. However, their principal influence was on the composition of the regional and the national lists of candidates. Since an individual was permitted to compete in the single member constituencies as well as on the regional lists and on the national list, the national leaders could almost guarantee election to those whom they wanted in Parliament. Furthermore, the application of "unused" votes in the constituencies and for the regional lists unexpectedly led to the election of ninety of the members of the new Assembly—nearly a quarter of the total—from among the national list candidates, those directly selected by the national leadership. Since the Democratic Forum had swept the constituencies, they gained only ten members from their national list; the Socialists and the Young Democrats received proportionately the largest number of these "compensation" mandates, as demonstrated in Table 2.4. Among the national list candidates selected by the national party leadership, it is not surprising that there were fewer members from the free professions and somewhat more members whose backgrounds were in managerial, interest group, administrative, and other semi-political professions.

Establishment of the New Leadership

Whether the new party system develops durable roots in Hungarian society and whether the new leaders that entered parliament in 1990 have prospects of establishing themselves as a new political class

TABLE 2.3 Educational Background of Members of the Hungarian National Assembly, by Party (in percentages)

Field of Highest Degree or Diploma	MDF	AFD	Small-holders	Socialists	FIDESZ	Christian People's
Law/ history	17	30	22	7	29	50
Philosophy	12	8	0	7	12	5
Medicine/ dentistry	20	9	0	7	0	0
Social sciences	10	14	16	39	30	1
Journalism	3	5	0	7	0	0
Natural sciences/ engineering	9	4	13	7	0	5
Horticulture/ agricultural sciences	3	1	13	0	6	5
Veterinary medicine	4	1	9	4	0	0
Theology	2	6	3	0	0	5
Business	2	0	6	0	6	0
Education	5	8	3	7	0	0
Other, none, not given	13	14	15	15	17	29
Total	100	100	100	100	100	100

depends on their representational links to the electorate as well as on their ability to demonstrate the political skills that make parliamentary government work. We turn therefore to a discussion first of their links to those whom they represent and then to some aspects of their behavior in parliament.

While it is possible to explain how a particular set of political leaders, drawn in considerable measure from among academic intellectual circles, managed to assume a dominant place in the Hungarian National Assembly, it is far more difficult to estimate whom they represent in Hungarian society, or whom they are seen to

TABLE 2.4   Types of Constituencies Held by MPs by Party (in percentages)

Types of Constituency	Democratic Forum (n=165)	Free Democrats (n=90)	Small-holders (n=44)	Socialists (n=33)	FIDESZ (n=21)	Christian Democrats (n=20)
Single-member	69	38	27	3	5	14
County list	25	37	36	42	38	38
National list	6	26	36	55	57	48
Total	100	101	99	100	100	100

represent. One clue may be found in voter attachment to the parties that succeeded in winning parliamentary seats. Low voter participation and the volatility of voter preferences demonstrated in voting shifts between the two ballots suggest that this attachment was weak in the election of 1990. Indeed it would not have been possible for voters to develop an identification with the new parties or, except for the oldest cohort in the electorate, to have had a residual identification with the "nostalgic" parties. Attachment to the previously ruling Hungarian Socialist Workers' Party may have been strong in some sections of the population, but the division of that party into three successor parties fragmented the loyalty of that part of the electorate that may have had affinity to the old government. By some analyses one-fourth of the electorate supported the socialist left parties (Racz 1991:124-25), but the electoral system translated that support into just thirty-three seats, 9 percent of the total. These MPs faced the challenge of demonstrating their difference from the old regime, while serving as the magnet for those sections of the population who continued to support that regime or who saw in the Socialists an alternative to the present governing coalition.

Another sort of evidence of the connections between the elected parliamentarians and their constituents comes from aggregate analyses of voting behavior in the 1990 election. These analyses indicate a distribution of support for the parties that fits historic alignments between urban and rural electorates and between the trans-danubian region in the west and the plains to the east, signs that the electorate's response to the parties reflected some durable attachments.

Finally, there is evidence that the candidates for parliament had local roots. In view of the deep geographic and social dislocations that occurred in Hungary over the past two generations, it is striking that 47 percent of the members for whom we have the necessary data represent constituencies located in the counties in which they were born. The relationship between county of birth and location of constituency was even stronger for the Hungarian Democratic Forum than for the other parties, in part because of the disproportionate number of victories it won in the single-member constituencies. MPs for single-member constituencies proceeded to regard constituency service as an important activity, an example that was emulated to some extent in their home areas by MPs who had won seats on the proportional lists.

The ability of the new leadership to establish itself depends not only on its ties to its constituencies in Hungarian society, but on its ability to acquire and exhibit the skill to make the parliamentary system work to resolve the problems that this society faces. We turn therefore to a discussion of some aspects of the behavior of the new elite in parliament. The experience of the negotiations at the round table between the governing party and the opposition movements, and the experience of the opposition movements in negotiating a consensus among themselves in an informal opposition round table, bred habits of compromise that were carried into the newly elected National Assembly. The opposition movements had concluded during the summer of 1989 that unless they stood together on the issue of the electoral law and on the constitutional revision that paved the way to a transition to a multi-party parliament, the governing party would prevail.

However, the opposition was divided on one significant issue, that of holding a presidential election prior to the parliamentary election, which the governing communist party set as the price for all other agreements. The communists expected to win that election with a popular leader of their reform wing, Imre Pozsgay. The Hungarian Democratic Forum took the pragmatic view that it was necessary to accept this price. However, the Free Democratic Alliance and the Young Democrats were not prepared to go along. In their one departure from the elites' general reluctance to appeal to the public, these two groups gathered the necessary signatures to hold a national referendum on this question, in which an early presidential election was rejected by the narrowest majority of 50.1 percent of the votes. This was a formative event for the new republic. This division among the opposition groups stood in the way of an all-party governing coalition after the election. It presaged the division in parliament between a governing coalition and a strong opposition. Furthermore, by avoiding the establishment of a popularly elected presidency, the outcome of the referendum led to the primacy of the cabinet and parliament in the new political system. The president subsequently elected by the National Assembly did attain unforeseen influence because of his ability to challenge the constitutionality of legislation by bringing it before the new Constitutional Court before signing it, but this did not alter the centrality of the National Assembly as the only popularly elected institution.

The division over the popular election of the presidency, between the Free Democrats and the Young Democrats on the one hand and the Hungarian Democratic Forum on the other, crystallized the alignment between government and opposition in the Assembly after the election. The Forum, with the largest number of seats, brought the Smallholders and the Christian Democratic People's Party into a governing coalition that held nearly 60 percent of the seats, a secure majority but short of the two-thirds vote required for constitutional changes and for a wide range of important legislation. Provisions in the parliamentary procedures that the new Assembly had inherited from the old required a two-thirds vote on many issues, a communist concession to the non-party minority that had entered the Assembly in 1985. Now these provisions compelled the governing parties to reach important accommodations with the opposition (Kònya 1992; Tölgyessy 1992). In return for changes in procedure that limited the need for two-thirds votes, the governing parties agreed to support a Free Democratic leader, Arpád Göncz, for the Presidency of the Republic, an office to be filled by a vote in the Assembly rather than in a national election. Furthermore, they agreed to allocate committee chairmanships among all parties in proportion to their strength. A constitutional change requiring a "constructive no-confidence vote" to oust the Prime Minister was part of the same compromise, a compromise widely criticized in the press because it seemed to have been a deal among party leaders arranged outside the parliamentary process.

The new Assembly was to some extent influenced by the evolution of the last parliament elected under the communist regime. In that Parliament a constitutional amendment had been adopted expanding the lawmaking competence of the Assembly and restricting the power of the government to issue decrees (Rácz 1992). The new Assembly insisted on exercising this recently expanded lawmaking authority extensively, encouraged by the propensity of the Constitutional Court to refer political questions to Parliament for resolution (Klingsberg 1993:44-48). It therefore approached the agenda of political and economic issues that it confronted with the determination to enact a large volume of new legislation. Consequently lawmaking became its principal activity, taking precedence over the supervision of administrative agencies, public deliberation, constituency service, and the range of other functions that European parliaments perform.

A large part of the legislative process naturally occurred in the committees, where the parties were represented in proportion to their strength. As in most European parliaments, a considerable number of members of the Assembly were in fact part-time politicians actively pursuing their private occupations; 100 MPs served on no committees at all. On the other hand, sixty served on more than one committee. Important committees were chaired by opposition parties. The Free Democrats chaired the appropriations and revenue committee, the committee on local government, and the special audit committee; the Young Democrats chaired human rights and national security; the Socialists chaired foreign affairs. Vice chairmanships were similarly apportioned among the parties, so that where a member of the governing parties chaired a committee its vice-chairs included an opposition party member. Furthermore, no party held a majority on any committee. Since parliamentary lawmaking is lawmaking by parliamentary committees, parliamentary lawmaking depended upon inter-party compromise. The pattern is closer to the German than to the British model.

The composition of the Assembly's committees reflected the common experience in specialized committee systems that members gravitate to the committees of their expertise. Not surprisingly, 90 percent of the members of the Committee on the Constitution, Legislation and Justice, were lawyers, as were nearly 50 percent of the members of the Committee on Local Government, Public Administration, and Internal Security. Lawyers also dominated the committee on procedure. Almost half of the members of the Committee on Budget, Taxes and Finances were economists by education, and nearly half of the members of the Committee on Social and Health affairs were physicians. Nearly 40 percent of the members of the agriculture committee were trained in the agricultural sciences. Theologians were strongly represented on the Human Rights committee. Thus parliamentary lawmaking was also lawmaking by specialists, and in that sense by special interests. Reconciling party interests with professional and group interests was therefore central to parliamentary lawmaking.

Finally, of course, parliamentary lawmaking required constant negotiation between cabinet ministries which initiated almost all important legislation and the Assembly which had to enact it. In confronting the enormous legislative agenda of a nation undergoing fundamental political, social, and economic changes, the style of the new elite has been a style of accommodation. It enabled parliament to enact a large volume of important legislation, often with the support of the parties in the opposition, in the environment of stable cabinet government (Ilonszki 1993:10). In the process it bred a cadre of experienced parliamentarians, at least some of whom developed the ambition to pursue parliamentary careers.

Conclusions

While Hungary shared with Poland and Czechoslovakia a peaceful transition from one-party to multi-party rule in 1989 and 1990, bringing new elites to power in all three countries, the manner of the transition was distinct in each, even if they influenced each other. The transition in Hungary was the most gradual of the three, for the communist regime in that country never returned to the oppressiveness it exhibited before the revolution of 1956. Apprehension about reigniting that revolution moved it gradually to a more liberal economic policy, a relaxation of travel restrictions, and greater tolerance for freedom of expression so long as it was not politically confrontational. This gradual relaxation of totalitarian control diminished the incentive to organize oppositional groups in the mass population. By the mid-1980s the political alignment that existed beneath the surface of communist rule was an alignment among four elite groups that expressed the reality of a political order that was no longer monolithic.

These groups were :

1. The established communist party bureaucracy;
2. The group of reform communists aware of the incompetence of the established bureaucracy;
3. An urban intelligentsia consisting of intellectuals and technical experts;
4. Members of the free professions and intellectuals who were local and regional notables.

None of these groups had deep roots in Hungarian society; there were no mass organizations that supported them, as Solidarity supported the trade union leadership in Poland. The four groups were united by a desire to negotiate the institutions that would make possible multi-party politics and by an aversion to mobilizing the public. And it was this negotiation among elites uncertain about their standing in the public but prepared to take their chances in multi-party elections that shaped the transition by which the old Hungarian communist elite was replaced in the election of 1990 (Bruszt and Stark 1992: 19). It also had a formative influence on the polity that emerged.

After the first free elections in 45 years brought a new political leadership into a newly powerful parliament for what turned out to be a full four-year term, the second free election will test how well that leadership has been established in Hungary. Though a substantial turnover in the composition of the National Assembly would fit the pattern of other newly democratized parliaments, the degree of continuity between the leadership composing the first two competitively elected assemblies will affect the institutionalization of that leadership in the newly democratic parliament. The political parties, which are the principal agents of leadership recruitment, the attitudes of the public toward candidates and issues, which will affect party strengths, and the general attachments of the public to the new political institutions will all influence the prospects of Hungary's new parliamentary elite and reveal the extent to which it has found roots in Hungarian society.

Unlike the experience in the neighboring states of Central Europe, the existing parties in Hungary exhibit durability as organizations. Divisions exist within some of the parties, notably within the Hungarian Democratic Forum, but they do not seem to portend disintegration. For example the conspicuous dissidence of Istvan Csurka, once deputy leader of the Forum, received only very limited support at the 1993 party congress and eventually led to Csurka's ouster from the party (*The Economist*, March 13, 1993, 5; *The New York Times*, June 8, 1993). Dissidents ambitious to form new political parties face the obstacles created by the electoral law.

Most of the political issues that were discussed in the electorate as the first term of the parliament neared its conclusion were issues with which parliament had grappled, including the privatization of industry and agriculture, the restructuring of state firms, the development of a social safety net for the dislocations accompanying the creation of a market economy, and compensation for former owners of land and property seized by previous regimes. In this respect the parliamentary agenda became the agenda of public political discourse.

The surprisingly rapid economic changes that occurred in Hungary since 1989, and public expectations about the consequences of these changes, only modestly affected public attachment to the party system and the new political institutions (Hibbing and Patterson 1993:13,15; Mishler and Rose 1993:9). These changes translated more substantially into shifts of support among the array of government and opposition parties. The Hungarian Socialist Party was positioned to be the beneficiary of voters distressed by economic reversals but it was not an anti-system party. The other "nostalgic" parties were part of the governing coalition and therefore less well placed to benefit from the normal pendulum swing against the government. The principal beneficiary of a normal electoral swing was the Federation of Young Democrats because of its unusual ability to appeal both to youthful idealism in society generally and to opponents of existing government policy. Thus economic change translated into changes in party strength rather than into changes of attachment to the new regime.

Mass movements challenging the new political institutions were evident only in isolated cases. There was widespread awareness that the fate of two million members of the Hungarian language community in neighboring countries was a potential issue around which extra-parliamentary action could crystallize. The new political leadership therefore made special efforts to support European efforts to protect minorities. For this as well as for economic reasons, Hungarian membership in the European community was an important goal of the new regime.

There is little evidence that the new political institutions and the political leadership which inhabits them are merely window dressing hiding the continuation of a communist regime, a reestablished *ancien regime*, or an unorganized mass public ready to be mobilized. The second freely elected parliament is certain to include a large number of new members, as parties now in opposition win new strength and as individuals who sacrificed their private careers to serve in the first democratic parliament resume these careers. Toward the end of the first parliamentary term only 40 percent of the members of the Assembly indicated that they wished to run for reelection (Ilonszki 1993:8-9). While the composition of Hungary's new leadership is bound to change and its intellectual eminence is likely to decline, that change would also add to the influence of those who continue into a second parliamentary term. They would constitute a cadre of experienced politicians to leaven a political class initially composed of political amateurs. In that way continuity and change in the new political class would mirror the pattern of development of democratic elites in other democratizing societies.

Hungary today is a state with drastically different boundaries from the Hungary of the interwar years. It is far more homogeneous ethnically. Its economic system has been changing steadily, at least since the 1970s, and far more quickly since 1989. The strength of the new Hungarian political leadership described in this chapter was its independence from the communist regime that this leadership wanted to reform. Its weakness was the looseness of its ties to a Hungarian society different from the pre-communist society and rapidly changing in the final decades of communist rule. As succeeding cohorts of leaders attempt to strike roots in the new society that is evolving, their effort is helped by the political institutions and the recruitment process that the first generation of political leaders created. Those institutions and processes make the establishment of the new political leadership possible though they cannot guarantee its success.

References

Bruszt, László. 1990. "1989: The Negotiated Revolution in Hungary." *Social Research* 57:365-87.

Bruszt, László, and David Stark. 1992. "Remaking the Political Field in Hungary: From the Politics of Confrontation to the Politics of Competition." In *Eastern Europe in Revolution*, ed. Ivo Banac. Ithaca, NY: Cornell University Press.

Goldfarb, Jeffrey. 1992. *After the Fall: The Pursuit of Democracy in Central Europe.* New York: Basic Books.

Heinrich, Hans-Georg. 1986. *Hungary: Politics, Economics, and Society.* Boulder, CO: Rienner Publishers, Inc.

Hibbing, John R., and Samuel C. Patterson. 1992. "A Democratic Legislature in the Making: The Historic Hungarian Elections of 1990." *Comparative Political Studies* 24:430-54.

Hibbing, John R., and Samuel C. Patterson. 1993. "Public Trust in the New Parliaments of Central and Eastern Europe." Presented at the meeting of the Research Committee of Legislative Specialists of the International Political Science Association, Paris, France.

Hibbing, John R., and Ivan Volgyes. 1992. "Political Elite Composition in the Wake of a Peaceful Revolution: Hungary 1990." Presented at the annual meeting of the Southern Political Science Association, Atlanta, GA.

Hungarian National Assembly. 1990. *Handbook.*

Ilonszki, Gabriella. 1993. "From Regime Change to Consolidation: An Institution in Search of Roles." Presented at the meeting of the Research Committee of Legislative Specialists of the International Political Science Association, Paris, France.

Klingsberg, Ethan. 1993. "Hungary: Safeguarding the Transition." *East European Constitutional Review* 2:44-48.

Kónya, Imre. 1992. "Oppositionelle und Reformer." In *Wandel durch Repräsentation-Repräsentation im Wandel*, ed. Uwe Thaysen and Hans Michael Kloth. Baden-Baden: Nomos Verlagsgesellschaft.

Körösényi, András. 1990. "Hungary." *Electoral Studies* 9:337-45.

Kovács, Mária M. n.d. "Intellectuals and Politics: A View from Hungary." Unpublished manuscript.

Kukorelli, István. 1991. "The Birth, Testing and Results of the 1989 Hungarian Electoral Law." *Soviet Studies* 43:137-56.

Loewenberg, Gerhard, and Samuel C. Patterson. 1978. *Comparing Legislatures.* Boston: Little, Brown.

Mishler, William, and Richard Rose. 1993. "Public Support for Legislatures and Regimes in Eastern and Central Europe." Presented at the meeting of the Research Committee of Legislative Specialists of the International Political Science Association, Paris, France.

Olson, David M. 1993. "Compartmentalized Competition: The Managed Transitional Election System of Poland." *Journal of Politics* 55:415-41.

Rácz, Attila. 1992. "Verfassungsrechtliche Veränderungen und die Durchsetzung des Parlamentarismus in Ungarn." In *Wandel durch Repräsentation- Repräsentation im Wandel,* ed. Uwe Thaysen and Hans Michael Kloth. Baden-Baden: Nomos Verlagsgesellschaft.

Racz, Barnabas. 1991. "Political Pluralisation in Hungary: the 1990 Elections." *Soviet Studies* 43:107-36.

Tökés, Rudolf L. 1990. "Hungary's New Political Elites: Adaptation and Change, 1989-90." *Problems of Communism* 39:44-65.

Tölgyessy, Péter. 1992. "Die "ausgehandelte" Revolution zwischen Apathie und Zivilgesellschaft." In *Wandel durch Repräsentation- Repräsentation im Wandel,* ed. Uwe Thaysen and Michael Kloth. Baden-Baden: Nomos Verlagsgesellschaft.

Weigle, Marcia A. 1992. "The Consolidation of Civil and Political Society in Post-Communist Regimes: Central Europe and Russia." Presented at the annual meeting of the Midwest Political Science Association, Chicago.

Tanchev, Evgeni. 1993. "Parliamentarism Rationalized." *East European Constitutional Review* 2:33-35.

Acknowledgments

I am indebted to Vera Alács, Office of Foreign Relations, Hungarian National Assembly, for making available the complete set of biographical information on members of parliament published in its biographical handbook, and the list of committee memberships. Professor Stephen L. Sass of the University of Iowa skillfully translated and interpreted the biographical sketches and did a preliminary coding. Professor John R. Hibbing of the University of Nebraska generously shared with me the complete election returns he had gathered in his own research on the elections of 1990.

For the analyses of these data I had the excellent assistance of Jean C. Willard, a graduate of the University of Wisconsin in sociology, and Brian D. McCuen, a graduate student in political science at the University of Iowa.

My interest in the Hungarian parliament developed out of my work in the East-West Parliamentary Practice Project. To the Hungarian member of its Steering Committee, Andras Baka, a former member of the National Assembly and now a Judge on the European Court of

Human Rights, I owe a particular debt of gratitude for his patient explanations of many aspects of the Hungarian political system.

As always I have depended on Michelle L. Wiegand, administrator of the Comparative Legislative Research Center of the University of Iowa, for editorial advice and for managing the facilities that are indispensable to research on legislatures outside the United States.

3

Professional Engagement
and Role Definition
Among Post-Soviet Legislators

Timothy J. Colton

This short essay offers a preliminary and schematic precis of some patterns turned up in an ongoing inquiry into comparative post-Soviet legislative politics. The focus of the work has been the attitudes and conduct of individual members of legislative elites in the early transitional era.* To use the methodological categories of the subfield in the United States, mine is a "behavioral study," as distinct from an "institutional study" or a "process-oriented study." Its main purpose is to discover and map principal aspects of legislators' activity, and thereby to facilitate the systematic description of that behavior, the formulation of hypotheses for in-depth testing, and the elaboration of a baseline for future developmental research. What follows is a discussion of certain phenomena uncovered in two specific areas: (1) lawmakers' engagement with their tasks and (2) their conceptions of their roles.

Data and Institutional Setting

My principal research tool has been a survey done in a span of nine months in 1991-92 among deputies in four legislative assemblies. The self-administered questionnaire was similar but not identical in the four legislatures. It was distributed and collected in the soon-to-be-extinguished Supreme Soviet of the Soviet Union in April-May 1991, almost simultaneously among members and affiliated deputies of the Supreme Soviet of the Russian Federation, in the Supreme Soviet of Ukraine in November-December 1991, and in the Supreme Soviet of

Kazakhstan in January 1992. Seven hundred and seventy-two deputies responded in total. Although the first two polls preceded the putsch of August 1991 and the collapse of Communist Party rule, enough had already changed in political conditions and processes for them to be reliably characterized as "post-Soviet."[1] Judiciously interpreted to take into account the turbulent historical context, the data gleaned can be a rich source of information and speculation.

In the USSR legislature, the questionnaire was directed to 115 deputies—a one-third random sample of those who had served in the Supreme Soviet for no less than a year—and returned, filled out, by 104 deputies, or better than 90 percent. In the other three legislatures, where circumstances made sampling impractical, the questionnaire was distributed to the entire population of deputies and lower response rates were accepted.

For the Russian Federation, the target was the 251 members of the Supreme Soviet and the approximately 400 other deputies in the Congress of People's Deputies at the time who were "participating in the work of the Supreme Soviet," i.e., sitting as members of its committees and subcommittees without having floor rights. Three hundred and seven responses were obtained, 159 from the plenary members and 148 from the associate members. Ukrainian Supreme Soviet deputies numbered 450 in all, although 40 to 50 of them were not so much as registering for sessions; 237 responses were received. Kazakhstan provided the thinnest yield by far—a disappointing 124 questionnaires returned out of 360 deputies.

Let me sketch for the non-specialist reader the legislative machinery in the governmental settings at hand in Moscow, Kiev, and Almaty.

USSR. Deputies were elected in 1989 from: (1) "territorial districts" partitioned on the basis of equal votes; (2) "national-territorial districts" drawn to reflect the ethnic composition of the electorate and administrative boundaries; and (3) officially approved "public organizations" such as the Communist Party and the Academy of Sciences. The Congress of Deputies met only several times a year until its dissolution in late 1991. The standing parliament it selected, the USSR Supreme Soviet, was bicameral, albeit with little differentiation in function between houses. All deputies from territorial districts served in the Council of the Union and all from national-territorial districts in the Council of Nationalities; deputies from public organizations were allocated equally to the two chambers. My sample of 104 was spread evenly between the two chambers, 52 deputies each; 32 deputies were from territorial districts, 44 from national-territorial districts, and 28 from public organizations.

Russia. As with the USSR, there was and is both an unwieldy Congress of Deputies and a relatively compact Supreme Soviet, bifurcated into two chambers. The 1,068 deputies in the congress were chosen from territorial and national-territorial districts, no seats being reserved here for organizations. Of the 159 Supreme Soviet deputies in my Russian sample, 90, elected in territorial districts, belonged to the Council of the Federation in 1991, while 69, from national-territorial districts, were members of the Council of Nationalities. Of the 148 associate deputies in the sample (members of the Congress but committee members only in the Supreme Soviet), 140 were from territorial districts and only 8 from national-territorial districts.

Ukraine. Constitutionally, Ukraine presents the simplest picture. Its Supreme Soviet is unicameral and without a parental Congress. All members were elected in 1990 from territorial districts.

Kazakhstan. Like Ukraine, Kazakhstan has a unicameral Supreme Soviet and no Congress. Like the USSR, however, its electoral law in 1990 mandated designation of one-quarter of the deputies by public organizations. Of my 124 respondents in Almaty, 103 (83.1 percent) were from territorial districts and the remaining 21 (16.9 percent) from organizations.

In sociodemographic terms, the deputies questioned were roughly representative of their legislative units. They were overwhelmingly male: 80.8 percent in the USSR Supreme Soviet, 96.2 percent in Ukraine, 89.5 percent in Kazakhstan (the gender question was inadvertently omitted from the Russian survey). They were mostly middle-aged, the modal age group in all four soviets being the forties. Healthy majorities had a higher education: 64.4 percent for the USSR parliament, 90.6 percent for Russia, 93.0 percent for Ukraine, and 75.0 percent for Kazakhstan. Occupational background was predominantly white-collar, with the USSR sample, as a residue of uncompetitive electoral procedures and quotas, having the greatest number of blue-collar members (42.3 percent workers and collective farm peasants, versus 8.5 percent of Russian deputies, 11.4 percent in Ukraine, and 19.4 percent in Kazakhstan).

I was not able to ask the USSR or Russian deputies their ethnic identification. In Ukraine, where this was allowed, 73.8 percent were ethnic Ukrainians, 21.9 percent Russians, and 4.2 percent other minorities. In Kazakhstan, 50.8 percent were members of the titular Kazakh nationality, 33.1 percent were Russians, and 16.1 percent belonged to other groups.[2] In the bitterly divided USSR and RSFSR Supreme Soviets, I was kept from posing detailed questions about electoral district (or organization), for fear it would compromise anonymity. In Ukraine and Kazakhstan, I gathered more such information.

The deputies polled were a mix of rank-and-file members and holders of leadership positions. Except for full members of the Russian Supreme Soviet, the proportion of the respondents who occupied a leadership post in a legislative commission or subcommission ranged from about 10 percent to about 30 percent. The abnormally high number of leaders among the Russian full deputies (almost 60 percent) reflects a selection bias in the survey; it also catches the Russian Supreme Soviet's tendency toward multiplication of commissions and subcommissions.[3]

Measures of Engagement

In getting a fix on post-Soviet legislators, it is crucial to know how they have engaged with their formally designated roles. The pre-*perestroika* soviets were notorious for being amorphous, amateur "rubberstamps" for the ruling party. Pivotal to Mikhail Gorbachev's scheme for political reform, enunciated and implemented at the USSR level in 1988-89 and carried forward in most of the successor states, was the desire to upgrade the soviets into bodies of dedicated professionals. This was to be done by freeing up elections from the tutelage of the party apparatus, elevating the status of elected officials, and improving their material welfare and working conditions. In theory, legislative activity was to be reconfigured into a full-time occupation and a lifelong career, capable of attracting and retaining the best and the brightest for public service.

Drawing on the production values of the traditional Soviet culture, Gorbachev and his allies construed the institutional re-engineering as a kind of labor reform: lawmaking was a form of work that had been undervalued in the past but henceforth would be properly recognized, rewarded, and orchestrated. To employ Nelson Polsby's well-known typology, the revived soviets were envisaged as effective "transformative legislatures," deliberative bodies with a capacity "to mold and transform proposals from whatever source into laws," as distinct from "arena legislatures" functioning as "formalized settings for the interplay of significant political forces," without emphasis on the end product (Polsby 1975:277).

Some of the effects posited have been realized, but far from all. If anything, my survey data overestimate the new deputies' involvement in transformative (and other) activity, as it is safe to assume that few returns were obtained, at least for the three soviets where I had to distribute the questionnaire broadside, from the least active of the members. Some inferences can, nonetheless, be drawn.

Caveats duly registered, the data do show the members to be busily enmeshed in many aspects of normal legislative activity. Almost without exception, they described taking part in floor debates, committee hearings, and drafting teams, interacting with constituents and social groups, conducting oversight of government bureaus, and interceding with state officials on behalf of voters. The commitment of time and energy is obviously far greater than for the *poslushnyi deputat*, the "obedient deputy" of the Soviet past.

Table 3.1 pulls together several indicators of commitment to assigned responsibilities. About three-quarters of the USSR deputies and of the full-fledged Russian deputies were committed full-time to legislative work and drew full-time salaries for it. Among the Russian deputies without Supreme Soviet seats, the proportion dipped below 50 percent. Among the Ukrainian and Kazakhstan deputies, it was considerably lower still. Even in the USSR Supreme Soviet, professionalization in the sense of five-day-a-week allocation of effort to parliamentary business was not fully attained. In Ukraine

TABLE 3.1   Deputies' Commitment to Deputy's Activities (in percentages)

	USSR	RUS (Mem)	RUS (Ass)	UKR	KAZ
Works full-time as a deputy in the given legislature	73.1	73.6	45.9	34.6	23.4
Serves simultaneously on another soviet	7.7	27.0	22.3	47.7	44.4
Member of a deputies' group or fraction	81.7	74.9	72.4	72.2[a]	19.4
Consults regularly and intensively on legislative business with fellow members of deputies' group or fraction	23.1	22.0	25.0	17.7	8.1
Consults regularly and intensively on legislative business with fellow members of legislative committee	64.4	34.6	31.1	41.4	37.9

[a]Reference is to membership in one or more of the relatively small and inactive "deputies' groups" in the Ukrainian Supreme Soviet. Only 39.2 percent of the Ukrainian deputies belonged to a "parliamentary bloc," a more important entity.

and Kazakhstan, substantial majorities were part-timers, with major work commitments elsewhere.

The second line of Table 3.1 picks up an echo of the French phenomenon of *cumul des mandats*.[4] Although relatively few USSR deputies held elective office at another plateau of government, approximately one in four of the Russian deputies did and very nearly a majority of the Ukrainian and Kazakhstan deputies did. In almost every instance, the cross-posting was to the local level, where it as a rule entailed a minor, part-time commitment only.

Table 3.1 also shows most of the deputies to be enrolled in a members' group or caucus, another channel of involvement with the institution and the wider world of politics. The Interregional Deputies' Group of westernizing liberals was the first such group to arise, in the USSR Congress and Supreme Soviet in July 1989. By one year later fractions with a dazzling array of ideological postures had proliferated in both the Soviet and the Russian legislatures. In Ukraine, almost three-quarters of deputies belonged to at least one small, specialized group in 1991, although enrollment in the more potent "parliamentary blocs" in the Supreme Soviet had plummeted due to the liquidation of the Communist Party bloc that August, leaving Narodna Rada (the parliamentary arm of the nationalist movement Rukh) as the only organized bloc in the legislature. Kazakhstan is the outlier, as there was only one deputies' group (Democratic Kazakhstan) in its Supreme Soviet, claiming around one-fifth of the members of parliament.[5]

As Table 3.1 goes on to indicate, membership in a parliamentary caucus was not equivalent to active participation in it. A mere 8 to 25 percent of the deputies reported consulting regularly and intensively on parliamentary affairs with colleagues in their group or fraction. Considerably more said they consulted members of the legislative committee to which they belonged, yet only among USSR deputies was this ratio more than half.

Table 3.2 presents an important piece of evidence, about plans for future political activity, that sheds further light on the post-Soviet legislators' engagement with their work. Pilot interviews indicated that general questions about career specialization would be of little use. Therefore, I asked concretely whether the deputy intended to seek nomination at the next general election for a seat in the assembly in which he or she was presently serving.

The thrust of the answers is that the Gorbachevian reform design has been crowned with but limited success and the barriers to professionalization remain formidable. Only for the Russian associate members did the number of respondents declaring a clear intent to run

TABLE 3.2   Deputies' Interest in Running for Re-Election to the Legislature[a]

Re-election Intentions	USSR	RUS (Mem)	RUS (Ass)	UKR	KAZ
Intends to run	3.8%	21.4%	29.1%	16.5%	24.2%
Intends not to run	45.2	28.9	21.6	42.6	31.5
Will decide later	39.4	47.2	46.6	35.9	35.5
Hard to say	8.7	2.5	2.7	5.1	8.9
No answer	2.9	0.0	0.0	0.0	0.0

[a]Question reads: "Do you intend to stand for election as a deputy of [ ] in the next elections?"

question provoke a strongly favorable response from as many as one-quarter of those polled. The paltry 3.8 percent of USSR deputies who were of a firm mind to stand again is an abysmal figure, considering the gushing hopes with which the remodelled Soviet parliament was inaugurated only two years before.

Table 3.3 summarizes deputies' answers to a query about efficacy in the legislative process, another indicator of engagement. The spectrum of responses is broad. More than 70 percent of the full members of the Russian Supreme Soviet believed that they always or usually made a difference in the shaping of legislative output, and more than 50 percent of the associate members of the Russian Supreme Soviet agreed. In the USSR and Kazakhstan parliaments, on the other hand, a majority felt that they rarely or never influenced the fate of draft laws. In Ukraine, the distribution was close to even, with a slight majority pessimistic.

Can the individual-level psychology of efficacy and frustration explain the differential levels of commitment to pursuing a legislative vocation? Table 3.4 arrays the re-election and efficacy variables against one another. Two striking patterns are revealed.

The first is that deputies with an elevated sense of efficacy and accomplishment were invariably more likely to be counting on re-election than deputies with low efficacy scores. There would seem, then, to be some positive correlation between retrospective self-evaluation and prospective career planning.

At the same time, differences between low-efficacy and high-efficacy deputies cannot plausibly account for all of the variance observed. Cross-parliamentary comparisons from Table 3.4 bring this

TABLE 3.3 Deputies' Sense of Efficacy on Legislative Questions[a] (in percentages)

Self-estimate of influence	USSR	RUS (Mem)	RUS (Ass)	UKR	KAZ
Virtually always	3.8	18.9	6.8	4.2	5.6
Most of the time	30.8	55.3	47.3	42.2	26.6
Rarely	51.9	25.8	42.6	51.5	59.7
Never	11.5	0	0.7	0.8	6.5
No answer	1.9	0	2.7	1.3	1.6

[a]Question reads: "Do you always manage to influence the course of working out a draft law in the [ ] Supreme Soviet?"

out in bold relief. Notice that the Kazakhstan MPs were not significantly more or less optimistic about their ability to affect draft laws than the USSR deputies—and yet, notwithstanding, they were 3.4 times as apt to be laying re-election plans as their USSR counterparts in Moscow. In fact, the share of *low*-efficacy Kazakhstan deputies intending to run again was 7 points higher than the *high*-efficacy USSR deputies aiming at re-election.

Conceivably, lapsed time in office accounts for some of the variation. The USSR Supreme Soviet might have had low re-election scores in May 1991 because its members had been in office two punishing years when surveyed, whereas their republic-level counterparts, elected only in the spring of 1990, had had less time to become disillusioned with political and legislative life.

Table 3.4 does not lend credence to such an interpretation. The scores for intent to seek re-election were highest for Kazakhstan's Supreme Soviet, which was the last of the republic legislatures surveyed. And the deputies there had in January 1992 been in office almost as long as the USSR deputies in May 1991. The low Ukrainian score is especially hard to square with the temporal explanation. Nor does this approach make it plain why Russian deputies not on the Supreme Soviet would have markedly greater re-election ambitions than deputies already sitting in the Russian Supreme Soviet.

Setting aside the defunct USSR Supreme Soviet, in which so tiny a minority evinced the desire to run for re-election, Table 3.5 tabulates for Russia, Ukraine, and Kazakhstan the intent to stand for re-election against several other possible explanatory variables. Occupancy of a leading position in the legislative structure, full-time immersion in

TABLE 3.4 Deputies' Re-Election Plans by Level of Efficacy on Legislative Questions (in percentages)

	Efficacy	
Re-election Intentions	*High[a]*	*Low[b]*
USSR		
Intends to run	11.1	0.0
Intends not to run	30.6	53.0
Russia (full members)		
Intends to run	23.7	14.6
Intends not to run	14.6	26.8
Russia (associate members)		
Intends to run	36.3	18.8
Intends not to run	11.3	34.3
Ukraine		
Intends to run	20.0	13.7
Intends not to run	40.9	45.2
Kazakhstan		
Intends to run	37.5	18.3
Intends not to run	25.0	34.1

[a]Combines "Virtually always" and "Most of the time" responses.
[b]Combines "Rarely" and "Never" responses.

parliamentary work, and simultaneous service at another level of government are associated with the propensity to run for re-election—but not in any uniform pattern across the three countries. In Russia, legislative non-leaders, part-time deputies, and deputies elected to another soviet were more likely to have the ambition to re-run. In Ukraine, it was exactly the reverse on all three scores. Kazakhstan resembled the Ukrainian lineup for leading position and full-time work, but Russia for dual electoral office. Ethnic affiliation, available for only Ukraine and Kazakhstan, was barely significant for Ukraine, and, counterintuitively, gave a slight advantage to non-Ukrainians over ethnic Ukrainians. In Kazakhstan, though, ethnic Kazakhs were more than twice as likely as non-Kazakhs to aspire to be returned to office.

The two variables in Table 3.5 that uniformly predict re-election intent relate to participation in organized subgroups within the legislature. First, the very act of belonging to a deputies' fraction seemed to increase the likelihood of a member wanting to extend his parliamentary service. The effect was weak in Russia, somewhat less so in Ukraine, but quite strong in Kazakhstan. Second, membership in

TABLE 3.5   Some Other Factors Associated with Intent to Run for Re-Election
(in percentages)

| | Intends to Run | | |
Variable	RUS	UKR	KAZ
MEAN	25.1	16.5	24.2
Leading position in legislature			
Yes	23.8	29.8	37.5
No	27.0	13.2	22.2
Works full-time in legislature			
Yes	19.0	18.3	27.6
No	29.3	15.5	23.2
Serves simultaneously on another soviet			
Yes	31.6	14.2	27.3
No	22.9	18.5	21.7
Member of deputies' group or fraction			
Yes	25.3	17.5	37.5
No	24.0	13.6	22.2
Member of a radical deputies' group			
Yes	31.5	22.7	37.5
No	22.5	14.0	22.0
Member of titular nationality			
Yes	ND	16.0	33.3
No	ND	17.7	14.8

ND = No data

one particular kind of group—radical "democrats," represented here
by Democratic Russia, Narodna Rada, and Democratic Kazakhstan—
was a better predictor than membership per se. (For Kazakhstan, the
two variables were coterminous, as Democratic Kazakhstan was the
only organized group in the soviet). To the extent that the liberal
groups have been the embryos of modern parties in the post-USSR, the
implication is that one key to professionalization of *legislative*
careers will be professionalization of *political* careers. The more that
political activists see themselves as cogs in machines for gaining
control of elective office—parties or quasi-parties—the more they
will tend to see service in those offices as a multi-year and multi-term
commitment.

Assessment of Ideal and Actual Roles

A major aim of the survey was to flush out the deputies' understanding of their responsibilities as elected officials. Several questions probed role conceptions as dichotomized in Edmund Burke's classic attack on imperative mandates in his "Speech to the Electors of Bristol," and referred to in nearly every work on legislative development since Burke's time. Do post-Soviet parliamentarians envision themselves as instructed "delegates," bound to carry out the instructions of their electors, or as more like the "trustees," following their own consciences, that Burke saluted?

Table 3.6 presents deputies' responses to a question about imperative mandate. As can be seen, in each of the four legislatures the trustee's role was favored over the delegate's role. Deputies saw themselves, not the citizens or organizations that put them in the legislature, as the best judges of the public interest. The USSR deputies were by a good margin the most inclined of the four groups to see themselves in this light, with almost three-quarters accepting the trustee interpretation of duty. In Kazakhstan, the difference in support between delegate and trustee interpretations was only 1 percent. Russia and Ukraine fell in between.

In preliminary runs of the data, I found three factors associated with deputies' inclination to define themselves as trustees or delegates. These are displayed in Table 3.7. The first was the reported experience of having or not having experienced an actual clash in opinion with voters on a policy question. Deputies who remembered having had such a disagreement were markedly more likely to see themselves as trustees than deputies who recalled no such experience.

TABLE 3.6 Deputies' Response to Question About Imperative Mandate[a] (in percentages)

Response	USSR	RUS	UKR	KAZ
Delegate (deputy should carry out the wishes of voters)	25.0	36.2	38.4	43.5
Trustee (deputy should do what he considers necessary)	70.2	48.9	51.9	44.4
Hard to say	3.8	12.1	6.3	3.2
No answer	1.0	2.9	3.4	8.9

[a]Question reads: "How do you think a deputy should act in the case of a divergence between his opinion and the opinion of his voters?"

TABLE 3.7   Some Factors Associated with Delegate/Trustee Interpretations of
Mandate (in percentages)

Variable	USSR	RUS	UKR	KAZ
Deputy's experience with divergence of his and voters' opinions on a specific question				
Has had this experience				
Delegate response	22.4	35.8	33.9	41.0
Trustee response	76.5	54.9	56.1	47.4
Has not had this experience				
Delegate response	43.8	43.2	54.9	53.8
Trustee response	43.8	40.0	37.3	41.0
Deputy belongs to a radical deputies' group				
Delegate response	9.1	19.1	18.2	29.2
Trustee response	90.9	59.6	75.8	50.0
Deputy elected from a public organization				
Delegate response	42.9	NA	NA	47.6
Trustee response	53.6	NA	NA	33.3

NA = Not applicable

A plausible interpretation is that relations with voters had some
formative influence on deputies' views of the imperative mandate
conundrum: a conflictual encounter, maybe triggering some underlying
attitude, pushed deputies toward the conviction that their own
reading of the public interest had to prevail.

As Table 3.7 indicates, members of radical deputies' groups ranked
far ahead of other deputies in their adherence to the trustee's
philosophy. The main reason would seem to be ideology. Deputies
subscribing to strong political programs and belonging, as we have
said, to proto-political parties, have been taking more cues from these
internalized value systems and fewer from voters. Election from a
public organization rather than a territorial district, which was
possible only in the USSR and Kazakhstan legislatures, had the
inverse effect. Deputies from public organizations were more likely to
imagine themselves as delegates than as impartial trustees. This
seems to flow from the applicable electoral rules and the nature of the
constituency: selection by an organization carries with it a stronger
sense of being custodian of a corporate interest than election in a
socially more diverse (and often physically more remote) geographic
district.

Related to the issue of the imperative mandate, but of greater interest and descriptive power, were questions concerning deputies' evaluations of the substantive roles they fulfill. Following the comparative literature on representation, these roles were laid out in the questionnaire in five specific categories:

1. *lawmaking* work at draft legislation;
2. *control* or oversight over the activity of government agencies;
3. *casework* on behalf of individual voters;
4. *advocacy* of the collective interests of the district, sponsoring organization, or some other social group; and
5. *informational* activity, keeping in touch with voters' opinions about what the government is up to.

There were complications in drawing up and executing these questions. The questionnaire in the Supreme Soviet of Russia presented the deputies with the five categories as given above, but without reference in the advocacy category to sponsoring organization (since all of the Russian deputies were elected from territorially-defined districts) or to social groups. In the USSR survey, the lawmaking category was broken down at the insistence of my research confederates into two subcategories, for committees and the Supreme Soviet. Advocacy was also parsed into two subcategories, the first for the interests of the district or of the electing organization, the second for "the interests of a social or occupational group," which could include an ethnic group. In Ukraine and Kazakhstan, advocacy was a double category, as with the USSR survey, but the lawmaking category remained unitary.

A further complication arose from the deputies' responses to the questions. They were asked first to read through the list of roles and to rank them *normatively*, in order of the place these activities ought to occupy in the work of a member of the given parliament. In the rush to get the research rolling, the question was not adequately pretested. Deputies often proved unwilling or unable to give a systematic, orderly ranking of the respective roles. The usual response was to cluster the answers, producing one or several tie scores and, often, omissions on the individual deputy's questionnaire. For example, a deputy might indicate in his answers that Role A was in "first place" in terms of desired importance, while Roles C and E were in "second place," Roles B and D were in "third place," and Role F was unranked.

In addition to the normative questions, respondents were also asked factual questions about the place that given roles *empirically* occupied in their day-to-day work as legislators. The same rosters of roles were used.

Despite the confusion, the answers to the questions about desired and actual roles produce some insight. The difficulties with the format were evident before the Ukraine and Kazakhstan surveys were done, but were not severe enough to force a change in strategy. I decided, in the end, that the costs of altering the form of the question would outweigh any benefits. Retention of the flawed original form maximized comparability of the Ukraine and Kazakhstan answers with the USSR and Russian results.

Table 3.8 presents average scores for deputies' evaluations of both their ideal and their actual roles, put on a five-point scale in which 1.00 represents the maximum and 5.00 the minimum. Table 3.9 shows how ideal and actual roles, respectively, rank in the estimation of the four samples of deputies. The rankings were for seven roles in the USSR Supreme Soviet, five roles for the RSFSR, and six roles for Ukraine and Kazakhstan.

Certain patterns jump out of the data on ideal, desired roles. The first is that lawmaking work, be it in committee or in the legislature at large, was again and again the deputies' top preference. In every country case, MPs believed that making laws as more or less disinterested agents of society as a whole was by far their most important duty.

In the USSR, Ukraine, and Kazakhstan parliaments, the second-ranking role in normative terms was defense of the interests of the electing district or organization. Russia was odd man out on this score, as oversight of the activity of government agencies was put second by deputies there. Deputies elected (in the USSR and Kazakhstan parliaments) from public organizations assigned greater value to defending the interests of their organization than territorially-elected deputies did to their districts. Importantly, members of radical deputies' fractions tended, by contrast, to downplay defense of constituent interests.[6]

The role of standing up for the interests of a social or occupational group, not the deputy's electoral constituency, tended to rank lowest of all the roles in terms of deputies' preferences (the exception was Russia, where this role was not listed). The informational role of keeping in touch with voters' opinions also ranked at or near the bottom of the heap. The exact ordering of the other roles varied from parliament to parliament. The USSR deputies gave an especially low rating to casework, helping voters who are encountering difficulties in dealing with government agencies; this role finished third among the Russian and Ukrainian deputies and fourth among the Kazakhstan deputies.

The ranking of actual roles performed falls out somewhat

TABLE 3.8   Deputies' Evaluation of Ideal and Actual Roles

Role	Average Score (5-point scale, with 1 high)[a]			
	USSR	RUS	UKR	KAZ
Lawmaking				
Work in commissions				
on draft laws and resolutions				
Ideal	1.15	NA	NA	NA
Actual	1.36	NA	NA	NA
Actual vs. ideal	+0.21	NA	NA	NA
Work in the Supreme Soviet				
on draft laws and resolutions				
Ideal	1.73	1.28	1.18	1.88
Actual	1.88	1.79	1.41	2.08
Actual vs. ideal	+0.15	+0.51	+0.23	+0.20
Control				
Control over the activity				
of government organs				
Ideal	2.24	2.73	3.04	2.98
Actual	2.97	3.58	3.24	3.07
Actual vs. ideal	+0.72	+0.85	+0.20	+0.09
Casework				
Helping voters who are encounter-				
ing difficulties in dealing with				
government agencies				
Ideal	2.50	3.16	2.66	3.06
Actual	2.49	2.29	2.44	2.93
Actual vs. ideal	-0.01	-0.90	-0.22	-0.13
Advocacy				
Defense of the interests of the				
district (or of the organization				
that elected the deputy)				
Ideal	2.12	3.24	2.65	2.50
Actual	2.28	3.11	2.74	2.52
Actual vs. ideal	+0.16	-0.13	+0.09	+0.02
Defense of the interests of a				
social or occupational group				
Ideal	2.82	NA	3.84	3.66
Actual	3.01	NA	3.75	3.44
Actual vs. ideal	+0.19	NA	-0.09	-0.22
Informational				
Keeping in touch with voters'				
opinions about the activity				
of the government				
Ideal	2.48	3.36	3.62	3.53
Actual	2.78	3.50	3.62	3.77
Actual vs. ideal	+0.30	+0.14	0.00	+0.24

[a]Scored as 1 (first place), 2 (second place), 3 (third place), 4 (fourth place), or 5 (fifth place, lower than fifth place, or no answer).

NA = Not applicable

TABLE 3.9   Ranking of Average Evaluations of Ideal and Actual Roles

	USSR	RUS	UKR	KAZ
Lawmaking				
Work in commissions				
on draft laws and resolutions				
Ideal	1	NA	NA	NA
Actual	1	NA	NA	NA
Work in the Supreme Soviet				
on draft laws and resolutions				
Ideal	2	1	1	1
Actual	2	1	1	1
Control				
Control over the activity				
of government organs				
Ideal	4	2	4	3
Actual	6	5	4	4
Casework				
Helping voters who are				
encountering difficulties				
in dealing with				
government agencies				
Ideal	6	3	3	4
Actual	4	2	2	3
Advocacy				
Defense of the interests of				
the district (or of the				
organization that elected				
the deputy)				
Ideal	3	4	2	2
Actual	3	3	3	2
Defense of the interests of				
a social or occupational				
group				
Ideal	7	NA	6	6
Actual	7	NA	6	5
Informational				
Keeping in touch with voters'				
opinions about the activity				
of the government				
Ideal	5	5	5	5
Actual	5	4	5	6

NA = Not applicable

differently. Legislative work is in each and every case the role that claimed the greatest time and effort. But some of the other roles gained on their idealized ranking, while others slipped. Deputies, in other words, found themselves doing some things with different intensity than their idealized conception of the representative's role would have led them to wish, and some with less. The rankings in Table 3.9 and the numerical measures in Table 3.8 (in the lines "Actual vs. ideal") are two ways in which the difference between actual and ideal roles can be depicted numerically.

The most common pairing (thirteen out of twenty times) finds the deputy giving a *lower* assessment of the reality of the role than of its idealized image. This is the deputies' way of saying, "Lawmaking [or controlling government agencies, or whatever] was not all I thought it would be," or "I have made less of a contribution in this sphere than I expected I would when I got started." The biggest negative displacements are in general those recorded for lawmaking roles and, less consistently, for control activity.

The numbers in bold typeface in Table 8 draw attention to differences in actual vs. ideal score in which the actual role gets a *higher* index than the ideal role. (That pairing is represented here by a negative number in the "Actual vs. ideal" line, since lower scores stand for a higher priority in the deputy's mind.) This result was achieved in seven pairings of roles. In all four Supreme Soviets, casework produced a higher actual than an ideal score. Advocacy of district/organizational interests generated one premium of actuality over ideal, and defense of the interests of a social or occupational group generated two higher actual scores.

One story these figures tell is that the gritty reality of post-Soviet legislative work differed from the deputies' ideal not only in terms of the relative downgrading of drafting and passing laws (although lawmaking remained the number one priority) and exercising control over state bureaucrats, but also in terms of the relative upgrading of varieties of representative activity toward which the legislators were not originally all that favorably predisposed. "I had not realized that people in my district would expect me to haul so many little loads for them," is how one Ukrainian deputy put it to me in an interview. "I was psychologically prepared for doing my part to write laws that would bring our nation out of its crisis, but not for this small change."

Conflicting Tendencies

Post-Soviet lawmakers are obviously having difficulty in integrating the reality of legislative life with their preconceptions. Only time will tell if this is a transient phenomenon or whether it reflects some deep-seated contradiction innate in post-Soviet or post-authoritarian transitions. Hypothetically, tension between idealized and actualized roles may be eased by altering expectations or by modifying behavior. Both possibilities should be watched for in future research.

This point may be related analytically to the earlier argument about the dynamics of, and the obstacles to, the professionalization of legislative careers. If Western experience is any guide, the re-election prospects of individual post-Soviet legislators—and not merely their re-election intentions, which were stressed above—will be directly affected by their willingness to take seriously the constituency-defense and personal-service functions that they have tended in the early going to turn up their noses at.

The most damaging contradiction here is that the members of the first cohort of post-Soviet legislative elites most inclined by temperament to conceive of political and parliamentary activity as a lifelong commitment—namely, the Westernizing democrats—are at the same time among the least favorably disposed to the purely representative strand of the elective politician's job. The forthcoming elections in Russia, Ukraine, and Kazakhstan will allow us to begin to judge whether would-be party-builders on the democratic and non-democratic sides of the aisle manage to reconcile themselves to the humdrum realities of "home style" politics even as they set out to pursue loftier images of social transformation and redemption.

Notes

* The study is part of a larger research project on political reform in the Soviet Union carried out from 1989 to 1993 with Jeffrey Hahn, Jerry Hough, and Blair Ruble. The project was funded by the Carnegie Corporation. I received additional generous support for work on the Ukrainian parliament from the Karl Popper Foundation. A monograph on my findings is in preparation.

1. The questionnaire was submitted by me directly and by my local research partners, who were a combination of legislative staffers and independent researchers. To encourage balky deputies to respond, most questions were put in a closed-ended, multiple-choice format. Strict guarantees of confidentiality had to be built in to gain the assent of the parliamentary leaderships. Ideally, the survey instrument should have been identical in every case. This proved impossible to achieve due to bargaining relations with research partners, logistical and communication difficulties, the quirks of local situations and personalities, and the swift flow of events (not least the crisis of August 1991). The questionnaire was essentially similar in the four legislatures, but with certain differences that impede sharp comparisons in some limited respects, especially for the Russian deputies. It was administered in the Russian language to the USSR and Russian deputies, in Ukrainian in Ukraine, and in both Kazakh and Russian in Kazakhstan.

2. Many ethnic Kazakhs—58.7 percent—chose to complete the Russian-language questionnaire, a strong indicator of linguistic assimilation. On some points of behavior, the Russified Kazakhs were quite different from native-speaking Kazakhs.

3. If 57.9 percent of the Russian full members polled held a leadership position (as chairman, deputy chairman, or secretary of a committee or subcommittee), only 23.0 percent of the Russian deputies not on the Supreme Soviet, 29.8 percent of the USSR deputies, 19.8 percent of the Ukraine deputies, and 12.9 percent of the Kazakhstan deputies held such a position.

4. This refers to the French tradition of local notables serving simultaneously as deputies in the national assembly and as leaders of local government. See John Frears, "The Role of the *Député* in France," in Vernon Bogdanor, ed., *Representatives of the People? Parliamentarians and Constituents in Western Democracies* (Aldershot: Gower, 1985), pp. 103-105.

5. Of the Ukrainian deputies, 58.2 percent said they had earlier belonged to a parliamentary bloc, 41.4 percent of them to the Communist Party bloc. In Kazakhstan, 13.7 percent said they had at some earlier time belonged to a deputies' fraction.

6. USSR deputies from public organizations gave defense of constituents an average score of 1.57, vs. an average for all USSR deputies of 2.12. Kazakhstan deputies elected by organizations rated constituent defense at 2.14 (average 2.50). Radical deputies from the Interregional Group in the USSR Supreme Soviet gave this same role an average score of 3.00; Democratic Kazakhstan deputies also scored it at 3.00.

References

Frears, John. 1985. "The Role of the *Député* in France," in Vernon Bogdanor, ed., *Representatives of the People? Parliamentarians and Constituents in Western Democracies* (Aldershot: Gower).

Polsby, Nelson W. 1975. "Legislatures," in Fred I. Greenstein and Nelson W. Polsby, eds., *Handbook of Political Science*, vol. 5, *Governmental Institutions and Processes* (Reading, Mass.: Addison-Wesley, 1975).

4

Political Cleavages in Yaroslavl Politics

Jerry F. Hough

The elections of 1989 and 1990 were the first free elections held in Russia in seventy years, and the legislative bodies that emerged differed radically from their predecessors in terms of both composition and activity. As a result, for the first time since the Duma, political scientists have the opportunity to analyze election results and the debates, coalitions, and voting patterns within the Russian legislatures with the same techniques used in the analysis of Western political institutions.

Any comparative analysis of Russian and Western legislatures must, however, be approached with the greatest of care. For example, the differences between Russian and American legislatures—especially at the local level—are far greater than the similarities. American institutions are settled in their traditions and procedures, while deputies in the Russian institutions have no professional experience as legislators, except perhaps in the old soviets which functioned in an entirely different setting.

More importantly, American institutions operate in the context of a non-revolutionary society, and city and state governments in particular deal primarily with the mundane questions of budgets, taxes, and detailed economic regulation. Russian society, by contrast, has been potentially revolutionary, and the creation of free legislatures allows that potential to become real. The Moscow and St. Petersburg legislatures and mayors see themselves as playing a transforming role in society that the mayors in New York and San Francisco would never imagine considering. Many deputies, both radical and conservative, are concerned not so much with the resolution of mundane economic questions (their powers of taxation and budgeting are still embryonic in any case), but with changing or defining the fundamental political structure.

Hence, the revolutionary character of Russian society in the early 1990s requires the scholar to analyze Russian legislatures, especially local government, in different terms than American ones. Moreover, it greatly complicates the task of analysis. When Russian scholars, journalists, commentators, and deputies describe the elections and legislatures, they generally do so not to answer abstract scientific questions, but to influence the course of the revolution. As a result, analysis often has a propagandistic, ideological, political character. Radicals—and their analysis predominates among scholars and journalists—characterize their opponents as nomenklatura and as unbridled conservatives, who represent no one but themselves. In the name of democracy, they call for the end or curtailment of democratic institutions if elections have produced the "wrong" result. They are very negative towards oblast institutions, because radicals have weak support in the countryside and therefore want to continue the lack of representation of the countryside that has prevailed in the entire communist period.

In fact, political life in Russia is much more complex than either the radical or conservative analysis suggests, and this chapter will explore a number of the nuances which need to be introduced into our political analysis. It will utilize a variety of kinds of information about the city and oblast elections in Yaroslavl and about the deputies who were elected, including: electoral support for different kinds of candidates, biographical data on deputies, a sociological survey of views of oblast and city deputies, and individual voting on a dozen questions in the first year of work in the city soviet. Further, we will consider the differences between the oblast and city deputies (and, therefore, the political character of the two soviets) and between the types of districts that elected different types of deputies.

Ultimately, however, this chapter will raise the question of the nature of the "radical" and "conservative" position in the summer and fall of 1990. In Moscow, those supporting the 500-day economic plan at that time were calling both for radical economic reform and strong decentralization of power to the republic level. But when questions to Yaroslavl city and oblast deputies on economic reform and on decentralization to the republic level were combined into an economic reform index and a decentralization index respectively, the correlation between the two was quite low (.13). Apparently the two issues were not as linked in the minds of the politically active members of Yaroslavl society as they were among the political elite in Moscow, and this difference deserves exploration.

The Oblast and City Soviets

The simultaneous elections to the oblast and city soviets began in March 1990 and, with subsequent runoffs and rounds of voting, they continued for several months. Originally there were to be 200 seats in each body, but because of the difficulty in obtaining the required 50 percent voter turnout in some districts, the oblast soviet finally contained 193 deputies and the city soviet 194.

According to the conventional wisdom in Yaroslavl, the members of the local popular front and their allies had done fairly well in the city soviet, electing as many as 35 percent to 40 percent of the deputies, while the oblast soviet was considerably more conservative. In part, it was said that this was due to the fact that the democrats had concentrated on the city and had not given sufficient attention to the oblast elections, even in districts for the oblast soviet located in Yaroslavl itself. In part, the districts outside Yaroslavl were said to be inherently more conservative or under the control of local party officials.

At first glance, the data on the deputies to the city and oblast soviets respectively confirm this general impression. Clearly officialdom was much more strongly represented in the oblast soviet than in the city soviet. As Table 4.1 indicates, political officials, governmental administrators, and directors of economic enterprises comprise only 26 percent of the deputies to the city soviet, but 51 percent of the deputies to the oblast soviet.

These differences are reflected in other statistics on the deputies. For example, only 68 percent of the city deputies were members of the Communist Party, compared with 82 percent of the oblast deputies (6 percent and 2 percent respectively were members of the Komsomol). The percentage identifying with the Communists of Yaroslavl and Democratic Yaroslavl (or the Deputies' Group) varied in like manner as Table 4.2 demonstrates.

On some questions the relationship between occupation, voting on issues in the city soviet, and membership in political groups is precisely that which is suggested by the stereotypes about occupation and politics. For example, one of the key votes in the city soviet occurred on September 12, 1990, and concerned the power of the city soviet to remove the chairman of the gorkom. Table 4.3 shows the results. If he could be removed by a simple majority, then the power of the soviet over him could be very great; if he could be removed only by a two-thirds majority, then the power of the soviet over him would be weak. The differences in the backgrounds of the deputies who voted

TABLE 4.1   Occupational Distribution of Deputies to Yaroslavl Oblast and
City Soviet, 1990 (in percentages)

Occupation	City Soviet	Oblast Soviet
Top political-governmental officials	6.2	19.7
Minor political-governmental officials[a]	11.9	10.4
Industrial directors[b]	7.9	11.4
Kolkhoz-sovkhoz directors	0.0	9.3
Directors, other institutions	9.3	7.3
Deputy heads, enterprises	8.2	6.2
Lower-level administrators	13.4	12.4
Non-administrative specialists	20.6	10.4
Workers & foremen	18.6	10.9
Miscellaneous	4.1	2.1

[a]Very low-level officials and non-administrative employees of political
institutions are included in the appropriate categories lower in the table.

[b]This category includes heads of construction and transportation enterprises

for each side of this issue were much in line with the conventional
wisdom about Russian politics.

Yet, when we begin to look at this data more closely and combine it
with the results of a sociological survey of deputies, the overall
picture looks very different, as Table 4.4 describes. First, while the
vote on the power to remove the gorispolkom chairman did correlate
very closely to membership in political groups, this example also
clearly demonstrates that the relatively large number of members of
the Democrats' Group in Yaroslavl and of the Deputies Group in the
city soviet gave these groups little ability to control the course of
events on this key test vote between the two groups. Every single one of
the "neutrals" supported the Communists of Yaroslavl position! On
other test votes in these early sessions, the radical position fared even
worse.

TABLE 4.2   Deputies' Membership in Political Groups, City and Oblast Soviet (in percentages)

Group	City Soviet	Oblast Soviet
Communists of Yaroslavl	11	20
Democrats (or deputies' group)	33	20
Neither	56	60

TABLE 4.3   Vote in City Soviet on September 12, 1990 on Requiring 2/3 Vote to Remove the Gorispolkom Chairman (by Political Group of Deputies)

Political Group	Those For	Those Against	Abstain
Communists of Yaroslavl	17	0	0
Democrats (or deputies group)	11	45	0
Neither	71	0	4

TABLE 4.4   Vote in City Soviet on September 12, 1990 Requiring a 2/3 Vote in the City Soviet to Remove the Gorispolkom Chairman By Occupation of Deputies

Occupation	Those For	Those Opposed	Abstain
Major political and governmental officials	9	1	1
Minor political and governmental officials	16	2	0
Factory managers	9	1	0
Directors other institutions	9	3	0
Deputy heads of enterprises	8	4	0
Lower-level administrators	12	9	0
Non-administrative specialists	16	6	1
Workers and foremen	18	7	1

By contrast, although the relative number of the communists in the oblast soviet was larger and that of the Democrats much smaller, the "neutrals" voted with the Democrats on the one roll-call taken at this time on a key symbolic issue. On August 11, 1990, a law was proposed to prohibit the chairman and deputy chairman of the oblast soviet from being elected into the leading organs of public-political organizations. This bill was passed 114 to 43, with five abstentions. Only forty-three deputies voted against it, and the neutral deputies took the other side. Certainly the oblast soviet seemed no more controlled by the Communist group than the city soviet was controlled by the Democrats.

Second, when an identical questionnaire was administered to deputies of the oblast and city soviet in the summer and early fall of 1990, the patterns of response were surprisingly similar to questions on economic reform. When an index on economic reform was created by adding the results of eight questions on private trade, cooperatives, agriculture, and foreign investment, the oblast deputies on the whole were a little more conservative than the city deputies, but not very much. On this scale, 100 was the most reformist position and 500 the most conservative possible. In practice, 388 was the most conservative score received. The oblast deputies averaged 184, but the oblast deputies elected in districts inside the city actually had a score (181) a bit more reformist than the city soviet deputies.

As Table 4.5 indicates, virtually identical proportions of both the oblast and city soviets (47 percent and 48 percent respectively) had index scores between 100 and 163, although the city soviet had a somewhat greater number of truly radical deputies. The key difference was that the conservative half of the deputies in the oblast soviet included a larger proportion of strong conservatives, while the city soviet conservatives were more moderate in their conservatism on the whole. However, the deeply conservative oblast deputies constituted a relatively small minority of the total. Behind the relative similarity in index scores of oblast and city deputies were more or less similar answers to most of the items on the questionnaire on economic reform as Table 4.6 highlights. The question about general approval for policies to develop various aspects of economic reform was supplemented by individual questions that tried to ascertain attitudes in a somewhat more sophisticated way. These questions showed that, in fact, attitudes were more cautious. For example, when given a choice between supporting private farming alone, supporting the maintenance of a strong collective and state farm sector, and the dissolution of weak ones over the next two to three years, the overwhelming majority favored a dualistic agriculture system. When asked about cooperatives in the city, only 35 to 40 percent gave unconditional support, while a

TABLE 4.5 Score on Economic Reform Index, Oblast and City Soviet Deputies (in percentages)

Index Score	City Deputies	Oblast Deputies	Oblast Deputies in City	Oblast Deputies in Oblast
100-125	29	22	29	18
138-163	19	25	23	25
175-200	20	13	10	15
213-250	16	19	24	16
263-388	15	22	14	27
Average	184	194	181	203

TABLE 4.6 "Yes" Answer to Question: "Do You Favor a Policy Supporting . . . ?" Oblast and City Deputies (in percentages)

Economic Reform Measure	City Soviet	Oblast Soviet	Oblast Deputies in City	Oblast Deputies in Oblast
Private trade	72	73	75	71
Cooperatives	79	66	78	57
Private farming	96	96	94	97
Joint venture	78	74	82	69

comparable percentage favored cooperatives with limits (usually on purchasing resale cooperatives) and a quarter took a more conservative position. The number who wanted a complete freeing of prices was tiny indeed. As Table 4.7 indicates, when the answers to these questions among oblast and city deputies are compared, the former do turn out to be somewhat more conservative, as has already been implied in their more conservative score on the economic reform index. However, the relatively minor degree of these differences is more striking than the differences themselves. Table 4.8 shows that only on the question of cooperatives (and urban cooperatives rather than rural) are the oblast deputies noticeably more conservative. Strangely, it was the deputies in the countryside who were most worried about the urban cooperatives, showing little concern about rural cooperatives.

TABLE 4.7 Attitude Toward Agricultural Reform Among Deputies to the Oblast and City Soviets (in percentages)

Attitudes	City Deputies	Oblast Deputies	Oblast Deputies in City	Oblast Deputies in Oblast
Private farming	20	14	13	14
Only collective sector	4	6	3	7
Both equally (write in)	12	9	9	9
Support strong collective farms, break-up weak	63	71	74	68
Hard to say	1	2	1	2

TABLE 4.8 Attitudes Towards Cooperatives, Deputies to City and Oblast Soviets (in percentages)

Attitudes	City Deputies	Oblast Deputies	Oblast Deputies in City	Oblast Deputies in Oblast
			cooperatives in city	
Support all types	42	37	44	32
Limit some types	34	35	39	33
We must be cautious	19	24	16	31
Cooperatives are dangerous	5	4	1	5
			cooperatives in countryside	
Support all types	56	59	60	58
Rural more desirable	26	27	27	27
Rural less desirable	7	9	9	10
I don't know	10	5	4	5

Presumably the urban cooperatives have become the latest symbol of the age-old view in the countryside that the city is a place where morality is under attack.

Finally, Table 4.9 demonstrates that on the question of foreign investment, attitudes of deputies in the city and the oblast soviets were virtually indistinguishable. All groups responded that it was "very necessary," and only negligible proportions opposed it on principle.

TABLE 4.9 Attitudes to Foreign Investment, Deputies to City and Oblast Soviets (in percentages)

Attitudes	City Deputies	Oblast Deputies	Oblast Deputies in City	Oblast Deputies in Oblast
Very necessary	58	57	63	52
Now experimentally	30	30	29	31
Now dangerous	1	4	3	4
We don't need it	2	2	1	3
Difficult to say	8	7	4	10

Occupation and Economic Reform

There are many reasons for the relative similarity in the views of the oblast deputies and the city deputies on economic reform. In the first place, of course, 42 percent of the oblast deputies were elected within the city of Yaroslavl. The Yaroslavl radicals perceive that oblast deputies are more conservative than city ones, but there are two groups more conservative than radicals: liberals and conservatives. It is true that the oblast soviet deputies selected in the city contain fewer radicals than the city soviet (only 10 percent of the oblast deputies elected in Yaroslavl can be identified as members of the formal Deputies' or Democrats' groups, compared with 33 percent of the city soviet deputies). However, on basic questions of economic reform the voters in Yaroslavl actually elected deputies of very similar views.

Secondly, however, the fact remains that the oblast soviet includes many more officials (51 percent versus 26 percent)and party members (82 percent versus 68 percent) among its deputies than the city soviet. Clearly if the oblast deputies are not that much more conservative than the city deputies on the average, then one conclusion is inescapable: deputies who are officials and party members are not that much more conservative than deputies who are not officials and/or members of the Communist Party.

And, indeed, that is precisely the result that emerges from the data when the attitudes of deputies are examined. For example, deputies who are party members are only marginally more conservative than those who are not members of the party—191 versus 187. The difference is greater among deputies to the city soviet—188 for party members versus 179 for those who are not in the party—but the party members among the oblast deputies are actually more reformist than those not in the party—193 versus 200.

Perhaps the most striking result in this entire analysis emerges when one looks at the economic reform index score of the hard-core Communist of Yaroslavl group among the deputies to the oblast soviet who voted to permit the chairman and deputy chairman of the oblast soviet to be members of the leading organs of political parties. This group was more strongly supportive of economic reform than the group of oblast deputies who voted on the other side of this measure—191 versus 197. As Table 4.10 indicates, the economic reform index scores for persons of different occupations also do not vary in any simple way by level of administrative post. Some of the results of Table 4.10 correspond with normal expectations.

The deputies who are top officials, especially in the city, are more conservative on the average, and most high obkom officials did not respond to the questionnaire and probably would have increased the index score of top officials among oblast deputies. Factory managers and farm directors also have conservative scores. And at the other end of the spectrum are relatively low level officials and non-administrative personnel with higher education.

Other results, however, do not correspond to the usual stereotypes.

TABLE 4.10 Economic Reform Index Score, Deputies to Oblast and City Soviets

Occupation of Deputy	Index Score City Soviet	Index Score Oblast Soviet
Top political officials	224	176
Minor political officials	159	197
Factory directors	214	186
Collective/state directors	—	221
Other enterprise directors	188	183
Dep. directors/enterprises	175	169
Mid-level administrators	174	195
Non-administrative specialists	171	181
Workers	204	226
Average	184	194

One non-administrative group of deputies, the workers, turn out to be only second to farm managers in their conservatism on economic reform. And although the middle-level governmental and economic managers certainly deserve the label "bureaucrats," they sit (on average) on the pro-reform side of the spectrum. Indeed, the pro-reform score of the "top officials" in the oblast soviet reflects the views of persons that most would call the most conservative in Russia—the first secretaries of the raikoms and small gorkoms, and the chairmen of the raiispolkom. Sixteen of such officials were elected, and fifteen filled out questionnaires. Their average index score was 175. If one highly conservative raiispolkom chairman is excluded, the average score of the others falls to 166.

The same general score is found, regardless of how the question is explored. Thus the economic reform index score for those with higher education is 183, while that for those with secondary education is 213. Similarly, and most surprising of all, the deputies who are over fifty-five years of age are most reformist (score of 177), while those under forty are also more reformist than average (score of 182). Indeed, the most radical deputies of all are the thirteen political officials or directors of enterprise who are fifty-five years of age or older. Their average economic index score is 139!

Often the sphere of employment of the deputies correlates more strongly with their views on economic reform than their occupation, as Table 4.11 shows.

TABLE 4.11 Economic Reform Index Score of Oblast and City Deputies, (by sphere of employment)

Sphere of Employment	Index Score
Government	184
Agriculture	201
Industry	198
Security	190
Health	202
Secondary and elementary education	185
Services	171
Higher education/science	167
Culture/media	150

If we break down occupation by sphere of employment, we see some of the reasons for the stereotypes about the correlation of occupation and views of economic reform. In the scientific-education realm that scholars know best, there does, indeed, seem to be a significant difference between the views of the top administrators, the middle-level administrators, and those without administrative responsibilities. In other areas, however, the sphere of employment seems more decisive than occupation. There are too few deputies in Yaroslavl to have a statistically significant number of deputies from each type of administrative level in most spheres of employment, but over 140 deputies are employed in industry. Here the results are quite interesting: factory directors score 195 on the index score; the middle-level administrators 181; the specialists without administrative responsibilities 201; the workers 213.

The general pattern of the support for economic reform found in Tables 4.10 and 4.11 actually corresponds reasonably well to the interests of various sectors and officials. Political officials have very broad knowledge of their city or region and a very broad set of contacts within it. They know how to deal with people and get them to reach agreement. They will do very well as organizers and facilitators in a market economy. There is also general agreement that privatization is likely to be controlled by officials for personal gain (the so-called nomenklatura privatization). The logical conclusion is that officials who understand their interests should support privatization. Similarly, many of those in higher education and scientific institutions—especially those with the communications skills to be elected deputies—will do well in a market economy.

By contrast, while many economic managers will adjust well to a market economy and become very wealthy, the production-oriented skills of the Soviet engineer and agronomist are not optimal ones for the future, and major adjustments will be necessary. Moreover, in the short run, radical reform will produce a major drop in production.

Workers, then, have special cause to be concerned. In many ways industrial workers were relatively privileged under socialism, and they did not need to worry about unemployment. Now they face both unemployment and a drop in real wages—in both relative and absolute terms. In the short run at least, the managers and workers in the defense industry have the most to fear from a radical change in policy. For this reason it is also unremarkable that the deputies of Zavolzhsk raion were more conservative on the average than those of other raions of Yaroslavl and that the defense city of Rybinsk sent one of the most conservative delegations to the oblast soviet, as Table 4.12 highlights.

TABLE 4.12 Economic Reform Index Score of Deputies of the City and Oblast Soviet (by district type)

Location of District	City Soviet	Oblast Soviet
Dzerzhinsk raion, Yaroslavl	175	178
Frunze raion, Yaroslavl	191	188
Kirov raion, Yaroslavl	163	156
Krasnopresnen raion, Yaroslavl	192	177
Lenin raion, Yaroslavl	191	172
Zavolzhsk raion, Yaroslavl	196	205
Rybinsk	—	208
Other cities	—	188
Worker's settlements	—	213
Settlements	—	216
Villages	—	201

As for agriculture, market reform in this sphere will end many of the subsidies and will make profitable agriculture virtually impossible. Health industry reform will sharply reduce the number of hospitals and hospital beds, and the directors of state hospitals will be caught in a very difficult competitive situation in which resources are difficult to find.

It comes as no surprise, then, that it is precisely deputies of these occupations—workers, agronomists, health professionals, and engineers—who tend to be conservative on questions of economic reforms. These facts about workers and bureaucrats are simple enough, but they are not reflected in much propagandistic description of legislative politics as a conflict between conservative bureaucrats and the reforming people. These survey results on the official-deputies and the worker-deputies remind us of facts we should not forget.

Elections and Democracy in Russia

The current conventional wisdom within the Moscow intellectual community—fully accepted in the American media—is that the majority of the deputies in the Russian legislature, let alone those in most of the local legislatures, reflect the interests of the party apparatus, who controlled the elections in 1990. In this view any opposition of the legislatures to the reform measures of the Gaidar government is, therefore, essentially undemocratic. In this view the "democratic" solution is to give the president the power to take emergency actions and to appoint heads of local administration.

It may well be that radical economic reform, and the long-term economic well-being of the Russian people, require some authoritarian measures in the near future. The countries with the most successful performance over the last two decades have been the Asian countries in the Pacific, and they have not been epitomes of Western democracy. Even Japan has had only one party in charge of its government for over forty-five years.

Yet if we are going to analyze the political system and political developments inside Russia from a scientific point of view, if we are going to create a real political science that is de-ideologized, we need to use words very carefully. We need to define democracy in objective terms, not just as a synonym for measures we personally approve. "Democracy" is a political process in which the majority of the population are able to influence decisions, and the experience of the west is that the majority often has a different position on issues than do the intelligentsia.

Thus, if we are to analyze on a scientific rather than propagandistic basis, the problem with the Russian legislature in 1992 from the perspective of the economic reformers is not that it is undemocratic, but that it is too democratic. Many of the districts are located in rural and small towns and are more naturally conservative (Smyth, 1990), while the workers in the cities are very worried by the deindustrialization policy suggested by the words of the Gaidar government. The policies that the majority in the Russian Congress is advocating may or may not be wise, but if they are unwise, that does not make them undemocratic.

This paper is about the first year of operation of the Yaroslavl city and oblast soviets, and it can say relatively little about the relationship of its decisions to public opinion in Yaroslavl and the oblast. The local soviets really did not have the financial base or the power of regulation over property to adopt the kind of budgets and legislative actions associated with a well-functioning legislature. Hence it is impossible to know whether they would have passed legislation that public opinion wanted. Only as time passes and as resources and control are decentralized to the local level will scholars be able to conduct sophisticated analyses about these questions.

Many Russian intellectuals have been critical of the defects of the

Russian elections of 1990, and have suggested that they were undemocratic to this or that extent. To an outside observer, however, the data suggest that the electoral process in Yaroslavl in 1990 functioned in a quite democratic way. To a large extent, the Russian intelligentsia's criticisms rest on utopian conceptions about the nature of democratic elections in the West, especially in the United States, and unrealistic expectations about them in Russia.

It is particularly encouraging to see the great similarity in the economic index scores of the deputies of the city soviet and the deputies to the oblast soviet who were elected from city districts. A Yaroslavl city electorate that was thinking about issues and that was making a free choice among candidates should have elected candidates of relatively similar views to the city and oblast soviet, and, in fact, they did.

Obviously voters do take other considerations into account, notably the personalities and qualities of the candidates. A state such as North Carolina in the United States can have one of its two Senators be extremely conservative (Jesse Helms)and the other be quite liberal (Terry Sanford). The variation in economic index scores for city deputies and oblast deputies in the same raion of Yaroslavl demonstrates that such factors are also at work in the Yaroslavl 1990 election, but it is encouraging that these differences basically averaged out. This suggests that they were relatively random.

There are three factors that might lead an observer to question the democratic character of the Yaroslavl election: 1) the level of turnout in the election; 2) the low number of candidates in some sections of the city, especially Dzerzhinsky and part of Lenin raions; and 3) the large number of officials elected. In reality, these criticisms stem more from unrealistic expectations about democracy than shortcomings in the Yaroslavl elections.

Thus, many are disturbed that only 62 percent of the registered voters in the city elections cast valid ballots in the March 4 elections, and only 50 percent in the April 22 election. After several rounds in which the turnout failed to reach the required 50 percent level, it was decided to leave six districts in the city soviet unrepresented and seven in the oblast soviet. Yet, an American is more impressed by how high the turnout was, not how low. Few American local elections could survive the requirement that 50 percent of the registered voters must, in fact, vote.

There is more serious reason to question whether the election was equally democratic in all sections of the city. In Kirov raion and the half of Lenin raion adjoining Kirov raion (districts 1 to 25 in Kirov raion and 26-40 in Lenin raion), there were 3.8 candidates in each district in the March 4 election, and only one district had a one-candidate election. Frunze raion was relatively similar, with 3.0 candidates and only three single candidate races. By contrast, the districts in Dzerzhinsky raion and the adjoining part of Lenin raion averaged only 1.7 candidates per district. Only one candidate ran in 52 percent of them. The situation in other raions fell between these extremes, as Table 4.13 illustrates.

Without question, the elections varied from raion to raion, and these differences were associated with differences in the views on economic reform of the deputies elected. One can imagine that the officials in the raions such as Dzerzhinsky and Zavolzhsk controlled the nominating process in order to elect more conservative candidates.

Future research might explore differences in political attitudes in various sections of Yaroslavl and on the socio-demographic characteristics associated with them. It is my hope to look at this question more closely in the future. However, the impression created by the data is that differences in political culture in the raions produced the differences in number of candidates and their views rather than differences in the degree of control over the process.

First, of course, the reader who refers back to Table 4.12 will be reminded that while the very active elections of Kirov raion did, in

TABLE 4.13 Number of Candidates and Voter Turnout in Yaroslavl City Elections of March 4 and April 22, 1990 (by raions)

	March 4, 1990		April 22, 1990	
Raion	*Average # of Candidates*	*Average Turnout*	*Average # of Candidates*	*Average Turnout*
Kirov & 1/2 Lenin (1-39)	3.7 (n=39)	65%	6.0	51%
Frunze (127-165)	3.0 (n=39)	60%	4.0	47%
Krasnopresnen (103-126)	2.3 (n=24)	56%	3.3	48%
Zavolzhsk[a] (166-200)	2.1 (n=35)	59%	1.8 (n=18)	49%
1/2 Lenin Dzerzhinsky (40-102)	1.7 (n=63)	62%	2.5 (n=19)	52%

[a]Turnout data were missing on four districts in Zavolzhsk raion.

fact, produce the deputies most dedicated to economic reform, the raion with the highest percentage of one-candidate districts— Dzerzhinsky—elected the second most reformist group of deputies. In addition, no evidence exists to suggest that the one-candidate elections diminished voter turnout in any raion, including Dzerzhinsky. When a larger number of candidates were nominated in the second round of the elections, this did not produce a larger turnout. As Table 4.14 depicts, turnout fell, and in the Dzerzhinsky-Lenin area turnout during the second round was negatively correlated with the number of candidates in the district.

Finally, we should not assume that the election of officials as deputies, rather than workers and scholars, demonstrates that the elections were undemocratic. On the contrary, this fact is more likely to mean that the legislatures are more democratic, not less. The old soviet legislatures were much more "representative" than Western legislatures in the social composition and occupations of their representatives, as the latter legislatures rarely include workers and peasants as legislators. However, the character of Western legislators does not mean that Western elections are controlled, but rather that the voters are seeking candidates who can represent them in the government. The deputy, particularly if he or she is elected in a district rather than from a list in a proportional representation system, is like a lawyer representing the interests of the district before higher authorities. A person choosing a lawyer seeks the most highly qualified, best educated one he can afford, as does a person voting for a "lawyer" in the legislature.

TABLE 4.14 Voter Turnout in Dzerzhinsky/Lenin Raions (by number of candidates)[a]

# Candidates in District	Turnout March 4	Turnout April 22
1	62% (n=32)	57% (n=5)
2	63% (n=22)	53% (n=5)
3	65% (n=7)	51% (n=7)
4	59% (n=2)	48% (n=1)
7	—	35% (n=1)

[a]This table refers to all of Dzerzhinsky raion and to the part of Lenin raion attached to it.

A detailed examination of the results in the elections to the USSR Congress of People's Deputies in the twenty-five areas for which newspapers were then available to a foreign reader showed that the electors seemed very interested in the quality of the representation that was to be expected. As Table 4.15 indicates, the electors seemed highly dubious that high party, state, and military officials, and top factory directors would have the time to be full-time legislators. Because of the two-stage legislature being selected, a district that elected such an official to the Congress would have little chance of having its representative elected to the more important full-time Supreme Soviet. Hence, it is not surprising that such candidates did poorly in contested elections. But by the same token, peasants and industrial workers were not likely to be skilled debaters or competent drafters of legislation, and they too received little support.

In Yaroslavl, the physical distance to the oblast and especially the city soviet was not as great as it was in the case of the USSR elections, the sessions of the soviets were much shorter, and the need to draft complicated legislation was significantly less. For this reason the electors seem not to have worried so much about electing high officials, and they were not quite as negative towards workers.

Yet, the status of the candidates appears strongly correlated with their chances of success. We have the electoral results for all electoral districts to the city and the oblast soviet in all rounds, and we can analyze the percentage of votes received by candidates of different occupations and levels of party membership. The data show that persons of low status often did very poorly. Managers and workers in heavy industry did much better than those in light industry and especially in trade and services. Women did very poorly, and since many of them were not members of the party, persons not in the Communist Party did much worse than party members.

Obviously the 1990 local elections were transitional in character. The soviets, and especially the city soviets, were larger than their counterparts in the West, and the initiation of the nomination from within the workplace ensured that many of the candidates would have similar occupations to those of the deputies of the past. In any case, the voters could not choose between candidates who had professional experience with electoral politics, for there had been no electoral politics in the past.

In the future the size of the legislatures will surely be reduced, and the candidates—especially the elected candidates—will increasingly become persons who want to be professional politicians. Questions about democracy will fade from the agenda, and those of road repair,

TABLE 4.15 Results of the March 1989 Elections to the Congress of People's Deputies By Occupation of Candidates

Occupation of Candidates	"Won"[a]	"Lost"
High[b] party, state, and military officials and top factory directors	8	18
Mid-level party, state, and military officials and factory directors	29	26
Chairmen of collective farms or directors of state farms	19	13
Persons in education, science, medicine, the law, or the media	61	24
Officials and specialists at industrial[c] enterprises	33	22
Officials and specialists at farms	21	21
Brigade leaders and foremen in industry	28	24
Industrial workers	23	50
Peasants	10	22

[a]"Won" means that the candidate received more votes than his or her opponent, even if both received less than 50 percent and hence both "lost."

[b]"High" officials denotes first and second secretaries of party committees and chairmen of soviets at the levels of oblasts, autonomous republics, krais, and cities (but not raions), commanders of military districts, and directors of plants that seemed among the largest in the city. "Middle level" means the other.

[c]"Industry" includes construction and transportation.

Sources: reprinted from Jerry F. Hough, "The Politics of Successful Economic Reform," *Soviet Economy,* Vol. 5, January-March 1989, p. 21. The figures are based on all two-candidate elections, including the runoffs, in Moscow, Moscow oblast. Leningrad oblast, all six krais, and all sixteen autonomous republics.

housing, zoning, budgets, and taxation will gain prominence. Politics will become less revolutionary, less ideological than it has been in the late 1980s and the early 1990s, and more "normal."

As this occurs, it will be necessary to move to a higher level of sophistication in our political analysis. One of the major causes of confusion in our discussion of the reform in Russia and the sources of support for democracy is that we use words such as "radical," "democrat," "conservative," and "reformer" in very idiosyncratic ways. Thus, a man such as Yegor Gaidar is called a "radical," and in some sense of the word he is. But in the West, a radical is a man of the right, at least in his language—a man who at least talks like a Chicago economist and whose policy is that of a Margaret Thatcher or a Ronald Reagan. On questions of economic reform, the true democrats today—the people whose policy is close to that of the majority of the population and who want elected legislatures to have strong power— tend to be relatively conservative on economic reform, comparable, say, to Swedish social-democrats who want a strong welfare state and governmental regulation of the economy. When the real Russian social democrats are called conservatives, and the avowed Russian social democrats want Thatcherite policy, we are still a long way from a "common European home" in our political analysis.

If we look at the background and general attitudes of deputies of the city soviet who took different positions on the level of taxes to be assessed on the resale of computers, we begin to see some of the complexities of political cleavages and coalitions that will have to be part of our analysis of Russian politics as those politics normalize.

For example, three votes were taken in the city soviet on February 19 and 22, 1991 on the level of taxes to levy on the sale of second-hand computers. The first was on a 20 percent tax, and the second on a 5 percent tax. The first of these measures received a plurality (ninety to forty-two with nine abstentions), but not a majority. The second failed fifty-eight to seventy-seven with ten abstentions. Then a compromise 10 percent tax passed with 108 to twenty-eight with nine abstentions.

These three votes gave deputies a chance to reject either the low tax or the high tax—and then to accept the compromise or not. All combinations were possible, but the overwhelming majority of deputies took one of four consistent positions: 1) yes on a high tax without compromise; 2) yes on high tax with compromise; 3) yes on low tax without compromise; and 4) yes on low tax with compromise.

Table 4.16 gives the breakdown of the voting on this tax by deputies with different attitudes towards economic reform. It suggests that Yaroslavl deputies are voting along ideological lines familiar in the West. Namely, those who are the most market-oriented tend to favor lower taxes, especially on items that are investment-oriented.

Yet, when one compares the pattern of voting on this tax with the socio-economic status of the deputies, one finds a result that is very different from the Western one. In the United States, political officials tend to be wary of tax increases, but in Yaroslavl the political officials favored a higher tax position by eighteen to five. In the United States, lower-income persons tend to support governmental spending—if not always higher taxes. In Yaroslavl the great majority

TABLE 4.16 Voting on Computer Tax in the City Soviet, By Level of Support for Economic Reform and Deputy Occupation

	High Tax No Compromise	High Tax Compromise	Low Tax Compromise	Low Tax No Compromise
	Level of support for economic reform			
Most supportive of reform (n=54)	3	23	10	18
Less supportive of reform (n=55)	4	32	14	5
	Occupation of deputies			
Political officials	2	16	3	2
Enterprise directors & deputy directors	1	11	9	4
Lower administrators & non- administrative personnel	5	31	28	16

of those with an uncompromising low tax position are lower-level officials, specialists, and workers.

The two results reported in Table 4.16 are not totally consistent. The political officials, as we have seen, are not opponents of economic reform on the average, and the workers who divide 12-13 on the tax question are not supporters of it. The officials would, no doubt, say that this vote shows the fundamental cleavage in the legislature—between those who are responsible and understand taxes must be raised and those who are irresponsible and populist and who play to the electorate. Others might argue that the pattern of voting would have been different if the object to be taxed were not used computers.

This is not the place to try to resolve such issues. The political cleavages in the Yaroslavl legislature were still in flux in 1990 and 1991 and will be for some time to come. What is important for the political scientist to understand is that as Yaroslavl politics normalizes, as the situation becomes less revolutionary, divisions on issues increasingly will arise along different lines than in the past. Former political enemies will become allies on some issues, while former political allies will come into conflict. The cleavages will vary from issue to issue. As Yaroslavl has to face up to fundamental questions of residential zoning, of taxation, of privatization, and of governmental regulation that have already been resolved in the West, it will become an exciting laboratory for political scientists. Our job now is to take the first steps to try to ensure that the analysis becomes more and more scientific and less and less ideological.

References

Smyth, Regina A. 1990. "Ideological Versus Regional Cleavages: Do the Radicals Control the RSFSR Parliament?" *Journal of Soviet Nationalities* 3: 112-157.

5

The Sundered State: Federalism and Parliament in Czechoslovakia

David M. Olson

Parliaments and elections, two of the critical features of democratic political systems, can help build unity within the state. These instruments help build societal unity out of diversity, as they simultaneously help build policy agreements out of disagreements.

These twin assertions about nation-building and conflict resolution in democratic political systems assume prior agreement upon the existence of a territorial state. Within decentralized and/or diverse states, federalism is an added instrument to help achieve the same objectives.

The current experiences of the former Warsaw Pact countries alert us to the limits upon these sweeping assertions. Post-communist transitions have been accompanied by disintegration of many of the states, especially those which are ethnically plural and which also had a formal federal structure (Comisso 1992). Democratization—or at least the ouster of former authoritarian rulers and collapse of the single party—has given regional elites and populations new opportunities to express their opinions on issues, not only political system and economic reform, but also of "stateness," of territorial definition of the sovereign national community.

The stateness problem has arisen in the "contrived federations" of the former Yugoslavia, the USSR, and Czechoslovakia (Linz and Stepan 1992: 123 and Lukic 1992: 598). An early review of these states suggested that Czechoslovakia presented a different set of circumstances than the others: the greater degree of democratization offered Slovak political elites a "greater voice within the system" than had the regional forces in the other countries (Frye 1992: 623). Accordingly, a split of the state was considered less likely.

Indeed, it could be argued that Czechoslovakia had many of the features of "consociational" democracy (Lijphart 1984). The parliament provided equal representation in one of its two houses for the two major ethnic-territorial segments of its population (Czech and Slovak), and further, had special decision rules requiring extra-large majorities on critical issues.

The failure to democratize at the federal level was cited as an impetus to regional fragmentation of the state in the USSR and Yugoslavia (Frye 1992). In Czechoslovakia, however, democratization at the federal level provided the opportunity to split the state.

The Slovak and Czech Republics, by contrast with the others, have become independent of the federation and from each other in a very different way than have the others: legislatures, elections and negotiations were the instrumentalities through which the decision to split the state was made and then implemented.

This chapter both examines the organization and functioning of the Federal Assembly of the former Czech and Slovak Federal Republic and also reviews the course of events through election and negotiation toward the sundering of the federal state. Particular attention will be given to the representational structure within the federal parliament and to the republic-centric formation of political parties. The Czechoslovak experience both supplements and modifies the electoral sequence hypothesis, that the timing of elections at different government levels has consequences for the newly democratized state (Linz and Stepan 1992).

The central argument is that the newly democratic political system, especially the structure of parliament and the organization of political parties within the ethnically regionalized federation of Czechoslovakia gave ample opportunity for regional separatism to be expressed, but little means by which those tensions could be resolved. There was a gap between the high intensity issue of ethnic separation and parliament's capacity to respond to that issue. One of the federal devices which could unite different regions and people into a common state, unequal representation in parliament, became an obstacle in attempting to find a basis for continued unity. The inherited structure and rules of the Federal Assembly and the newly formed democratic political parties were overwhelmed by the issue of ethno-regional separatism.

This analysis does not presuppose that a continued federation was preferable to the formation of two new states. This case does suggest, however, first, that the question of "stateness," when and if it becomes salient, is hard to resolve in favor of continued federation, especially in the aftermath of the transformation of an authoritarian system, and second, that under those circumstances, democratic and peaceful means can be utilized to achieve a "velvet divorce."

Parliament and Transition

Though the authoritarian political systems of Central Europe collapsed within a single year, the construction and development of a democratic political system is taking much longer. Everything is in flux. The new constitutions are largely unwritten, leaving relationships among president, parliament, and government undefined.

The new parliaments in the early post-communist transition of Central Europe are at the heart of both policy decisions and the institutionalization of the new democracy. Legislatures are often the only available site within which major political actors meet, and from which major political actors emerge. Legislatures are often the locale, the "central site," within which the nascent democracy's party system is defined (Liebert and Cotta 1990; Agh 1993).

There is an enormous variation among the post-communist countries of Central Europe and the former Soviet Republics, both in the transitional process itself and in how their respective legislatures are organized and function. In some countries, the transitional process was slow and deliberate, while in others, the communist system imploded late and precipitously. Some countries are ethnically homogeneous, while in many, ethnic tensions threaten not only the stability, but the existence, of the state, as in the former Czechoslovakia. In some, political parties have become organized both in the country and in parliament, while in others, parties are only embryonic.

The opportunities for legislatures to be active and influential in their political systems are probably much greater in new than in established democracies, for the external constraints (such as powerful executives and well-organized interest groups and parties) are not yet in place. Yet, the capacity of parliaments to act responsibly are probably at their lowest, for the new members have not had the time to develop the complicated internal structures of political parties and committees.

In Czechoslovakia, as a result of the collapse of the communist system the parliament underwent four stages since the beginning of communist rule. First, during the communist period of forty years, the National Assembly was inactive. Its few functions were performed by the Presidium. This forty-year period was then succeeded by several brief stages. In retrospect, however, in this long period of inactivity, one crucial decision was made: the state was officially federalized and the parliament converted into a bicameral body and renamed "Federal Assembly" (Skilling 1976: 481-89; Wolchik 1991: 61-67).

In its second stage of a half-year, the old parliament was "reconstructed" immediately following the collapse of the communist government in November 1989, at both the federal and republic levels. Almost half of its members left the parliament, and the new members were appointed through agreement between the Communist Party and the regime transition movements of the Civic Forum and Public Against Violence. Similar changes were made in the two National Councils (Reschova 1992, 1993; Syllova 1992a).

This temporary body served until the new democratic parliament could be elected in June 1990, to begin its third stage as an active and democratic legislature lasting until the 1992 election.

During the fourth stage, lasting for the half-year from the June 1992 election until the official dissolution of the federal state on January 1, 1993, the Federal Assembly declined from democratic vitality toward irrelevance and finally dissolution. During this fourth stage, however, the two National Councils were transformed from provincial bodies to parliaments of sovereign nation-states.

This chapter will concentrate on the last two periods of the Federal Assembly, from the first election of the new democracy in 1990 through the sundering of the state on January 1, 1993.

The Federal Assembly

In newly active legislatures of post-authoritarian countries, especially critical elements include committees, rules, and procedures, and relationships with the government. This review of the Czechoslovakian Federal Assembly will begin with its distinctive bicameral and party structures (Olson, Syllova and Reschova 1993; Olson 1992).

One , Two, or Three Chambers?

The most unusual feature of the Federal Assembly was its practice of bicameralism. Bicameralism was based upon the federal structure of the state. It was not bicameralism itself but its practice which was unusual in Czechoslovakia.

Though bicameral in structure, the Federal Assembly typically met in joint session, suggesting a unicameral system in practice. But on the other hand, for certain issues such as constitutional amendments votes were tabulated separately within three voting sections, suggesting the reality of a tricameral system. This complicated arrangement has been characterized as a "three-chambered" parliament, with two of the chambers located within one house (Pehe 1992a:31).

Structure and Composition

The two chambers of the houses were of equal size—150 seats each. Seats in the Chamber of People were allocated on the basis of the distribution of the population in the whole country, two-thirds to the Czech Republic (101 seats), and one-third (49 seats) to the Slovak Republic. Seats in the Chamber of Nations, by contrast, were equally divided between the Czech and the Slovak Republics, with 75 seats each. The presidia as well as the legislative committees reflected both the two-chamber and three voting section structure. Table 5.1 shows that the inter-republic difference of only twenty-six seats between the two chambers, joined with a different party configuration in the two Republics, resulted in major political and policy differences between the two chambers on one of the major issues facing the new democracy—federalism.

The practices of bicameral structure were unicameral in many respects but tricameral in other critical respects.

Unicameralism

The unicameral practices of the Federal Assembly began with their equal powers. The two chambers were equal in their legal authority and scope. Neither chamber had special powers in a no-confidence vote, confirmation of presidential appointments, or in treaty ratifications. Bills required the approval of both chambers. Neither chamber acted as only a delaying body for the other. The equality of action makes it inappropriate to refer to one chamber as "upper" and the

TABLE 5.1   Bicameralism in the National Assembly: Seats by Republic

Republic	*Chamber*	
	of People	*of Nations*
Czech	99	75
Slovak	51	75
Total	150	150

other "lower"; neither is it accurate to refer to one as "the confidence chamber." The complete equality of the two differently constituted chambers was a departure from usual democratic systems (Bogdanor 1987).

Their equality was also expressed through identical terms of office, simultaneous elections and integrated election campaigns. The two houses were directly elected at the same time, using the same system of proportional representation (Wightman 1990, 1991, 1993; Syllova 1992b). The elections and their impact upon division of the state will be discussed in a subsequent section.

Unicameral practices of the bicameral structure also characterized both the committees and floor sessions. The committees existed in parallel form in the two chambers, and most often met together to consider legislation. The two chamber components at a common committee meeting usually agreed upon a single legislative text. For most purposes, the dual committees functioned as a single unit. Two rapporteurs from the dual committee, one per chamber, presented the committee report to the floor.

On the floor, most bills were debated and voted in a single common session of the two chambers. The two chambers voted together, but quickly, through an electronic vote tabulation system. One chamber could meet by itself for either an election of its own members to committees of other parliamentary organs, or, on occasion, to reconsider an earlier vote in which the two chambers disagreed.

Tricameralism

The tricameral feature, by contrast, was based on the requirement of a "double majority" within the Chamber of Nations. On constitutional and certain other questions, a majority must have been separately obtained from each of the two Republic voting sections in the Chamber of Nations, as well as from the whole Chamber of People. Furthermore, the requirement on some questions was a three-fifths majority, not a simple majority. These majority requirements were usually based upon the whole membership, not only those present and voting.

The double majority requirement within the Chamber of Nations, with varying sizes of the needed majority, covered three categories of decision: 1) constitutional amendments and "constitutional laws"; 2) a set of constitutionally specific topics; and 3) votes of no-confidence.

Constitutional protections to minorities are a common feature of democracies (Banton and Simeon 1985). In a federal state, the bicameral structure of parliament is, itself, a protection for the lower levels of government (Lijphart 1984). In the Czech and Slovak Federal Republic, the relatively small size of the Chamber of Nations, divided into two equal voting sections, each of which required a 60-percent majority of all members on sensitive questions, provided a small number of members (thirty), if they were so determined or merely absent, with a veto power within the Assembly.

This constitutional rule, inherited from the 1968 Communist Constitution, was vitally important to Slovakian political forces, but was simultaneously regarded by others as an overly-rigid feature of the Assembly. As federalism grew in importance, increasingly the Slovakian section of the Chamber of Nations withheld 60 percent support. Increasingly, the Federal Assembly could not adopt proposed legislation on the most important question before it, the question of stateness.

While the Slovakian section of the Chamber of Nations sometimes vetoed decisions endorsed by the Czech section and the other chamber, there are examples of negative votes in the other section and chamber as well. While the Slovakian Section did not agree to the referendum bill, the Czech section did not approve the Judiciary bill. The Chamber of People, too, voted against proposed legislation that had been approved by the other Chamber. On a wide range of "ordinary" issues, Slovakian and Czech deputies voted similarly to one another, thus making the Assembly a functioning unicameral body. It was on federal issues that the double majority requirement increasingly expressed, and blocked, effective decisions (Ciganek 1992: 187-198).

During the Federal Assembly's fourth stage, of institutional decline, major decisions were repeatedly delayed and/or defeated by the double-majority and the 60-percent rules. Those decisions increasingly concerned the means by which the federation could be legally dissolved. During this decline stage, to be discussed more fully below, the Federal Assembly was reflecting and reacting to decisions made elsewhere.

The unicameral versus tricameral practices of the Federal Assembly reflected the two dimensions of issues and conflict in post-Communist Czechoslovakia. The full range of issues faced in all of the new democracies, such as foreign policy, economic reform, and crime, that is, the "normal" issues facing a country, were handled by the Federal Assembly on a unicameral basis, both in committee and on the floor. The second dimension, however, the stateness issue, provoked the Assembly to function as a tricameral body. Equal representation of the two portions of the country, coupled with the double majority requirement, blocked solution of questions on the stateness dimension.

Political Parties and the Party System

Political parties in the post-Communist period in Central Europe are tentative and fluid (Agh 1992; Olson 1993b). This characteristic, perhaps typical of a new political system, is illustrated by the constantly changing configuration of political parties. The initial election of early 1990 was a regime change election, in which the major question was a referendum on a new political system. The leading group, the Civic Forum (OF) in the Czech lands and the Public Against Violence (PAV) in Slovakia (VPN), were mass social movements, not political parties (Skala and Kunkel 1992).

Once in office, the newly elected Members of the Federal Assembly soon began to split into smaller parliamentary clubs, which became the early political parties of the new democracy. Not only was the number of party groups always subject to change, but so was their size, for members would both join and leave, and in addition, the very concept of membership was open and fluid. By the time of the 1992 elections, eighteen such clubs had been created in the Federal Assembly, while an additional set of Members were "unorganized." There was similar party fluidity in the two National Councils as well.

At the same time, political parties were formed outside of parliament, so that in early 1992, well over one hundred parties had officially been registered, though only thirty-five offered candidates for the Federal Assembly in the June 1992 elections (*Lidove Noviny*, April 22, 1992). As the elections approached, both the party clubs in parliament and the party formations outside parliament slowly formed new parties among each other. The most prominent illustration of this broader tendency was the agreement that Alexander Dubcek, then Chairman of the Federal Assembly, would join the Social Democratic Party of Slovakia as both its chairman and as its election leader (*Rude Pravo*, March 16, 1992; Obrman 1992a).

The fluidity of party formation in the Assembly was matched by their voting patterns (Ciganek 1992: 192-198; *Respekt*, June 1, 1992). Party discipline changed over time and also varied among parties. As new parties were created, they formed ad hoc coalitions on individual bills. Some members did not vote with their parties. With the exception of the traditional discipline of the Communist Party, no deputies reported a strong sense of party discipline or recrimination from their party clubs.

The fluidity of the party system and the tentative character of political party organization was duplicated in both Poland and Hungary during the 1989-1992 period (McQuaid 1991; Wiatr 1992).

This plasticity may be a typical feature of parliaments, and of democratic political systems more broadly at their beginning.

The tentative and changing party system in Central Europe is itself partly a consequence of the previous communist period, dominated by a single hierarchical party. The very concept of political party has been clouded by the experience. The new parties tended to emphasize participation rather than leadership. Most of the new parties lacked the kind of organization which could direct its members within parliament. In addition, numerous new parties did not even use the term "party" in their own names (Olson 1993b; Olson and Fried 1992).

Yet, the essential feature of this party system is that it was a dual-party system, a republic-centric party system. Each republic developed its own set of political parties. Parties rarely formed across republic boundaries. Those few which made the attempt were repudiated in the 1992 election. Even the initial regime-change movements were separately organized in each republic and received different levels of voter support in the regime change election of 1990. While the leaders of the two regime change movements cooperated, apparently smoothly, in government, those leaders were repudiated in the 1992 elections.

After the 1992 elections, the parliamentary parties appear to have gained cohesion, at least in parliamentary floor votes. Those elections gave decisive power to one party in each republic, which came to embody republic-level solidarity in relationship to the other republic. The agreement between the two republic-leading parties to split the state became the basis of their governing coalition at the federal level during the final and declining stage of the Federal Assembly.

It was the diverse opposition parties which tended to split at critical junctures in the Federal Assembly during this final stage. They provided some votes—enough—for major decisions to finally be made by the Federal Assembly to split the state in a legal manner (Pehe 1992d).

Committees

The structure of the committees was another inheritance from the communist institution. Their small number, wide jurisdiction, and lack of staff support were continuing features in the new democratic Assembly continued from the communist era (Races 1989: 472-77; Olson and Simian 1982).

Draft bills were usually referred to several committees, one of which was designated as the lead committee for each bill. The other committees reported their views to the lead committee, which was responsible to report to the floor the conclusions of the other committees, along with its own. Though the jurisdiction of the legislative committees had not been defined in the rules, the chairmen usually requested bills consistent with the scope of the committee's concerns.

The Committee on Constitutional Law and Legislation had a unique function, in common with several of the other post-Communist parliaments. Most bills, with the exception of treaty ratifications, were considered by this committee as well as the substantive committees. On bills of shared jurisdiction, it usually limited itself to review of the compatibility of a draft bill with the existing legal code. On those bills on which it was the lead committee, however, it acted autonomously. Constitutional matters were within its jurisdiction, elevating the importance of this committee in the formative stages of a new democracy and in the growing controversy over the shape of the federation.

Members were placed on committees initially in accordance with at least two criteria. One was party ratios, to allocate committee seats among the parties proportionally to their numerical strength in each chamber. This criterion lost relevance as the old parties disintegrated and the number of new party clubs grew. In addition, the committee seats within the Chamber of Nations were, like the Chamber itself, evenly divided between the Czech and Slovak sections.

The other criterion consisted of the preferences and skills of the members as judged primarily by their education and occupation. Thus, most members of the Committee on the Constitution and Law were lawyers if not also professors of law. Most members of the Committee on Social Affairs and Culture, as another example, were trained in professions relating to both fields.

During most of the 1990-92 session of the Federal Assembly, committees worked on "normal" legislation free of obvious conflicts and constraints stemming from the Czech-Slovak distinction. So long as federalism was not the main issue, the members, especially in committee, functioned as one could find in a "normal" legislature at the beginning of a new political system, typifying the unicameral practice of the bicameral legislature.

Legislative Rules and Procedures

One of the difficulties facing a new legislature is the task of defining its rules of procedure. New members, especially in the first post-authoritarian years, often are not familiar with collective decision-making within deliberative bodies, and thus are not prepared immediately to define the rules which they will need for effective and fair procedures. On the other hand, a legislature which is the legal continuation of a communist institution inherits, among other things, its rules and procedures. Those rules can be awkward and inadequate to a fully democratic parliament, for in an authoritarian system, the rules had little practical effect. They were neither tested nor refined in practice. Though new rules were adopted in Spring 1991, many procedures for the first Federal Assembly were specified by the still-existing communist era constitution, and thus could not be changed by amendment of the internal rules.

Steps in Legislation. Draft bills flowed through several clearly defined steps. Government bills were presented to the Chairman of the Federal Assembly and the presidia of the two chambers. The chairmen of the two chambers consulted with committee chairmen and referred bills to the committees. From the Assembly committees, bills went to the floor. In the few cases in which the two chambers disagreed, a special inter-chamber negotiation committee was formed to work out a compromise.

Committees. Procedures within the committees were informal but regularized. Ministers or their delegates presented and explained government bills, as did deputies who sponsored their own bills. Two committee rapporteurs, one for each chamber, kept track of the committee amendments and prepared the committee report. Votes were by show of hands but were counted separately for the two sets of members within the common meeting of the two chamber committees.

Plenum. Floor procedures could be more complex. At the beginning of each session, the agenda prepared by the presidium was debated and voted on by the plenum. There was an increased load of floor business as adjournment of the term drew near. The preliminary discussion of the agenda for a two-week floor session sometimes took a half-day, thus delaying proceedings from the very beginning.

During consideration of bills, questions have been raised from the floor about proper procedures of debate, amendments and voting (Reschova,1992). At times, members argued over the chairman's rulings and actions, while chairmen have left the post in frustration. Some members have felt offended more than once by comments by individual presiding officers in the chair (personal interviews). It is striking, in retrospect, that few of these episodes have involved the federal question, but rather, concerned other types of disputes.

To shorten debate, a ten-minute limit on individual statements has sometimes been adopted at the beginning of floor discussion of complex bills. Most bills were debated and voted on quickly. Bills to which many floor amendments have been offered have been frequently postponed following debate to the next day, so the committee rapporteurs could write and arrange the amendments for voting. Postponement overnight also permitted the lead committee to formulate its position on the floor amendments.

The complicated voting procedures discussed earlier were facilitated by a new electronic display board on both sides of the chamber, which was instituted in Fall 1990. For each vote, there was a clear indication of the voting units—two chambers or three voting sections—and also of the needed margin of vote. Not only could members vote "yea" or "nay," but they could also officially abstain, or simply not vote. Given the need for each of the two sections of the Chamber of Nations, any vote other than "yea" counted against the immediate proposal.

Almost 2,000 roll-call votes were taken on the electronic equipment. It was possible to conduct two votes per minute. In rapid voting, however, it was apparently difficult to identify the exact topic of the votes in the electronic record. There was also sometimes confusion over the exact wording of an adopted amendment, for often amendments were offered orally.

Sources of Legislation

Bills could be proposed by the Government, the Members, the committees, the two national councils, and the President.

Though most bills were proposed by the government, and most of them were adopted in some form, the proportion initiated by members was also fairly high in comparison to other democracies. The government appeared weaker in relation to the parliament than in other democratic systems.

Members sometimes initiated bills which the government considered, but did not offer. Other member bills were alternatives to bills submitted by either the government or the president. Still others were opposition party drafts which as such had little possibility of adoption.

The members, however, were handicapped in bill preparation, for the parliament lacked a bill drafting staff to support the members. There were many complaints about the quality of draftsmanship in both government and private members' bills, but there was no agreement on whether or not parliament should develop its own bill drafting staff.

The republic national councils and the president proposed few but major constitutional bills. The councils were more successful with the Federal Assembly than was the president.

Parliament and Government

One characteristic of the Federal Assembly at the democratic beginning was a blurring of the distinction between government coalition parties and the opposition parties. Members of the Assembly, as well as members of the government, observed that the government sometimes obtained more support from opposition parties than from its own party groups. Furthermore, there was little consensus during this first parliament about which parties could properly be considered "government" parties in distinction to opposition parties.

The question of confidence was never brought to the floor to test parliamentary support for the continuance of the whole cabinet in office, and only once against individual members (Ciganek 1992: 188). The cabinet members themselves were leaders of the newly forming parliamentary parties. The regime-transformative movements were splitting into new parties within the cabinet, but the continuance in office of the cabinet as a whole was not questioned. The government continued to function as a whole and to propose government bills to parliament.

As new parties formed, the government parties lost seats. By themselves, the parties with ministers in government became a minority. Though there was no cohesive opposition to challenge the government in office, the fate of its legislation was always contingent. The federal dimension did not appear to be important in this respect. The Slovakian members could not, by themselves, either unseat or form a government, even if they had been united on such issues.

In summary, this legislature functioned through a complicated set of internal structures of bicameralism, parties, and committees. It was a parliament at the beginning of a democratic existence. Its internal structures had a tentative, beginning quality. No one was quite sure of how committees should be composed or should function. No one was sure what legislative parties should be or do. Procedures on the floor were unclear. Yet, the Federal Assembly met full time, handled a complicated agenda of legislation, and did make decisions for the new democracy. At the same time, however, the federalism question was increasing in salience in parliament, became the vital issue in the 1992 elections, and culminated in the dissolution of the common state. The following sections trace this growing development, both in and outside of the Federal Assembly.

Elections and Political Parties

Czechoslovakia experienced a sequence of two elections after the authoritarian system transition. The initial election, 1990, was the "founding" election of the new democratic political system. The second election, only two years later, could have been an integral element in consolidation of the democratic system. While it may have had that effect at the republic level, the more immediate significance has been to lead directly to the dissolution of the federation (Wightman 1992 1993; Olson 1993a).

The initial, founding election in 1990 followed the street demonstrations and the "velvet revolution" of November-December 1989. The election continued the street demonstration process, for it was a referendum on the continuance of the communists in power. This election was dominated by the regime-transformative movements of the Civic Forum and the Public Against Violence. That election brought the transformative movements into governmental power in the Federal Assembly and also into the two National Councils (Wightman 1990, 1991; Wolchik 1991; Brokl 1992).

The transformative movements were explicitly not political parties. They were much broader in scope and more amorphous in organization (Skala and Kunkel 1992; Olson 1993b). Political parties did form, both in the country but especially within the Federal Assembly, as recounted in a previous section, so that over thirty-five parties contested the 1992 Federal Assembly elections. At the republic National Council level, twenty parties ran for the Czech, while twenty-two ran for the Slovak legislatures.

The displacement of the regime-transformative movements by political parties offered the possibility that Czechoslovakia would experience its first "normal" democratic election in 1992 with a contest for power and office among rival parties and candidates, rather than a referendum on the character of the regime.

In Slovakia, however, the 1992 election retained the character of a referendum—this time, on continuation of the federation. The winning party, like the original regime-transformative movements, attracted a diverse membership to broad goals rather than a more limited membership concerned with more specific issues.

The parties were republic-specific. The structure of the Federal Assembly required the election results to be calculated in three sections, to ascertain the likelihood of any one party or coalition being able to obtain not only a simple majority but a 60% majority in each. In an initial normal democratic election, the question would be the shape of the party system in the whole federation, and especially in the Chamber of People. In Czechoslovakia, however, the question became the shape of the party system in each Republic. Thus a second question followed. Would the winners in each republic be able to form a cross-republic coalition to govern the federation? The country was officially a federation, but operated politically as a confederation.

At the beginning of the election year, no party was organized across republican boundaries. Even the Communist Party, beginning in the 1990 parliament as a single country-wide party, split into two republic-level parties. Some parties did attempt to build coalitions with parties in the other republic, as did both the Social Democrats and Civic Democratic Party. Neither the cross-republic parties nor those in Slovakia advocating federation did well in the election results.

The importance of Republic boundaries was both recognized and emphasized by the election law (Zakon 1992; Syllova 1992b). Election districts, for the proportional representation system of voting, were the large provinces, all of which were contained within a single republic. Further, the threshold clause was defined as 5% of the vote in a single republic. In addition, the distribution of seats in a second round was calculated on a republic, and not a federation, basis. Finally, the election was administered through three election commissions, one federal, the others republican.

Economic reform was the major issue in the Czech Republic, in contrast to federalism in Slovakia. Federalism was hardly noticed as an issue in the Czech Republic, while all of the major Slovakian parties argued for greater Slovakian autonomy. The most separatist views were advocated by the Slovakian National Party (SNS) and the Slovakian Christian Democrats (SKDH). The winning party, Movement for Democratic Slovakia (HZDS), internally divided on the issue, took a less explicit position.

Slovakia differed in economic conditions from the Czech Republic. Unemployment was higher, and the heavy industry and military orientation of its manufacturers became liabilities in the post Cold War era. In its disadvantaged economy, Slovakia differed from the economic position of separatist regional movements in both Spain and Yugoslavia (Frye 1992).

That Slovakia and the Czech lands differed politically was clear from the beginning of the velvet revolution. Each republic created its own regime-transformative movement. Furthermore, in the 1990 regime-change referendum, Public Against Violence received only 32 percent of the vote in Slovakia, while the Civic Forum received 52 percent in the Czech Republic (Wightman 1991).

In the 1990-1992 period, the dynamics of Slovakian politics differed from the Czech. Several Slovakian parties split, the Prime Minister was removed, and the Slovakian National Council was more internally divided than the Czech (Pehe 1991a). At the Slovakian National Council, dissatisfaction was often expressed about Slovakian status in the federation (information obtained from personal interviews). Furthermore, the dynamic of Slovakian politics was in the National Council at Bratislava; the Slovakian representation in the Federal Assembly reflected but did not originate the splits and tensions within Slovakian politics.

The 1992 campaign was fully integrated between the two government levels within each republic. Candidates for the two levels regularly campaigned together, presenting a common party, rather than a more specific office-oriented view. The most prominently displayed graphics were party symbols and party numbers (for the ballots) rather than images of the candidates for office. The party campaigns were centrally organized, funded, and scheduled, as were the campaign literature and posters.

The election results either reflected or justified the central party campaign strategy. Party results between the Federal Assembly and the two National Councils were very similar to each other. As Table 5.2 demonstrates, each republic had one clear plurality-winning party: the Civic Democratic Party (ODS-KDS) in the Czech lands and the Movement for a Democratic Slovakia (HZDS), at about 33 percent each.

The 5-percent threshold requirement had an important effect on the results. It completely eliminated the moderate center parties in both republics, and thus undermined pro-federalist parties in the Slovak Republic's National Council. Many of the leaders of Czechoslovakia's first post-communist government were thus removed, not only from government, but also from the Federal Assembly and the national councils.

The election results, at the intersection of electoral law and party system were converted from country-wide elections into republic-centric contests, as has also been noted in Canada (Gibbons 1982b).

That the most likely federal leaders assumed republic office was the clearest of all signals that what could have been the federation's first "normal" democratic election, had, instead become the major event in sundering the state. Instead of choosing parties and filling offices, it became a referendum on the meta-political question of "stateness."

TABLE 5.2 Election Results for the 1992 Federal Assembly and National Councils, by Party Votes and Seats

Republic and Party	Federal Assembly					National Councils		
	Chamber of People		Chamber of Nations					
	Votes (%)	Seats (N)	Votes (%)	Seats		Votes (%)	Seats	
				(N)	(%)		(N)	(%)
Czech Lands:								
Civic Dem (ODS-KDS)	33.90	48	33.43	37	49.33	29.73	76	38.00
Left Bloc (LB)	14.27	19	14.48	15	20.00	14.05	35	17.50
Czech Soc Dem (CSSD)	7.67	10	6.80	6	8.00	6.53	16	8.00
Rep Assoc (RPR-RSC)	6.48	8	6.37	6	8.00	5.98	14	7.00
Chr. Dem Union (KDU-CSL)	5.98	7	6.08	6	8.00	6.28	15	7.50
Liber. Social Union (LSU)	5.84	7	6.06	5	6.67	6.52	16	8.00
Civic Dem Alliance (ODA)	4.89	—	4.08	—	—	5.93	14	7.00
Civic Movement (OH)	4.39	—	4.74	—	—	4.59	—	—
Moravian/Silesian Movement (HSD)	4.23	—	4.90	—	—	5.87	14	7.00
Subtotal	87.74		86.94			85.48		
All others	12.26		13.06			14.52		
Republican Total	100.00	99	100.00	75	100.00	100.00	200	100.00
Slovakia:								
Dem Left (SDL)	14.44	10	14.04	13	17.33	14.70	29	19.33
Slov Nat (SNS)	9.39	6	9.35	9	12.00	7.93	15	10.00
Chr. Dem Mov (KDH)	8.96	6	8.81	8	10.67	8.88	18	12.00
Coexistence	7.37	5	7.39	7	9.33	7.42	14	9.33
Sl Soc Dem (SDSS)	4.86	—	6.09	5	6.67	4.00	—	—
Civic Dem Union (ODU)	3.96	—	4.04	—	—	4.03	—	—
Dem Coalition (DS-ODS)	3.95	—	3.66	—	—	3.31	—	—
Sl. Chr. Democ Mvmt. (SKDH)	3.45	—	3.24	—	—	3.10	—	—

(*continues*)

TABLE 5.2   *(continued)*

	Federal Assembly					National Councils		
	Chamber of People		Chamber of Nations					
	Votes	*Seats*	*Votes*	*Seats*		*Votes*	*Seats*	
Republic and Party	*(%)*	*(N)*	*(%)*	*(N)*	*(%)*	*(%)*	*(N)*	*(%)*
Subtotal	89.91		90.47			90.63		
All others	10.09		9.53			9.37		
Republic Total	100.00	51	100.00	75	100.00	100.00	150	100.00
Federation Total		150		150				

Notes: Includes all parties over 3.2% in one Republic per chamber or council. The entries "all others" include all parties under 3.2% for any one chamber per Republic Council. Parties listed by size for Chamber of People by republic.
Sources: Svobodne Slovo, June 8, 1992; *CSTK,* "Volby 92," June 7, 1992; *Federal Election Commission* "1992 Report Disk"; and *Rude Pravo,* June 11, 1992.

Dissolution of the State

The fourth and final stage of the Federal Assembly followed the 1992 elections. As a result of those federal level but republic-centric elections, republic leaders decided to dissolve the federation. The Federal Assembly thus had the task of legalizing the dissolution, while at the same time facing its own marginalization as part of the decline of all institutions of the federal state.

The Federal Assembly, with respect to the critical issue facing the country, returned to its status under communism: it acted in response to major decisions made elsewhere. But unlike the communist period, its members and party composition had been decided through free elections.

During this period, there were at least three sets of divisions within the Assembly:

1. Slovak versus Czech. This dominant division led to the governing caretaker cabinet after the 1992 election, formed by the unlikely coalition of opposites, whose leaders could agree only upon one objective, to dissolve the state. The Slovakian voting power, augmented through the double majority requirement, was one basis for the negotiations between the leaders of opposites;
2. Government versus Opposition. The opposition parties had little

in common. They could vote against proposals of the government. At critical stages, they split their votes. Not only did the opposition parties vote differently from each other, but individual members sometimes voted differently from their own parties as well;

3. Intra-party. Each party was beset by its own internal divisions. One source of division, however, cross-cut all parties with membership in both the national councils and in the Federal Assembly: how to deal with the Federal Assembly members? Would they simply be out of office upon the dissolution of the federation? Or should they become members of the National Councils, which would then have to be reorganized (Pehe 1993)?

The Federal Assembly, in its final stage, was dominated by its inability to act. It could neither elect a President of the federation, nor adopt legislation legally permitting the formal dissolution of the state.

The presidential election was characterized above all by the Slovakian members' refusal to reelect Vaclav Havel as President. In the end, no one was elected, for by that time, dissolution of the state was a certainty. The refusal to reelect Havel was, however, by itself, an important step toward state dissolution, occurring within about a month of the 1992 election (Obrman 1992c).

Legislation to dissolve the state was proposed by the caretaker government, but the governing parties by themselves lacked a 60 percent majority in each of the three voting sections of the Assembly. The opposition parties voted against, preferring a referendum on the issue (Obrman 1992d). The bill was twice defeated, after which it was referred to a committee. The committee accepted two amendments to gain a sufficient margin of votes from the opposition. One amendment was accepted on the floor, thus leading to adoption of a constitutional law by which the federation could legally be sundered. Some deputies from several opposition parties provided the missing votes for the three separate three-fifths majorities (Pehe 1992d).

By the time of the third and successful vote on the constitutional law to dissolve the federation, November 25, the only remaining question for the Federal Assembly to decide was the means by which the state would be sundered. The decision to split the state had long since been made and acted upon at the republic level. If the Federal Assembly did not act, the federation would split in a cloud of legal ambiguity. If it did act, the federation would split in a much clearer and simpler legal manner.

Republic-centric decisions led to the dissolution of the state. The critical bargains were between two leaders; what they could not agree upon—federation versus confederation—led to the next best argument, sundering of the federation (Pehe 1992c:36). Their decisions had the support of a majority within. Their agreements usually required the formal adoption by the national councils, and some agreements were in the form of bilateral treaties which required formal ratification. Their initial meetings between two party leaders in the federation soon became meetings between republic-level governments.

The Slovakian government took unilateral action to force the pace of the federal dissolution. It adopted a declaration of sovereignty, enacted a constitution, and moved toward election of its own president (Obrman 1992c; Pehe 1992b; Sivakova 1993).

The republics had continually grown in decision-making importance in the 1990-1992 period as well. The question of the constitutional status of the republics was negotiated for months, in 1991 and early 1992, by the republican leaders elected through the Civic Forum and Public Against Violence. Their agreement was rejected, not by the Federal Assembly, but by the Slovakian National Council (Pehe 1991b). That action both reflected the changing party configuration within Slovakia and was precursor to the sovereignty campaign appeals adopted by most Slovakian parties in the subsequent 1992 elections (Brokl and Mansfeldova 1992; Gal 1992).

Assent by the Federal Assembly to the inter-republic leader agreements was, in each case, useful but not essential during the last stage of the federation. When the republic leaders could not agree, action by the Federal Assembly did become more important. Of those disagreements, the question of division of federal assets was by far the most critical. A bill on that question was adopted shortly before the Federal Assembly finally accepted, on its third try, the law on dissolution of the federation; adoption of the former was one important prerequisite to adoption of the latter.

The Federal Assembly, along with the entire federal level governmental structure, became marginalized as the stateness issue grew in importance. While this decline was obvious following the June 1992 elections, the trend had begun earlier. The direct republic-level negotiations in 1991 and early 1992, somewhat like the Canadian First Ministers' Conferences (Smith 1993), became an important means of expressing and resolving critical policy disputes between regions. Thus it displaced the Federal Assembly.

Parliament, Elections, and Federalism

The dissolution of Czechoslovakia appears a deviant case, one not explicable by existing theories. One review of several cases found that regional and ethnic groups which separated from a larger federation tended to have two characteristics in common: clear ethnic differentiation and a relatively prosperous economy. The Slovakians were an exception to both conditions (Frye 1992).

Czechoslovakia does not fit comfortably with the elections sequence thesis (Linz and Stepan 1992). Countries in which country-wide elections were held before the regional level elections tended to preserve unity. If, however, elections were held first at the regional level, separatist political forces would gain the initiative. The initial democratic elections in Czechoslovakia, by contrast, were held simultaneously to both the federal and republic legislatures.

The logic of the electoral sequence hypothesis, however, does apply to Czechoslovakia. Regional elections, if held before the all-union level, are seen to provide regional elites the opportunity to define region-wide identities which differentiate them from other ethnicities and regions in the country. This republic-centric dynamic did occur in Slovakia, but more in the second (1992) than in the founding (1990) election.

Spain is the classic case in which the initial elections were country-wide. Several country-wide elections and referenda were held to write and adopt a new democratic constitution. After the new country-level democratic institutions had been defined and filled, the regional autonomy was discussed, negotiated, and legislated. During the almost decade long period, the regional separatist parties lost strength in their own regions to the union-oriented parties, and public identification with the country grew (Linz and Stepan 1992).

At least five circumstances differentiate Czechoslovakia from Spain, which suggest additional factors in considering the "stateness" issue.

First, the number of ethnicities and regions is important. In the post-World War II era, Czechoslovakia consisted of only two subgroupings, the Slovaks and the Czechs (hence the name of the country), while Spain was composed of many regions and potential regional identities. The growing separatist views of Slovakia engaged a full one-third of the country, while the Catalan and Basque regions constituted a much smaller proportion of Spain.

Secondly, the two cases differ in terms of age and experience of unity. Spain had been a single political unit for close to 500 years. Like many countries of Central Europe and the Balkans, Czechoslovakia was a successor state to older empires formed only at the end of World War I. If the symbols associated with the name "Spain" have positive emotive power among Spaniards, the symbols associated with the name "Czechoslovakia" had much less time to develop similar positive identifications (Rose 1992).

Thirdly, there is the issue of the authoritarian inheritance. Each newly democratized regime worked within an inherited regional structure from the recent authoritarian past. There were no regional governments in Spain at the death of Franco, while the Slovakian Republic structure was already in place at the time of regime change as a result of communist-era federalization of the state. The regime-transformative movements in each country emerged within a received governmental structure. Thus, in Czechoslovakia the regime-transformative movements were two—one in each republic. The inherited regional structure of Spain permitted all-union elections to be held first, while in Czechoslovakia, two inherited levels of government required democratization and free elections. Each step of the regime-transformative process occurred simultaneously at the two governmental levels (Reschova 1992; Sivakova 1992; Syllova 1992).

Fourth, there were different policy burdens in the two countries. Democratic transition from communism involves a political transformation in combination with reform of the economy. Previous authoritarian system transitions have occurred in countries with private ownership and an underlying legal system already in place (Offe 1991).

Finally, economic conditions are a source of difference. In Spain, and in several other countries, the separatist regions were more prosperous than the Czech lands. It is not entirely clear that the sense of nationalism, however, would have been lessened by more equal economic conditions , and neither is it clear that separation would improve the Slovakian economy more than would continued federation. An added economic consideration was the presence of the European Common Market. Slovakian political leaders seemed perfectly willing to substitute Brussels for Prague as the source of both economic support and constraint.

As both the Canadian and Belgium experience suggest, separatist ethno-regional tensions place severe strains upon central governments and their parties (Olson and Franks 1993; Rudolph 1989).

Authoritarian governments, however, perhaps create special vulnerabilities in the social fabric and special liabilities in the governmental structure and political parties. The Czechoslovakian federal institutions were overwhelmed by their tasks. The Federal Assembly as a beginning legislature, and perhaps also the federal government as a newly democratized entity, lacked the experience and the resources of internal structure and procedures to process the highly volatile issue of regional separatism. The federal state was underdeveloped in its capabilities but overwhelmed by its responsibilities.

One key development occurred within the party system of Czechoslovakia. In full conformity with the logic of the electoral sequence hypothesis, the new political parties, though emerging within the Federal Assembly, were formed solely within republic boundaries. Though there was full discussion, interaction and bargaining between Czech and Slovak deputies, both in committee and on the floor of the Federal Assembly, their primary political identities were shaped within the pre-existing republic boundaries.

Within Slovakia itself, the initiative was seized by the separatists—who came in many different varieties. The clear pro-union group, the regime-transformative movement, split, lost deputies and was eliminated in the 1992 elections. No new pro-union party was successful in those elections, though the leading Czech party did attempt to form a Slovakian affiliate during the 1992 campaign. Quite apart from the sequence of elections, however, moderate and unionist parties around the world run the risk of being undercut by local and ethnic particularist appeals (Horowitz 1985; Comisso 1992).

The intricate balancing of Slovakian with Czech representation in one chamber of the Federal Assembly, coupled with intricate decision rules about double majorities in three voting sections, would seem to be examples of consociational arrangements to protect minorities and to create the conditions for consensus (Lijphart 1984). The Czech and Slovak Federation, however, did not meet one of the essential conditions for either creating or keeping a federation: its constituent parts, or at least the leadership elected within each part, did not desire continued union as a good in itself.

Under these circumstances, the elaborate representation balance and rules of decision-making proved more a source of irritation and confusion than a means of arriving at shared decisions. The structure and rules of democratic governance were used to encourage regional separatism rather than to build country-wide unity.

Those elaborate structures and rules were used, however, to

accomplish separation through a negotiated settlement. The negotiations were not between military commanders, but through elected party and thus government leaders. When extra-large and differently composed majorities could not be negotiated within parliament, the critical decisions were made through extra-parliamentary negotiations between separately elected leaders.

Acknowledgments

The author expresses appreciation to the many members and staff of the Federal Assembly and the two National Councils, and to candidates and party workers, who have contributed generously of their time for interviews, field trips, and documents. A particular note of appreciation goes to my two co-authors on a larger project on the Federal Assembly, Dr. Jana Reschova, Higher School of Economics, and Dr. Jindriska Syllova, Parliamentary Institute of the Federal Assembly. The section of this paper on the Federal Assembly is based on portions of our joint work (Olson et al. 1993). This research is based upon a Fulbright appointment at Charles University.

Dr. Vladimir Balas, Dr. Zdenek Zboril and Dr. Petr Mares have been particularly helpful in providing access to data and in their interpretations. In addition, Ian Fried, of Johns Hopkins and Komenius Universities, and Dr. Danica Sivakova of the Slovak Academy of Sciences, Institute of Sociology, have been most helpful in understanding the electoral situation in Slovakia. Thanks are also owed to the author's colleagues in the two Departments of Political Science and the Institute for Political and Social Research at the Charles University, and to the members of the Institute of State and Law, and the Institute of Sociology, both in the Academy of Science. My research assistant through the MPA program at UNCG, Gregory Ferguson, has labored long and hard in support of this research.

References

Agh, Attila. 1992. "The Emerging Party System in East Central Europe," *Budapest Papers on Democratic Transition*, No. 13. Budapest: Hungarian Center for Democracy Studies Foundation.
————. 1993. "Bumpy Road to Europeanization: Policy Effectiveness and Agenda Concentration in the Hungarian Legislation (1990-1993)," *Budapest Papers on Democratic Transition*, No. 50. Budapest:Hungarian Center for Democracy Studies Foundation.
Banton, Keith, and Richard Simeon. 1985. *Redesigning the State: The Politics of Constitutional Change in Industrial Nations*. Toronto: University of Toronto Press.

Bogdanor, Vernon (ed.). 1987. *The Blackwell Encyclopaedia of Political Institutions.* New York and Oxford: Basil Blackwell.

Brokl, Lubomir. 1992. "Mezi Listopadem 1989 a demokracii-antinomie nasi politiky," *Sociologicky Casopis* 28:2 (April) 150-164.

Brokl, Lubomir and Zdenka Mansfeldova. 1992. "Die Tscechische und Slowakische Foederative Republik nach den Wahlen 1992." Czech Academy of Science, Institute of Sociology (August), manuscript.

Ciganek, Frantisel (ed.). 1992. *Kronika Demokratickeho Parlamentu, 1989-1992.* Praha: Cesty.

Comisso, Ellen. 1992. "Federalism and Nationalism in Post-Socialist Eastern Europe," paper read at symposium on "Federalism for the New Europe," Cardozo School of Law, New York, September 10-12.

Federalni Statisticky Urad (FSU). 1992. "Volby do Federalniho shromazdeni Ceske a Slovenske Federativni Republike, 1992,"Czech and Slovak Federative Republic: Report of the Federal Election Commission on disk under the program name "Infofsu" June 10.

Frye, Timothy M. 1992. "Ethnicity, Sovereignty and Transitions from Non-Democratic Rule," *Journal of International Affairs.* (Winter) 599-623.

Gal, Fedor (ed.). 1992. *Dnesi Krize Cesko-Slovenskych Vztahu.* Prague: Sociologicke Nakladatelstvi.

Gibbons, Roger. 1982. *Regionalism and Territorial Politics in Canada and the United States.* Toronto: Butterworths.

Horowitz, Donald L. 1985. *Ethnic Groups in Conflict.* Berkeley: University of California Press.

Leff, Carol S. 1988. *National Conflict in Czechoslovakia.* Princeton New Jersey: Princeton University Press.

Lidove Noviny. 1992. Prague (January-June).

Liebert, Ulrike and Maurizio Cotta (eds.). 1990. *Parliament and Democratic Consolidation in Southern Europe.* London: Pinter.

Lijphart, Arend. 1984. *Democracies: Patterns of Majoritarian and Consensus Government in Twenty-One Countries.* New Haven: Yale University Press.

Linz, Juan and Alfred Stepan. 1992. "Political Identities and Electoral Sequences: Spain, the Soviet Union, and Yugoslavia," *Daedalus* (Spring) 123-139.

Lukic, Reneo. 1992. "Twilight of the Federations in East Central Europe and the Soviet Union," *Journal of International Affairs* (Winter) 575-598.

McQuaid, David. 1991. "Poland: The Parliamentary Elections A Post-mortem," *Report on Eastern Europe* . RFE/RL Research Institute, 2:44 November 8, 15-21.

Obrman, Jan. 1992a. "Dubcek Joins the Social Democrats in Slovakia," RFE/RL Research Report, April 3, 16-19.

———. 1992b. "Czechoslovakia's New Governments" *RFE/RL Research Report* (July 17), 1-8.

———. 1992c. "Slovakia Declares Sovereignty: President Havel Resigns," *RFE/RL Research Report* (July 31) 25-29.

———. 1992d. "Czechoslovakia: A Messy Divorce After All," *RFE/RL Research Report* (October 16) 1-5.

Offe, Claus. 1991. "Capitalism by Democratic Design? Democratic Theory Facing the Triple Transition in East Central Europe," *Social Research* 58:4 (Winter) 865-892.

Olson, David M. 1993a. "Dissolution of the State: Political Parties and the 1992 Election in Czechoslovakia," *Communist and Post-Communist Studies* 26:3 (September) 299-312.

————. 1993b. "Political Parties and Party Systems in Regime Transformation: The Inner Transition in the New Democracies of East-Central Europe," University of North Carolina at Greensboro: manuscript.

————.1992. "The New Parliaments of New Democracies: The Experience of the Federal Assembly of the Czech and Slovak Federal Republic," *Budapest Papers on Democratic Transition* No 24. Budapest: Hungarian Center for Democracy Studies Foundation, Department of Political Science, Budapest University of Economics.

Olson, David M. and C.E.S. Franks (eds). 1993. *Representation and Policy Formation in Federal Systems: Canada and the United States.* Berkeley: Institute of Governmental Studies.

Olson, David M. and Ian Fried. 1992. "Party and Party System in Regime Transformation: The Inner Transition in Poland and Czechoslovakia," paper read at the American Political Science Association, Chicago, Illinois.

Olson, David M. and Maurice D. Simon. 1982. "The Institutional Development of a Minimal Parliament: The Case of the Polish Sejm," in Daniel Nelson and Stephen White (eds.). *Communist Legislatures in Comparative Perspective.* London: MacMillan Press.

Olson, David M., and Jindriska Syllova and Jana Reschova. 1993. "Prvni volebni obdobi demokratickeho parlamentu v CSFR: Federalni shromazdeni 1990-92: komparacni pohled," Pravnik 132:2, 125-41. ("The First Term of the Democratic Parliament of the Czech and Slovak Federal Republic: A Comparative Perspective")

Pehe, Jiri. 1991a. "Bid for Slovak Sovereignty Causes Political Upheaval," *RFE/RL Report on Eastern Europe* (October 11) 10-14.

————. 1991b. "Czech and Slovak Leaders Deadlocked Over Country's Future," *RFE/RL Report on Eastern Europe*, (November 28), 7-13.

————. 1992a. "Scenarios for Disintegration," *RFE/RL Research Report* (July 31) 30-33.

————. 1992b. "Czechs and Slovaks Prepare to Part," *RFE/RL Research Report* (September 18)12-15.

————. 1992c. "The Referendum Controversy in Czechoslovakia," *RFE/RL Research Report* (October 30) 35-38.

————. 1992d. "Czechoslovak Parliament Votes to Dissolve Federation," *RFE/RL Research Report* (December 4), 1-5.

————. 1993. "Constitutional Imbroglio in the Czech Republic," *RFE/RL Research Report* (January 29) 1-5.

Racz, Barnabas. 1989. "Political Participation and the Expanding Role of the Hungarian Legislature," *East European Quarterly* 22:4 (January) 459-493.

Reschova, Jana. 1992. "Nova politika s novymi ludmi: Federalne zhromazdenie v roku 1990," *Sociologicky Casopis* 28:2 (Duben) 222-236.

Respekt, March-June 1992.

Rose, Richard. 1992. "Czechs and Slovaks Compared," *Studies in Public Policy*, No. 198. Glasgow: University of Strathclyde, Centre for the Study of Public Policy.

Rude Pravo, January-June 1992.

Rudolph, Joseph. 1989. "Belgium: Variations on the Theme of Territorial Accommodation," in Joseph R. Rudolph and Robert J. Thompson (eds.), *Ethnoterritorial Politics, Policy and the Western World*. Boulder, CO: Lynne Rienner Publishers.

Sivakova, Danica. 1992. "Slovenska narodna rada: Analyza struktury a cinnosti v roku 1990," *Sociologicky Casopis* 28:2 (Duben) 247-263.

————. 1993. "New Slovak Parliament: The Recent Changes in Its Structure and Activities," paper read at conference on "Europeanization of Parliamentary Research in Central Europe," Budapest, May 1993.

Skala, Josef and Christoph Kunkel. 1992. "Auf dem Weg zu einem Konsolidierten Parteiensystem?," *Geschichte and Gesellschaft*, 18:3, 292-308.

Skilling, H. Gordon. 1976. *Czechoslovakia's Interrupted Revolution*. Princeton: Princeton University Press.

Smith, David E. 1993. "Representation and Policy Formation: The Canadian Provinces," in David M. Olson and C.E.S. Franks (eds.) *Representation and Policy Formation in Federal Systems: Canada and the United States*. Berkeley: Institute of Governmental Studies.

Syllova, Jindriska. 1992a. "Ceska narodni rada v roce 1990: Analyza slozeni a cinnosti," *Sociologicky Casopsis* 28:2 (Duben) 237-246.

————. 1992b. "The Transition to Democracy in Czechoslovakia in the Field of Electoral Law," in Ziemowit J. Pietras and Marek Pietras (eds.), *The Transitional Future of Europe*. Lublin: Maria Curie-Sklodowska University Press.

Wiatr, Jerzy. 1992. "Fragmented Parties in a New Democracy: Poland," paper presented at conference on "Political Parties in the New Democracies," Vienna, April 24-26.

Wightman, Gordon. 1990. "Czechoslovakia," *Electoral Studies* 9:4, 319-326.

————.1991. "The Collapse of Communist Rule in Czechoslovakia and the June 1990 Parliamentary Election," *Parliamentary Affairs* 66:1 (January) 94-113.

————. 1993 "The Czechoslovak Parliamentary Elections of 1992," *Electoral Studies* 12:1 (March) 83-86.

Wolchik, Sharon. 1991. *Czechoslovakia in Transition*. London: Pinter Publishers.

"Zakon o volbach do Federalniho shromazdeni" 1992. Sbirka zakonu, Castka 60 (28 unora), 340-346.

6

Voting Behavior in the Ukrainian Parliament: The Language Factor

Dominique Arel

Since the beginning of perestroika, Ukraine has been one of the most stable former Soviet republics in terms of minority relations. Its greatest challenge to date—the drive for secession by Crimea, Ukraine's only province (out of twenty-six) with a predominantly non-Ukrainian population—was temporarily staved off in mid-1992, at least for the short term, when Kiev granted Crimea a great deal of political, economic and linguistic autonomy.[1] Moreover, to the surprise of many, Ukraine's referendum on independence, in December 1991, was seemingly endorsed by all of its minority groups living outside Crimea.[2]

The fact that Ukraine has been able to maintain stability in the *politics* of its minorities does not mean, however, that it has inherited a stable sociopolitical minority *structure*. The opposite is actually the case. Ukraine is the only former Soviet republic where severe regional cleavages are aggravated by a serious identity problem for the titular nationality, i.e. the Ukrainians.[3] Ukrainians are unsure of the boundaries of their group, since a great many of them have linguistically assimilated to Russian in the Eastern and Southern regions, where ethnic Russian minorities are heavily concentrated. Linguistic assimilation is greatly unsettling to nationally-conscious Ukrainians because, as is the case for most East European nationalities, it is ultimately *language* which constitutes the core ethnic marker for the Ukrainian group, especially in the Eastern and Southern regions, where Ukrainians have the same Slavic Orthodox background as the Russians.[4]

If the language is the soul of the nation, as Ukrainian writers are fond of repeating, then the loss of language means ethnic assimilation.

As we saw previously, this did not *officially* happen, however, among linguistically assimilated Ukrainians because of the peculiar Soviet internal passport policy, established in 1932, according to which nationality (i.e. ethnic background) became a bureaucratic category separate from citizenship, strictly determined by biological descent: Children of Ukrainian parents became Ukrainian, irrespective of the language spoken at home.[5] Thus officially, large-scale *ethnic* Russification did not take place in Eastern and Southern Ukraine, despite the fact that linguistic Russification greatly increased in the post-war decades. How Russified Ukrainians actually perceive themselves as group members, and how they will behave politically in a post-independence environment in which the Ukrainian state is likely to emphasize its Ukrainian identity vis-à-vis the intimidating Russian neighbor is perhaps the most crucial question to be addressed not only in contemporary Ukrainian politics, but in post-Soviet ethnic politics. The internal stability of Ukraine is important for the entire region, given its growing geo-strategic importance.

Language as such has not been an issue in Ukraine since a language law was adopted in the fall of 1989, proclaiming Ukrainian the sole state language, and making Ukrainian mandatory for all those working in state offices, industry or higher educational institutions. Russian-speaking minorities in Eastern and Southern Ukraine have not mobilized in protest to date, like their counterparts in Estonia and Moldova, because, at the time of this writing, the law had yet to be implemented (unlike Estonia and Moldova, it anticipated a long transition period, of five to ten years). Ukrainian nationalists, for their part, have not focused on language, as they did prior to the adoption of the law, because of the unexpectedly rapid accession of Ukraine to independence. Their attention has been directed at building the state apparatus, and attempting to wean Ukraine away from the influence of the Russian state, by 'nationalizing' all military assets on Ukrainian soil, establishing border control, strengthening diplomatic links with East European states, and so forth.[6]

To state that language has remained off the agenda in terms of state policy (i.e. language policy as a dependent variable: DV) does not necessarily imply, however, that language has not played a major role in determining other state policies (i.e. language of social actors as an independent variable: IV). To date, Ukraine has been spared group conflicts over language policy, but has it been spared language cleavages at the *elite* level over policy-making? In other words, could it be that policy-makers in post-Communist Ukraine actually split along linguistic lines over certain specific issues? If so, what does that portend for the future cohesion of the Ukrainian state? Or is language wholly overshadowed by other more significant cleavages, such as occupational, generational or urban/rural?

Thanks to the Gorbachev-induced shift in decision-making from the Communist Party to reborn legislatures, and also to a pervasive *passive* bilingualism among residents of Ukraine, the proposition that language (IV) impacts on policy-making (DV) can actually be tested. Since May 1990, Ukraine has had a standing parliament, the *Verkhovna Rada* (Supreme Soviet), acting as the highest, although not unchallenged,[7] legislative authority in the land. Parliamentary debates are open to the public (and broadcast in full on state radio) and quite lively, since the opposition in the chamber (pro-independence and anti-Communist, although with only approximately one-fourth of the seats) is so much more mobilized than the conservative majority that it actually monopolizes half of the time allowed for discussion.

Two practices, crucially important for our purposes, have been adopted by the parliament since its recent rejuvenation: Most key votes are taken on a roll-call basis, and speeches in parliament are reproduced in stenographic reports *in the language in which they were delivered.*[8] Thus, if a deputy says something in Russian, and the next one responds in Ukrainian, the stenographic report will not translate anything, enabling the observer to establish the language used by deputies.[9]

Thanks to the availability of roll-call votes, and the creation of the database *language spoken by Deputy x,y...,* this paper will thus investigate the effect of language on voting behavior in the Ukrainian parliament, and attempt to address two interrelated questions:

1) Did language (or ethnicity) play a significant role in the way elites joined the "sovereignty" bandwagon in the year preceding the collapse of the USSR? The sovereignty movement was first championed by an overwhelmingly Ukrainian-speaking "Popular Movement" (*Rukh*), and staunchly resisted by the Communist Party elite, until a faction of the elite, led by future President Kravchuk, began to coopt the movement in early 1991. On which basis did the so-called "national communists," i.e. the Kravchukites, form themselves? Did the split occur along linguistic (or ethnic) lines, or was the division due to other sociopolitical factors?

2) In addition to votes related to sovereignty, did language significantly affect voting results on other *specific* issues, and if so what were they, and how important are they in assessing middle- to long-term internal developments. With Ukraine, like all successor states, experiencing an extremely painful transition to a post-Soviet,

post-Communist economy, is language in any major way linked to economic strategies?

The investigation of these questions will tell us a great deal about the inner dynamics of multiethnic Ukraine, but it may also bear interesting insights for broader theoretical questions pertaining to the rise of ethnic/linguistic conflicts. Instrumentalists explain popular mobilization over ethnic issues mainly through strategic behavior by political entrepreneurs, whose interest it is to displace elites of another ethnic group from positions of influence. In other words, it pays to politicize ethnicity, because the elite ends up getting the good jobs. What does the recent Ukrainian experience tell us about the applicability of this theory? As to whether language significantly influences discrete voting in Ukraine, this paper may contribute to a broader interest in the conditions for political stability, when a state is being established with large 'accidental minorities' (i.e. minorities that did not consider themselves to be minorities before a change of borders) in its midst.

In the first part of the paper, we will provide background information about the first post-Communist parliament of Ukraine. We will then analyze the voting index of deputies, and assess the significance it may yield in terms of regional, occupational and ethnic/linguistic cleavages. The last part will be devoted to the rise of the national communists, attempting to establish the bases of their support in parliament, and whether language played a role in determining the outcome of certain key votes.

Ukrainian Parliament: The Setting

The elections to the unicameral *Verkhovna Rada* took place in March 1990, using a two-round majoritarian system.[10] The elections were not multi-party yet (the "leading role" of the Communist Party had only been abrogated a month before during a Central Committee Plenum in Moscow), but they were genuinely multi-candidate, with two or more individuals on the ballot in each of Ukraine's 450 constituencies. Most candidates, and most deputies elected (85.6 percent), were Communist Party members, but Communist *affiliation* was less the issue than Communist *power*, since more than half of the deputies supporting the umbrella opposition movement, the *Rukh*, were themselves card-carrying members of the CPSU, although mostly at the rank-and-file level. The elections were far from being fully democratic. The *Rukh* was only officially registered *after* the nomination of candidacies was over (candidates could only be nominated by "public organizations" registered by the authorities, or by "workers' collectives"), the media were still largely in the hands of the party-state apparatus, and many reformists were prevented from running in districts still ruled by hardline Communist functionaries.[11] The fact that the *Rukh* could only officially claim 27.7 percent of the deputies in the early weeks of the first parliamentary session (125 deputies out of 450), while Yeltsin's supporters claimed more than 40 percent in the Russian parliament, and the Baltic opposition movements actually won a majority in their respective republics, does not necessarily mean, however, that the *Rukh* was robbed of a victory. Unlike the Balts, the *Rukh* was not merely waging an electoral battle against an entrenched Communist establishment, it was also involved in an uphill battle against a submissive Ukrainian peasantry, and a Russified urban population in the Eastern and Southern regions.

One-third of the population of Ukraine lives in rural areas and, as in Russia, it returned, almost systematically (except in one region), conservative deputies with Communist-era rates of participation (in the 90-97 percent range). The problem here seems one of *resolve.* The independent-minded peasantry was destroyed by the brutal collectivization and artificial famine of the 1930s, and is now wholly dependent upon the local potentate, the collective farm chairman, for its material well-being. As for the cities of Eastern and Southern Ukraine, they are home to close to 40 percent of the entire population of Ukraine, a majority of which declare themselves ethnically Ukrainian, although speaking mostly Russian, either as a self-declared mother tongue, or as the actual language of daily use at home. Hardly a word of Ukrainian can be heard in the streets of the major cities of the East and South: Kharkiv, Donets'k, Dnipropetrovs'k and Odesa. With the *Rukh* emphasizing the symbols of *Ukrainian* history, and relying exclusively on the use of the Ukrainian language in its public forums, its attractiveness to Russified constituencies is, to say the least, far from being a given.

As a result of these structural impediments, the *Rukh* ended up with a geographically lopsided representation in parliament. It reaped most of the seats in the Western region, which had never been part of the Russian/Soviet state before its annexation in 1939-1945, and whose peasantry did not experience the famine of the 1930s; and spectacularly carried the capital, Kiev, where the central institutions of the Ukrainian intelligentsia (media, creative unions, scientific institutes) are concentrated. The *Rukh* also did well in the urban areas of the Central agricultural region, but it got only scattered support in the Russified East and South, and virtually no support among the peasantry outside Galicia. Whether the *Rukh* was able to broaden its base in the actual voting support it received in parliament in the first two years after the elections, and whether it was able to maintain bloc discipline among its own ranks of early supporters will be examined in the next section.

As for the deputies not elected on a *Rukh* platform, although they were almost all, to a man, Communist Party members (97 percent), many presumably ran personalized campaigns, since up to one-fourth of them actually displayed a much more centrist attitude in parliament than the bulk of their conservative colleagues.

Table 6.1 shows that, not surprisingly, once broken down by occupations, the largest contingent of deputies were full-time Communist Party functionaries or *apparatchiks*, from the Central Committee down to the party cells in enterprises (ninety-six, or 21.3 percent). The very top officials, though, frightened by the debacle of the 1989 elections at the all-union level, tended to shun the elections, and most *apparatchik*/deputies emanated from the middle-to-lower tier of the party hierarchy (regional party second-in-command, city and district officials).[12] *Industrial managers* came in second (fifty-five, or 12.2 percent), followed closely by representatives of the *state apparatus* (fifty, or 11.1 percent), and the *agrarian bloc* (fifty, or 11.1 percent). The latter group, it must be noted, was strictly comprised of collective farm chairmen and agro-industrial managers. Not a single peasant was elected, a point to bear in mind when parliament is debating land reforms. The *working class*, on the other hand, does have its own representatives (twenty-five, or 5.6 percent), although well below its relative weight in society. Half of the *worker*/deputies are miners from the Donbas (Eastern region), undoubtedly the most politicized branch

TABLE 6.1   Occupation of Deputies

Occupation	No. of Deputies	% of Deputies
Apparatchiks	96	21.3
State Apparat	50	11.1
Industrial Managers	55	12.2
Agrarian Bloc	50	11.1
Security Apparat	28	6.2
Workers	25	5.6
Liberal Professions	43	9.6
Technical Intelligentsia	45	10.0
Humanist Intelligentsia	38	8.4
Others	20	4.4
Total	450	100

Source: Compiled and coded by the author from data published in *Pravda Ukrainy* (March 12 and March 24, 1990).

of the working class. *Security officials*, from the army, interior ministry and secret police also managed to get themselves elected (twenty-eight, or 6.2 percent), with the bulk coming from the army (seventeen).

The biggest winners of the contest, however, were arguably the intellectuals, whom we have subdivided into three groups: the *liberal professions* (doctors, lawyers, teachers, journalists, priests), the *technical intelligentsia* (professionals with a degree in engineering or pure science, working in an institute or a university), and the *humanist intelligentsia* (the educated strata working in cultural institutions, social science institutes or university departments). Privileged under the old regime, as long as they conformed to the party line, but kept far away from the real levers of power, these groups emerged with a combined total of 126 deputies (28 percent), a total that actually underestimates slightly their real strength, since many of the deputies listed as "unemployed" at the moment of their registration as candidates (here counted under our last rubric, "others") were intellectuals/former dissidents whose work was not recognized by state functionaries.

Ukraine is basically a bi-ethnic state, comprised of the titular group, the Ukrainians (72 percent), and a large Russian minority (22 percent), with no other ethnic group forming more than one percent of the population. Remarkably enough, the ethnic breakdown of deputies mirrored the ethnic breakdown of the population of Ukraine almost exactly, with 75 percent of the deputies Ukrainian, 22 percent Russian, and 3 percent from non-Russian minorities. The Russian group managed to achieve proportional representation, despite the fact that the electoral system was not proportional, due to its great territorial concentration: 80.2 percent of the Russians of Ukraine live in the Eastern and Southern regions. Although they constitute a majority only in the Crimean *oblast*, they form large pluralities, and often majorities in several urban electoral districts.

Since many Ukrainians (and non-Russian minorities) use Russian as a mother tongue, the Russian-speaking, or Russophone, group in Ukraine is much larger than the ethnic Russian minority. If 22 percent of the population is Russian, 30 percent are classified as Russophones, according to 1989 census data. In the Eastern and Southern regions, that proportion exceeds 50 percent in general and 65 percent in urban areas, meaning that, even if most cities outside of Crimea have an ethnic Ukrainian majority, when the ethnic Russian and Russified Ukrainian groups are counted together as Russophones, they are predominant in virtually all cities of these regions.[13] (It should be emphasized here that the term Russophone does not connote *ability* to speak Russian, but *claim to speak Russian as a first language*, i.e. as a mother tongue.

Virtually all Ukrainians are fluent in Russian, but not all are more comfortable in Russian than they are in Ukrainian.[14])

Data on the mother tongue of deputies are not available, but since stenographic reports of parliamentary sessions record speeches in the language in which they were delivered, the actual *language spoken* publicly by the deputies can be ascertained. These data are actually a much better indicator than mother tongue, since they demonstrate language *use*, whereas mother tongue can be interpreted either as language used or the language spoken as a child, the latter of which may no longer correspond to the language used as an adult.[15] These data were compiled by the author by looking at all the stenographic reports for the first four sessions of the Ukrainian parliament (May 1990 to January 1992), and coding deputies by language spoken, either Ukrainian or Russian (no other language was spoken).[16]

Interestingly, despite the fact that all deputies can understand both languages (which explains why no simultaneous translation is used in parliament), the overwhelming majority of deputies (391, or 86.9 percent, or 93.7 percent of those whose language could be ascertained) spoke one or other of the languages on an *exclusive* basis, and only a tiny minority (26, or 5.7 percent) used both languages in the course of these four sessions.[17] This finding highlights the crucial difference between *passive* and *active* understanding of a language: Everybody understands Ukrainian, but several deputies, including many ethnic Ukrainians (74, or 24.6 percent of those using either Ukrainian or Russian), do not feel comfortable addressing an audience in that language. The point is that, while similar languages might facilitate understanding, they do not necessarily make active use easy—especially when the languages involved are confusingly similar—unless one acquires a mastery at an early age. And language conflicts in the modern world arise precisely over the question of *active* use (language requirement at work, language of instruction in schools), not passive understanding.

For nationally-conscious deputies, mostly from the West and Kiev, speaking Ukrainian is a political statement. Despite the fact that they all have an active fluency in Russian, they would *never* use Russian, even when engaged in a dialogue with a Russian-speaking deputy who clearly cannot use Ukrainian actively. Russian-speaking deputies have a more functional approach to language. They stick to Russian presumably because they feel they cannot express themselves sufficiently well in Ukrainian, even if it is politically advantageous for them to use Ukrainian in parliament, although speaking Russian may become a political statement as Eastern and Southern Ukraine get mobilized. Remarkably enough, fewer than five of the deputies actually changed his/her language in these first two years (and the last session coded took place after the August 1991 declaration of independence), thus contradicting expectations by some analysts that Russified Ukrainians would switch to Ukrainian after a short period of adaptation.[18]

Table 6.2 displays the linguistic picture of the *Verkhovna Rada*. Somewhat more than half of the deputies are exclusive Ukrainian-speakers (Ukrainophones), while close to 40 percent are Russophones. However, as Table 6.3 highlights, the regional breakdown is even more telling. Almost all deputies from the West and Kiev, and three-fourths from the agricultural Center are Ukrainophones, but this proportion drops dramatically to one-fourth or less in the East and South. Russification is most severe in the mining province of Donets'k, with only one Ukrainophone among its twenty-two Ukrainian deputies. Only one ethnic Ukrainian deputy out of three from the Eastern and Southern regions actually speaks Ukrainian in parliament, while all but one of the Western Ukrainian deputies, and 88 percent of those from the Central region do. Regional

TABLE 6.2   Language Spoken in Parliament

Language	No.	%
Ukrainian	226	(50.2%)
Russian	165	(36.7%)
Both	26	(5.7%)
Unknown	33	(7.3%)

Source: Compiled by the author from stenographic reports of the Ukrainian Parliament, May 1990-January 1992.

TABLE 6.3   Language Spoken in Parliament per Region (in percentage)

Region	Ukrainian	Russian	Both
East	21	72	7
South	25	56	19
Crimea	5	91	5
Center	75	19	6
Kiev	91	9	0
West	95	4	0

Notes: Crimea was counted separately, and was thus not included in the Southern region. (significant at the .01 level.)
Source: compiled by the author from stenographic reports of the Ukrainian parliament, May 1990-January 1992.

cleavages along linguistic lines are thus much more severe than census data would suggest.

Since we are drawing from a sample that over-represents the traditional *elites*, i.e. deputies from the party, state, security, industrial and agrarian apparatuses, is it perhaps the case that the language figures presented above actually exaggerate the actual state of Russification of language use in society? Perhaps, considering that the three least Russified occupational groups represented in parliament (the three non-elite intellectual groups—liberal professions, technical and humanist intelligentsia) are somewhat under-represented. However, as Table 6.4 shows, their relative weight in parliament (close to 30%) is probably not too far below their proportion of the societal workforce. The absence from our sample of the peasantry, a totally Ukrainophone group, also distorts the linguistic picture somewhat, since 22 percent of the collective chairmen and rural party officials taking its place are Russified. On the other hand, Russification among the working class *exceeds* that of the traditional elite groups, and the workers in parliament, as indicated earlier, are seriously under-represented (5.5 percent of deputies). Admittedly, our sample of Ukrainian *worker*/deputies is quite small (N=14), but the figure (71 percent Russification) is certainly indicative of a general trend. As for the traditional elites themselves, Russification is much more pronounced among industrial managers and security officials than among party, state and agrarian officials, because many of the latter groups came from rural areas.[19] We will have to await reliable sociological surveys or new census data on language *use* to assess the linguistic representativeness of the Ukrainian parliament. Because of the trade-off between under-represented Ukrainophone peasants and under-

TABLE 6.4   Language Spoken among Ethnic Ukrainian Deputies by Occupation

Occupation	Ukrainian	Russian	% Russified
Party	52	14	21.2
State	23	10	30.3
Agrarian	25	7	21.9
Managers	14	19	57.6
Security	6	5	45.5
Workers	4	10	71.4
Liberal Profs.	22	4	15.4
Technical Int.	26	3	10.3
Humanists	36	0	0.0

Source: Compiled by the author from stenographic reports of the Ukrainian Parliament, May 1990-January 1992. (Significant at the .01 level.)

represented Russified workers, however, the difference between sample (parliament) and population is not likely to be significant.

Voting Index

In the period covered by this study (the first four sessions of parliament, between May 1990 and January 1992), only the *Rukh*-sponsored opposition officially organized a parliamentary bloc, the *Narodna Rada* (People's Council), whose membership (125 deputies) was made public.[20] As a reaction to the mobilised *Rada*, a large group of mostly Communist deputies began to refer to themselves as the "Group of 239," after Communist Party of Ukraine (CPU) Second Secretary Leonid Kravchuk received 239 votes to secure his election as Chairman of parliament in July 1990 (on a secret ballot boycotted by the *Rada*).[21] The expression "Group of 239," however, became a term of opprobrium later in the fall, when 240 deputies voted for the arrest of a radical deputy from Western Ukraine.[22] The "239" group then began to call itself simply the "parliamentary majority," and gave itself a spokesman, Oleksandr O. Moroz, a regional party official in charge of agriculture. No list of deputies from this 239/parliamentary majority group was ever made available, however, and it is quite likely that such a list never existed. Assuming, however, that 239 deputies did register with the Moroz group, then it would mean that 86 deputies remained unaffiliated, perhaps acting as centrists, shifting their support from bloc to bloc depending on the issues.

The best way to find out how imposing this "parliamentary majority" was, to what extent the Moroz and Rada groups acted as cohesive blocs, and whether a parliamentary centre did indeed form, is to build a voting index based on roll calls. During our field research in Ukraine, we collected all roll call votes published in stenographic reports between May 1990-January 1992. The list was fairly comprehensive, although it did omit roll calls taken on three particular days.[23] Following a close scrutiny of each vote, in the course of which procedural, minor and purely symbolic votes, as well as votes whose purpose remained obscure, were discarded, we retained 94 votes, and established the direction of each of those votes, i.e. whether a "Yes" or a "No" was indicative of a radical, or a conservative vote in each case. For example, a "Yes" to the question "Are you in favor of a referendum on the nationalisation of the property of the Communist Party" was interpreted as a "radical" vote, whereas a "Yes" to a resolution calling for hoisting of the Ukrainian *Soviet* flag in Parliament was interpreted as a "conservative" vote. All conservative votes were then coded as "1" and radical votes as "3," while abstentions were given a

"2," on the grounds that a person who abstains has presumably not made up his/her mind, and finds himself between the two camps.[24] A voting index score was obtained by adding up all the scores ("1s," "2s," "3s") of a given deputy, and dividing them by the number of votes in which s/he participated. An index of 3.00 would thus indicate pure radicalism, and an index of 1.00—pure conservatism.

The mean of all 450 voting scores was 2.09. As predicted by theorists of modernization, who link *urbanization* with demands for greater political pluralism and, in multiethnic areas, with rising nationalism (two indicators of radicalism), deputies from urban constituencies yielded a much higher score (2.26) than their colleagues from the countryside (1.97) or small towns (1.99). *Place of birth*, however, did not seem to be a factor. Deputies born in rural areas, small towns, and big cities obtained virtually the same score (between 2.07 and 2.10). *Generational* differences, on the other hand, could be observed, with deputies below 40 years of age markedly more radically minded (2.32 for the 30-39 cohort, 2.43 for the 20-29) than the deputies over 40 (2.01 for the 40-49 cohort). Educational data were not available.

Regional cleavages, as was to be expected, were quite pronounced between the nationalist West (2.55) and the capital Kiev (2.64) on the one hand, and the agricultural Center (1.94) and industrial East and South (1.97 and 1.82) on the other. Unsurprisingly, Crimea was by far the most conservative (1.61) of all of Ukraine's twenty-six provinces.[25] The most nationally-conscious areas—Ukrainian: the West, Russian: the Crimea—thus found themselves at polar ends of the spectrum. Within each region, moreover, urban deputies obtained a score much higher than the one obtained by deputies from rural areas or small towns, although only in the West did deputies from rural areas and small towns register a score superior to the mean (they were actually quite superior: 2.49 and 2.59, respectively).

On the indicator of *ethnicity*, Ukrainian deputies obtained a more radical score (2.13) than their Russian colleagues (1.89), although this discrepancy is to be explained almost entirely by the pronounced regional differences noted above, since 97 percent of deputies from the radical West and Kiev are Ukrainian. Outside of these two regions, Ukrainian and Russian deputies obtained virtually the same score (1.91 and 1.90, respectively). In terms of *language spoken*, however, the gap between Ukrainian-speaking and Russian-speaking deputies was not only more significant (2.29 vs 1.84), but even outside of the radical West and Kiev, Ukrainian-speaking deputies registered a higher score (2.29) than both Russified Ukrainian deputies (1.81) and Russian deputies (1.89).

Finally, on the *occupational* scale, the technical and humanist intelligentsia were by far the most radical groups (2.67 and 2.75, respectively), followed by the liberal professions (2.67), and the working class (2.29). Party *apparatchiks* were the most conservative group (1.65), which is hardly a revelation, considering that a great number of votes were aimed specifically at the "departization" of society. Party officials from the youth organization and the enterprise party cell—only very few in our sample (6 of 94)—registered a much higher score, 2.62 and 2.18 respectively. The other traditional occupations—state and security officials, industrial managers and the agrarian bloc—all had scores below the mean, with the bulk of their contingent located in the 1.75-2.00 range. Table 6.5 summarizes the voting index by each indicator.

The *median* of our 450 voting scores was exactly 2.00, meaning that an equal number of deputies found themselves below and above the middle score on a scale of 1 to 3. The mean, as we saw, was quite high (2.09), as a result of a great concentration of deputies (94, or 20.9

TABLE 6.5   Summary of Voting Index by Indicators

Indicator		Score	Indicator		Score
Urbanization	Rural	1.97	Nationality	Ukrainian	2.13
	Town	1.99		Russian	1.89
	City	2.26		Others	2.13
Region	East	1.97	Language	Ukrainian	2.29
	South	1.82		Russian	1.84
	Center	1.94		Both	1.98
	West	2.55		Don't	1.99
	Kiev	2.64		know	
	Crimea	1.61			
Occupation	Party	1.65	Age	<30	2.43
	State	1.76		30-39	2.32
	Security	1.83		40-49	2.01
	Managers	1.87		50-59	1.99
	Agrarian	1.94		60-69	1.91
	Workers	2.29			
	Liberal Profs	2.35			
	Technical Int.	2.67			
	Humanists	2.75			

Source: Compiled by the author from stenographic reports of the Ukrainian Parliament, May 1990-January 1992.

percent, most of them from the West and Kiev) at the very radical end of the spectrum (2.75 and above), while no such concentration could be found at the other end, and only very few (3, or 0.06 percent) qualifying as extreme conservatives (1.25 and below). Most deputies below the median 2.00 were located in the 1.50-2.00 range.

The absence of a polarization at *both* ends of the spectrum is a result of the group dynamics engendered by the sovereignty movement, and the total discredit suffered by the Communist Party in the aftermath of the failed putsch. In the first two sessions of parliament (May 1990 to February 1991), the polarization was much greater, but once Ukraine asserted a very critical stance vis-à-vis the new Union Treaty proposed by Gorbachev, following a close vote (see next section), most, though not all, subsequent votes on the Treaty and on Ukrainian sovereignty tended to reap huge majorities. The failed putsch of August 1991 led to the banning of the Communist Party of Ukraine, the dissolution of its cells, confiscation of all its property, and other "radical" measures. Relatively few deputies dared to oppose these measures publicly, and many presumably just went with the flow, while others preferred not to vote, or not to attend. Unfortunately, this sort of protest cannot be reflected in the voting index.

Because of the unusual nature of this distribution (demonstrated in Table 6.6), and in order to keep the discussion of voting blocs as simple as possible, it was decided to include all deputies with scores lower than 2.00 in the "conservative bloc," all those with scores equal or superior to 2.00 and inferior to 2.50 in the "centrist" bloc, and all those with scores equal or superior to 2.50 in the radical bloc. While this categorization loses specificity at the edges, it does enable us to make valuable observations about voting bloc behavior within an acceptable margin of error. (The decision to establish the border of the radical group at 2.50, and not 2.75, was made on the grounds that most deputies in the 2.50-2.74 range belonged to the original list of *Rada* deputies.)

The size of the two opposing blocs is similar to those advertised by the Moroz and *Rada* groups. Our conservative bloc has 244 deputies (five more than the "239"), while the radical bloc has 129 (four more than the original list of 125). Seventy-seven deputies thus ended up as centrists. Since only thirteen of the 125 original *Rada* deputies did not make it to our radical bloc (eleven had centrist scores and two, conservative scores),[26] one can say that the radicals voted quite cohesively as a bloc. The voting cohesion of the Moroz group cannot be estimated, of course, because its membership was never publicized.

TABLE 6.6   Distribution of Deputies on the Voting Index

Voting Index	Number of Deputies
2.75–3.00	94
2.50–2.74	35
2.25–2.49	27
2.00–2.24	50
1.75–1.99	85
1.50–1.74	95
1.25–1.49	61
1.00–1.24	3
Total	450

Source: Compiled by the author from stenographic reports of the Ukrainian parliament, May 1990-January 1992.

Using the indicators discussed above, a profile of the three voting blocs can be established:

1) The Radical Bloc is formed essentially of *intellectuals*—technical and humanist intelligentsia, liberal professions—who, taken together, account for 69.8 percent (ninety of 129) of the group.[27] Its hard core comes from humanist intelligenty (writers, literary scholars, museum workers), thirty-two of whom (of thirty-eight, or 84.2 percent) have scores higher than 2.75. Testifying to the absence of a Gorbachevian wing in the party-state apparatus, only one party official at the level of district party secretary or above (out of ninety-two!) and three state officials (out of fifty) showed radical scores. Industrial managers (three of fifty) were also largely absent from the group. Radical deputies are overwhelmingly Ukrainian (113 of 129, or 87.6 percent), and exclusive Ukrainian speakers in parliament (107 of 127,[28] or 84.3 percent). Only five Russified Ukrainians (of seventy-four, or 6.8 percent) and eight ethnic Russians (of eighty-one, or 9.9 percent) are radicals.

A solid majority of radicals (seventy-seven of 129, or 59.7 percent) are from the West and Kiev, with their more impressive political base in the three Western provinces of Galicia, a region that had been part of the Polish/Hapsburg sphere of influence for 500 years before its annexation by the Soviet Union in 1939. In Galicia, *all* but three deputies (of forty-six) are radicals, and all but four have scores higher than 2.75. In the Central region, radicals represent less than one-fifth of the districts, although they did capture close to two-thirds of the *urban* seats. The Central region is the breadbasket of Ukraine, however, and purely urban ridings only account for a small portion of the total (14.8 percent). Radicals representing small towns or villages from the Center can be counted on one hand (four of 109, or 3.7 percent), a startling contrast with the West, where two-thirds of the deputies representing small towns and rural areas (forty-six of sixty-seven) have radical scores. The Orthodox Ukrainian peasantry has thus been immune to *Rukh* appeals (Western Ukrainians tend to be Catholic Uniates). In the industrial East, most radicals also come from urban constituencies (eighteen of twenty-six, or 69 percent), but, unlike the Central region, most urban seats were not carried by radical deputies (only about one-fourth, eighteen of sixty-nine). Outside of the cities, the representation of radicals is quite poor (eight of eighty-one, or 9.9 percent). As for the South (including Crimea), radicals were practically shut out, with only three deputies (out of sixty-six, or 4.5 percent).

To summarize, the radical bloc dominates the West, urban and rural ridings included, did well in the urban Center (sweeping Kiev), made inroads in the urban East, but was shut out of the South and of all rural areas outside of the West.

2) The Centrist Bloc is not dominated by any occupational group, although it does comprise two-fifths of the workers (ten of twenty-five), close to one-third of the industrial managers (sixteen of fifty-five), and close to one-fourth of representatives from liberal professions (ten of forty-three). Its ethnic breakdown closely mirrors that of the general population (69.2 percent Ukrainian, 27 percent Russian), but only two-fifths of its deputies (twenty-nine of seventy-three) are exclusive Ukrainian speakers in parliament, a sharp contrast to the radical bloc (84.2 percent). The centrists have a strong presence in the big industrial cities of the East (nineteen of sixty-nine, or 27.5 percent)—particularly Dnipropetrovs'k and Donets'k—and of the South (six of twenty-one, or 28.6 percent). Their demographic base is much broader than that of the radicals, however, since three-fifths of their contingent (forty-six of seventy-seven) represent small towns and rural constituencies. In the Central region, perhaps not coincidentally, deputies from agricultural areas contiguous to the Western regions (Khmel'nyts'kyi and Vinnytsia provinces) have a higher score than their rural colleagues further east.

3) The Conservative bloc is unquestionably the preserve of (now former) party officials. Three statistics stand out: Party *apparatchiks* formed almost one-third of the conservatives (eighty-one of 244); almost nine party *apparatchiks* out of ten from the *raikom* (district committee) upward (eighty-one of ninety-two) were conservatives;

and a little over half of the hard conservatives (score lower than 1.50) were party *apparatchiks*. It is noteworthy that Leonid Kravchuk, who began his parliamentary career in May 1990 as Ideology Secretary in the Ukrainian Politburo, was promoted to Second Secretary a month later, and was elected Chairman of Parliament in July 1990, before he radicalized his position in early 1991 on the issue of Ukrainian sovereignty, was one of the very few party officials— and the only one among Central Committee secretaries with a seat in parliament—who obtained a score superior to 2.00, thus qualifying as a centrist. The bulk of deputies from the elite occupations—state and security officials, agrarian bloc and industrial managers—also obtained conservative scores, although, as we mentioned previously, most of these wound up in the 1.50-2.00 range, unlike party officials. Industrial managers, an interest group often touted as a potential constituency for reform, had two-thirds of their representatives among conservatives. On the other hand, few roll call votes were taken on strictly economic issues, so the conservativeness of industrial managers reflected mostly their attitude vis-à-vis political (departization) and national (sovereignty) issues.

The conservative bloc is 70 percent ethnic Ukrainian, but only 40 percent exclusively Ukrainian-speaking (compare with the radical bloc: 88 percent Ukrainian vs. 84 percent Ukrainophone). Two-thirds of all Russified Ukrainian deputies (fifty of seventy-four) are conservatives. Conservatives represent three-fourths of the seats from the South, two-thirds from the Center, and three-fifths from the East, but they do not dominate the big cities of the industrial East, where more than half of the seats (thirty-seven of sixty-nine) were taken by centrists and radicals. The poor performance of party officials in urban centers, already noticed in the 1989 quasi-free *All-Union* elections, convinced the great majority of higher-ups in the party-state hierarchy that it would be safer to have themselves elected in far-away rural ridings.[29] The countryside, except in Western Ukraine, is indeed safely conservative. Table 6.7 outlines the parliamentary blocs by region, while Table 6.8 shows the support for parliamentary blocs outside of West Ukraine.

The voting index tells us a great deal about regional, demographic, ethnic/linguistic and occupational cleavages among the deputies of the Ukrainian Parliament, but how truly representative of the general population are these deputies? The opposition in the *Narodna Rada* has consistently claimed that the parliament is not representative, because the 1990 elections took place before parties were allowed to organize, and the elections themselves were far from democratic.

TABLE 6.7   Parliamentary Blocs by Region

Region	Conservative	Centrist	Radical
East	90	34	26
South	51	12	3
Center	86	19	23
West	14	10	60
Kiev	3	2	17
Total	244	77	129

Source: Compiled by the author from stenographic reports of the Ukrainian parliament, May 1990-January 1992. (significant at the .01 level.)

TABLE 6.8   Support in Areas Outside of West Ukraine

Areas	Conservative	Centrist	Radical
Big cities	55	29	50
Small towns	71	19	12
Rural areas	104	8	7
Total	230	56	69

Source: Compiled by the author from stenographic reports of the Ukrainian parliament, May 1990-January 1992. (significant at the .01 level.)

It has thus called three times for a referendum on an early dissolution of parliament.[30] Although it is quite plausible that a freer electoral campaign would have yielded better results for the opposition, the fact that Ukraine is severely divided regionally along linguistic lines (East/South vs. Center/West), and between rural and urban districts (everywhere but in the West) suggests that more than mere cheating was at work. The results of two of the popular consultations which took place since 1990—the March 1991 referendum on the preservation of the Soviet Union, and the December 1991 Ukrainian presidential election—seem to substantiate this cautionary observation.

The March 1991 referendum, which took place throughout the Soviet Union, asked voters whether they were in favor of "the preservation of a renewed USSR...". The *Narodna Rada* explicitly campaigned for a "No" vote, but only 30 percent of the population followed that call. If the referendum results, broken down by provinces (twenty-six), are correlated with the average voting score in each province *as of March 1991*, then a r^2 correlation of 0.79 is obtained. (A correlation of 1.00 would mean *perfect* correlation, i.e. identical results.) The analysis shows that only one province, the Western oblast of Chernivtsi, produced significantly different results (it scored the second lowest voting index, out of twenty-six, but the seventh highest anti-Union vote). Chernivtsi is a predominantly Ukrainian oblast (province) which, like Galicia, had never been part of Russia/Soviet Union before 1945. That seven of its eight deputies are in the conservative bloc probably means that the 1990 elections in that region *were* unfair, considering how appealing the *Rukh* had been in the other Western oblasts. If we exclude Chernivtsi from the correlation, then the correlation r^2 jumps to 0.89, quite a high figure. In other words, the way electors voted in March 1991, province by province, does not differ very much from the voting behavior of deputies elected one year before.

A second correlation can be conducted between the results for the December 1991 presidential election and the voting index of deputies *as of December 1991*, again taking the province as our unit of analysis. The presidential election pitted Leonid Kravchuk (score 2.04), then Chairman of Parliament, against five candidates, all with radical scores, and all but one clearly identified with the *Rukh*. The issue then was no longer independence, since all candidates campaigned for independence, but rather whom the population trusted the most—a candidate from the opposition, or someone who originated from the traditional *apparat* (Kravchuk). The correlation r^2 between Kravchuk supporters and average voting score, per province, was 0.59. Again, Chernivtsi, alone, was an outlier. Excluding Chernivtsi, we obtain a correlation r^2 of 0.72, a lower figure than before, although still quite high. These tests can be disputed as a reliable measure of the representativeness of parliament, but they do reasonably suggest, as shown in Table 6.9, that the radical bloc does not seem to be able to penetrate the industrial/Russified and rural areas.

Support for Sovereignty

Ukraine achieved independence with extraordinary rapidity, barely two years after the nationalist movement *Rukh* held its founding congress, and not even a year and a half after parliament first convened. The key chronological events were the following: The Russian Republic, under the new chairman of its parliament, Boris Yeltsin, declared sovereignty in June 1990, claiming that its laws had supremacy over federal laws, and the conservative Ukrainian parliament followed suit a month later. The Ukrainian Declaration of Sovereignty remained a paper tiger in the fall of 1990, despite repeated attempts by the opposition *Narodna Rada* to give it

TABLE 6.9   Representativeness of Parliament

Oblasts	Union Vote March 1991 (in %)	Voting Index to March 1991 (on a scale of 1.00–3.00)	Kravchuk Vote Dec. 1991 (in %)	Voting Index to Dec. 1991 (on a scale of 1.00–3.00)
East				
Donets'k	85	1.90	71	2.07
Luhans'k	86	1.65	76	1.87
Kharkiv	76	1.96	61	2.11
Dnipropetrovs'k	78	1.90	70	2.09
Zaporizhzhia	80	1.81	75	2.00
South				
Crimea	88	1.51	57	1.75
Mykolaiv	84	1.79	72	1.92
Odesa	82	1.69	71	1.86
Kherson	81	1.80	70	1.97
Center				
Kiev City	45	2.49	56	2.54
Kirovohrad	82	1.90	75	2.03
Sumy	79	1.75	72	1.94
Chernihiv	83	1.82	74	1.99
Kiev oblast	67	1.79	66	1.97
Poltava	79	1.80	75	1.95
Cherkasy	77	1.72	67	1.90
Zhytomyr	82	1.70	78	1.92
Vinnytsia	81	1.99	72	2.12
Khmel'nyts'kyi	78	1.99	75	2.15
West				
Volyn'	54	2.25	52	2.33
Rivne	54	2.28	53	2.43
Ivano-Frankivs'k	18	2.63	14	2.69
L'viv	16	2.80	12	2.79
Ternopil'	19	2.58	17	2.62
Zakarpattia	60	2.19	58	2.34
Chernivtsi	61	1.52	44	1.78

r^2: 0.79
r^2 minus Chernivtsi: 0.89

r^2: 0.59
r^2 minus Chernivtsi: 0.72

Sources: Pravda Ukrainy, 23 March 1991; Peter J. Potichnyj,"The Referendum and Presidential Elections in Ukraine," *Canadian Slavonic Papers,* Vol. 33, No. 2 (1991); voting indexes compiled by the author.

constitutional status. The attempted army-led coups in the Baltics in January 1991, and Gorbachev's decision to force a referendum on the preservation of the Union in March, led to a split within the conservative majority in the Ukrainian parliament. Parliamentary

Chairman Kravchuk emerged as a defender of Ukrainian sovereignty, and wisely suggested that a second question be added to the ballot, asking people if they wanted a renewed Union "on the basis of Ukraine's Declaration of Sovereignty." The *Narodna Rada* went along with this compromise—other republics simply refused outright to conduct the referendum in their territory—along with an unknown portion of the conservative bloc. This group began to be referred to in the Ukrainian press as the "sovereign communists." Analysts later suggested that technocrats, i.e. industrial managers, formed the main power base of the Kravchukites. Factory directors, fed up with growing economic turmoil, were throwing in their lot with the sovereignty movement, on the grounds that a Ukrainian republic would be more economically viable than an overextended federal state.[31] The split inside the ruling elite, it was alleged, took place largely along occupational lines, although the leader of the sovereign communists was himself a former Central Committee Secretary.

Is this picture accurate? Was occupation the main factor accounting for the rearrangement of forces over republican-federal issues? ("Sovereignty" at that point was not interpreted as outright independence, but as an increasingly assertive stance by Ukraine in the negotiations over the Union Treaty.) Were regional, ethnic and *linguistic* cleavages also operative? In other words, might not the conservative deputies split also, or instead, along linguistic lines, with the Ukrainian-speakers going with Kravchuk, and the Russian-speakers remaining loyal to Gorbachev?

To test these propositions, we have divided our database of ninety-four roll call votes into three broad categories: Nationalism, Politics, and the Economy. The national votes (thirty-six) were those addressing republican-federal relations (sovereignty, union treaty, conscription quotas for the Red Army, declaration of independence), minority issues (language policy, Crimea), or questions of state symbols (flag). Two-thirds of these votes were taken during or after the appearance of the sovereign communist group. The political votes (forty-five) dealt mostly with the dismantlement of the Communist Party (opposed by the majority before the putsch, then accepted), but they also touched upon other issues, such as the performance of the government, and the rehabilitation of political prisoners. The economic votes were few in number (thirteen), and two-thirds of them (nine) dealt with the land issue, with eight of these votes taken on the same day. A voting index was constructed for each of these categories.

Results show that deputies were more radical on political issues (2.21) than on national issues (2.04), with the economic category (largely attitude towards the land question) solidly conservative

(1.79). There was no regional variation in this rank-ordering: *All* provinces, including the Western ones, yielded lower scores in the national category than in the political one, and the relative distance between the three scores on our conservative-radical continuum was strikingly similar from one province to the other, since a correlation of all scores broken down by provinces yielded a correlation r^2 of 0.94. What this suggests is that the sovereign communists appear to have originated from more or less *all* regions.

What about occupation? A more precise index was constructed for the purpose of measuring the support for the Kravchuk votes of February 1991, which provoked a split in the ruling elite. Seven votes were then taken over whether there should be a second sovereignty question on the ballot, and what the formulation of the question should be. An index was built for all roll call votes taken before the Kravchuk votes (i.e. before May 1990 and early February 1991), and another one for the seven Kravchuk votes. The results, as seen in Table 6.10, were then broken down per occupation. Industrial managers did increase their score tremendously, from 1.67 to 2.15, seemingly confirming the view of analysts that technocrats had joined the nationalist bandwagon, *but so did all other occupational groups.* A correlation of the two indexes, per occupation, once again produced a startlingly high r^2: 0.92. In other words, the sovereign-communists seemed to have come from all walks of life, including party and security sources. There do not seem therefore to have been significant regional or occupational cleavages in the broadening parliamentary base for sovereignty in 1991.

TABLE 6.10 Comparison Between Voting Index to February 1991 and Seven Votes on Referendum March 1991

Occupation	Index to Feb. 1991	Index 7 Votes March 1991
Party	1.47	1.93
State	1.54	2.14
Managers	1.67	2.15
Agrarian	1.60	2.15
Security	1.61	2.22
Liberal profs.	2.27	2.50
Technical int.	2.63	2.84
Humanists	2.74	2.81
Workers	2.15	2.70

Source: Compiled by the author from stenographic reports of the Ukrainian parliament, May 1990-January 1992.

Did ethnicity, and/or language, play a role? Hardly, it seems. To be sure, Ukrainian deputies had a higher score (2.39) than Russian deputies (2.21) for the seven Kravchuk votes, but *both* groups increased their radical score by a similar proportion, if compared to their scores for all votes taken *before* the Kravchuk votes: Ukrainians increased from 1.99 to 2.39, Russians from 1.72 to 2.21. The same pattern obtains by language spoken: Ukrainophones increased their score from 2.18 to 2.49, but Russophones increased theirs with a similar intensity, from 1.66 to 2.15. So the Kravchukites, it seems, were spread out among ethnic, linguistic and occupational groups, and came from all regions. The drive for sovereignty in the Ukraine of 1991 appears to have been quite an inclusive phenomenon.

The Effect of Language as an Independent Variable on Key Votes

Language then was not a factor significantly influencing the outcome of the Kravchuk votes on sovereignty in February 1991, nor did it seem to affect how deputies voted on national issues. But if language had no influence on the aggregate national votes, did it nonetheless play a role on certain *key* votes, whose political importance is perhaps underestimated by the voting index?

In order to investigate this question, we calculated the chi-squares of all ninety-four votes of our general index with *language spoken in parliament* as an independent variable and *voting outcome* (conservative, centrist, radical) as a dependent variable. The chi-square is a statistical test establishing whether two variables are related. If two variables are deemed unrelated by the test, then the voting outcome obtained is statistically no different than a random distribution. Over twenty votes passed the significance test, meaning that there was a relationship between language and outcome. Three, in particular, stood out, indicating a very strong relationship between the two variables:

1) *A vote on language use in parliament*—the only vote ever taken on a language issue during the period of study, on June 12, 1990. (The language law was adopted in the fall of 1989, *before* the elections.) A Russian deputy from the city of Kharkiv (East), Volodymyr Hryn'ov (future presidential candidate), had just been selected as Deputy Speaker, and in that capacity had to preside over plenary sessions. Hryn'ov did not speak Ukrainian, although he promised he would learn. Nationalist deputies, however, objected to his use of Russian in the conduct of official responsibilities, since Ukrainian had been proclaimed the sole state language a year before. A vote was taken

and, predictably, only 2 percent of Russophone deputies supported the nationalist motion. The Ukrainophones themselves were split on the issue along regional lines.

2) *A vote on potential territorial autonomy for certain regions of Ukraine.* The actual vote, taken on October 23, 1990, was on a resolution outlawing parties and movements that advocate violence in order to change the territorial integrity of Ukraine. But there were disagreements as to whether the resolution should emphasize *"any kind of change* in the territorial integrity" [emphasis mine], or simply refer to the territorial integrity of the republic. As the debates made clear, the point was of course not whether violent means were acceptable, but whether the *unitary* nature of the Ukrainian republic could be questioned. Nationalist deputies insisted that to omit stating that "any kind of change" in the territorial integrity of the state is forbidden would open the door to separatist movements, especially in the Russified regions.[32] The central issue of the very nature of the Ukrainian state—unitary or federal—has yet to be directly addressed, since the new Ukrainian Constitution was still not adopted at the time of writing, but several political parties and social movements, based in the Russified East, are increasingly advocating federalism (with official language use in the regions as the main issue on the agenda).[33] The October 1990 vote was an early indication of the federal-unitary issue, and the Russian-speaking deputies voted en masse for the resolution merely emphasizing the territorial integrity of Ukraine. Ukrainophones once again split along regional lines.

3) *A vote on the Treaty of Economic Union,* proposed by Gorbachev and his economic chief Yavlinskii in the last weeks of the Soviet Union, on November 6, 1991. The vote, as it turned out, was less on economics, than on nationalism. The *Narodna Rada* was, as a matter of principle, against *any* kind of treaty offered by the Soviet government, irrespective of economic rationale. (Ukrainian independence had been proclaimed six weeks earlier, but the vote still had to be ratified by referendum on December 1st.) Conservative deputies argued that, independence or not, Ukraine was still in the Soviet economic sphere, and that it had to take coordinated measures to redress its collapsing economy. Russophone deputies voted en bloc for the Treaty (only 6.3 percent objected), while, once again, Ukrainophones were split in two. The Treaty itself became history within a few weeks, but the vote, we believe, remains significant as an indicator of *future* trends.

Table 6.11 analyzes the three votes whose outcomes were most affected by language as an independent variable. These votes dealt with three issues whose importance may well become paramount in the next few years: language use in an official setting; territorial autonomy, first and foremost on language matters; and the degree of economic integration with Russia, with communities culturally close to Russia—ethnic Russians *and* linguistically Russified Ukrainians— advocating closer links. The language law, calling for Ukrainian as the sole administrative language in all state offices, is supposed to be implemented by 1994, but the Eastern and Southern regions are calling increasingly for bilingualism (a euphemism for the maintenance of Russian). Discussion over the second draft of the constitution keeps being postponed, and Ukraine has yet to decide whether it is a state of the "people of Ukraine" (a territorial conception that implies that there are no majorities and minorities, only citizens, and that the status quo on official language use should be maintained), or a state of the "Ukrainian people" (implying that there is a difference between the *indigenous* ethnic Ukrainians and the *minorities*, and that Ukrainian should be the sole state language used everywhere in official institutions); and if it is the latter, whether a *unitary* or *federal* form of state should be adopted (federalism would imply that minorities concentrated in certain territories would be granted various autonomous rights, such as official language use in their regions). As for economic integration with Russia, in light of the economic

TABLE 6.11 Overall Results of Three Key Votes

	Conservative	*Abstention*	*Radical*	*Absent*	*Total*
Vote on Use of Russian by Deputy Speaker (June 1990)					
Ukrainophones	79	5	80	62	226
Russophones	136	2	3	24	165
(Chi-square: 114.3, degrees of freedom: 9, significant at .01 level)					
Vote on Potential Territorial Autonomy (October 1990)					
Ukrainophones	100	14	73	39	226
Russophones	129	5	7	24	165
(Chi-square: 69.3, degrees of freedom: 9, significant at .01 level)					
Vote on Treaty of Economic Union (November 1991)					
Ukrainophones	84	11	82	49	226
Russophones	116	3	8	38	165
(Chi-square: 71.3, degrees of freedom: 9, significant at .01 level)					

Note: The table above is extracted from a larger 5×4 table, which explains why there are nine degrees of freedom.

Source: Compiled by the author from stenographic reports of the Ukrainian parliament, May 1990-January 1992.

catastrophe which has befallen Ukraine since 1992, the issue is most pressing.

That the language spoken by deputies significantly affects the outcome of the three votes tapping these issues is an indication that, despite conventional wisdom (most observers of the Ukrainian political scene are of the opinion that "there are no problems with language in Ukraine"), language would appear to be quite central to the internal dynamics of independent Ukraine.

Ukrainian-speaking deputies were split for each vote, presumably along regional lines, since most radical deputies are Ukrainophones and come from the West or Kiev. But the important issue is how the *Russophones* voted. In each case, we saw that they voted *en bloc*, with only a dozen or so abstaining or opposing. But could it be that these dissenting voices represent groups that might play a much more influential role in a revamped parliament? Since parliament is overly dominated by people from the traditional command positions (*apparatchiks*, state officials etc...), what we should really be focusing on perhaps is the voting behavior of groups whose parliamentary weight may increase if more democratic elections take place in the near future.

The key group to consider is the parliamentary faction representing the *Party of Democratic Renaissance of Ukraine* (PDVU, in Ukrainian), a political formation created in December 1990. The PDVU deputies, thirty-six in total,[34] represent a variety of occupations, who have in common their decidedly non-elite character (the fact that most were Communist Party members is beside the point), while not being a party of poets and literary scholars: Eleven are from technical intelligentsia (from institutes or factories), six from liberal professions, five from the working class, three were lower-tier party officials etc... Even more interestingly, only six of them are from the West or Kiev, and no less than twenty originate from the industrial East. Unlike the *Rukh*, they are thus broadly based geographically, except in the cradle of nationalism, Galicia (West). Significantly, only half of them (seventeen of thirty-four; the language of two could not be ascertained) are exclusive Ukrainian speakers in parliament, even if two-thirds are ethnic Ukrainians. Most appeared on the original list of *Narodna Rada* members, and indeed thirty of them (of thirty-six) received scores superior to 2.50 on the voting index, and thus qualified as radicals (although almost half—14—were moderate radicals, i.e. between 2.50-2.74). In early 1992, the PDVU was a founding member of the coalition "New Ukraine," a one-issue pressure group advocating market reforms in Ukraine.

The PDVU is thus no conservative offshoot. If conservative deputies are to be replaced by a new cohort in a forthcoming election, the types of deputies to be elected outside of West Ukraine and Kiev would most probably fit the sociological profile of the PDVU deputies: pro-reform, anti-Communist, from a non-elite occupational background, and with every other deputy being a Russophone. The question becomes: Does language also affect the voting outcome of the PDVU deputies on the three key votes that we just analyzed above, or do the PDVU deputies side with Ukrainian nationalists on these issues? This question is crucially important, since it could indicate whether rising tensions over the issues of official language use, territorial autonomy and economic integration are mainly provoked by former Communist elites attempting to cling to their positions in a changing political environment, or whether they have much deeper roots in society.

Before analyzing the voting outcome of PDVU deputies for the three key votes discussed above, let us first focus on three "test" votes in each category (political, economic, national) in order to put the parliamentary branch of the PDVU in clearer perspective. The first test vote, a classic attempt at "departization" (political dimension), held on October 15, 1990, was over the instauration of a referendum on the nationalization of the property of the Communist Party of Ukraine. The resolution was defeated 192-130, but the PDVU deputies voted in favor 25-1. The second test vote, in the economic category, dealt with the sensitive question of private ownership of the land. It was taken, on December 7, 1990, over a resolution by radical deputy Barabash that the "right to individual ownership of land plots be recognized with a restricted usage." The resolution was defeated 172-130, but the PDVU once again voted sweepingly in favor, 26-2. The third test vote was the most important of the seven Kravchuk votes of February 1991 referred to in the previous section. The issue was whether there should be only *one* question on the referendum, i.e. the Gorbachev question on the preservation of the Union (and thus a Ukrainian sovereignty question should not be added). The resolution received more positive than negative votes, 181-143, but fell short of the parliamentary majority of 225.[35] The PDVU once again voted en bloc, *against* the resolution, 28-1.

Judging by these three important votes therefore, the PDVU deputies were firmly allied with the radical Ukrainian deputies from the West and Kiev on questions of anti-Communism, land reform, and Ukrainian sovereignty. Despite their strong Russian and Russophone background, and their Eastern base, they were massively behind what eventually became Ukraine's *independence* movement.

On the three specific questions of language, territorial autonomy and economic integration, however, the voting pattern of the PDVU was drastically different: PDVU deputies voted 17-5 *in favor* of allowing Hryn'ov (himself a PDVU member) to speak Russian when presiding over sessions of parliament (radical Western deputies voted against); but they split on the questions of territorial autonomy (17-12 against, while Western radicals voted against), and economic integration (15-11 against, with radical Westerners voting against). The last two votes are particularly insightful. If PDVU deputies are separated by language spoken in parliament, then a polarization occurs *along linguistic lines* in the actual voting outcome. PDVU deputies altogether may have been narrowly against territorial autonomy (17-12), but Ukrainophone PDVUs were massively against (13-3), while Russophone PDVUs were strongly in favor (9-4). Similarly, on the question of signing the Treaty of Economic Union, all PDVUs were narrowly opposed (15-11), but Ukrainophone PDVUs were overwhelmingly opposed (12-3), while Russophone PDVUs were solidly in favor (8-3).

It would appear that, within a sample of non-elite deputies, with impeccable pro-reformist credentials, *language cleavages* manifested themselves over precisely the two questions that may well dominate the agenda in the next few years: economic rapprochement with Russia, and autonomy for the Russified regions. (On the issue of language use, the PDVU deputies were more tolerant, with Ukrainophones voting 9-5, and the Russophones 8-0, in favor of allowing use of Russian.)

The same analysis was repeated on a larger sample, i.e. that of all the deputies who were classified as centrists by our voting index (77), and all radical deputies who are not exclusive Ukrainian-speakers from Western Ukraine or Kiev (36, for a total of 113). The idea is to compare the voting behavior of Ukrainophones, outside of the West and Kiev, who are not conservatives, with Russophones from all regions who are not conservatives. (Most of the PDVU deputies are in this category, and are thus included again, but this time forming only one-third of the sample.) The sociological profile of this group could be described as "open-minded representatives of traditional elite occupations," plus non-elite representatives of the PDVU type.

The deputies from our sample showed strong progressive credentials on all three test votes, voting 69-18 in favor of the nationalization of CPU property, 61-18 in favor of private property of the land, and 68-11 against placing the single Gorbachev question on the referendum ballot (they were thus in favor of the sovereignty

TABLE 6.12 PDVU Votes

	Conservative	Abstention	Radical	Absent	Total
Vote on Nationalization of CPU Property (15 October 1990)					
PDVU/all	1	0	25	9	35
Vote on Private Property of the Land (7 December 1990)					
PDVU/all	2	1	26	6	35
Vote on Gorbachev Referendum (13 February 1991)					
PDVU/all	1	0	28	6	35
Vote on Use of Russian by Deputy Speaker (12 June 1990)					
PDVU					
Ukrainophones	9	0	5	5	19
Russophones	8	1	0	7	16
Total	17	1	5	12	35
Vote on Potential Territorial Autonomy (23 October 1990)					
PDVU					
Ukrainophones	3	0	13	3	19
Russophones	9	0	4	3	16
Total	12	0	17	6	35
Vote on Treaty of Economic Union (6 November 1991)					
PDVU					
Ukrainophones	3	2	12	2	19
Russophones	8	0	3	5	16
Total	11	2	15	7	35

Source: Compiled by the author from stenographic reports of the Ukrainian parliament, May 1990-January 1992.

question). But again, the voting pattern was totally different for the three votes on language, autonomy and economic integration. The deputies voted 67-12 in favor of Hryn'ov speaking Russian, with the Ukrainophone non-conservative deputies from outside the West and Kiev showing tolerance by also voting in favor 21-11 (while their Russophone colleagues voted 46-1 in favor). On the issue of territorial autonomy, as with the PDVU, the deputies split along linguistic lines, with the Ukrainophones opposed 22-16 and the Russophones in favor 49-8. An identical polarization could be observed over the Treaty of Economic Union: The deputies from our sample altogether were in favor of the treaty (49-28), but Ukrainophones rejected it (21-14) while Russophones threw their support behind it (35-7). In terms of voting behavior, our larger sample thus yielded the same results as the smaller PDVU sample. This means that the language background of a deputy does count for some important issues.

Conclusion

This chapter was based on an analysis of ninety-four roll call votes taken in the Ukrainian parliament during the four sessions (May 1990 to December 1992) following the first free elections in Ukrainian history, which took place in March 1990. A voting index, on a scale of conservative to radical, was constructed for all 450 deputies, allowing the author to identify radical (129), centrist (77) and conservative (234) blocs, whose membership approximates the size of proclaimed blocs in parliament. Radicals are extraordinarily concentrated in the Western provinces and in the capital Kiev. They also have roots in urban areas of the Center, and to a lesser degree in the industrial East, but have almost no support among the Ukrainian peasantry. They are overwhelmingly ethnic Ukrainians and Ukrainophone. Almost half of all centrists and conservatives are Russophone, and have relatively the same occupational profile.

The chapter sought to establish a causal link between language spoken in parliament—a variable coded by the author from stenographic reports—and voting outcome. No such link was found on the issue of general support for Ukrainian sovereignty (based on an aggregate measure of thirty-six national votes). Nor were there linguistic undertones in the formation of the so-called sovereign communists, i.e. elites who decided to throw their support behind Leonid Kravchuk in his quest to wrest more sovereignty for Ukraine in the negotiations over the Union Treaty. The proposition that Kravchuk's political base was among industrial managers could also not be substantiated, and no particular occupational group was over-represented among the newly-born "sovereign communists." An instrumentalist explanation of the nationalist conversion of a segment of the Ukrainian elite is thus not borne out by the data, since it is not clear which social groups among the traditional elite began to capitalize on nationalist appeals. Over three specific national issues, however—language use in an official setting, regional autonomy (regarding, among other things, the official use of language), and economic integration with Russia, the relationship between language and voting outcome was significant. And with the implementation of the language law, the forthcoming debate over the constitution, and the economic ruin of Ukraine, these three issues in particular are emerging at the head of the political agenda.

In the Russified industrial regions, candidates with a sociological profile similar to that of the PDVU deputies—a non-communist elite past, technical education, largely Russian-speaking, and pro-economic reform—are likely to represent the only truly democratic alternative to the former apparatchiks. The fact that, among deputies associated with the PDVU, a linguistic polarization was observed over three crucial issues, especially territorial autonomy and economic integration, suggests that, despite the paramount importance accorded to economic matters, the *language* factor is very much central to the shaping of post-independence Ukrainian politics.

Acknowledgments

The author would like to thank David Laitin, Bohdan Harasymiw, Andrew Wilson, Thomas Lancaster, Jerome Black and Andrea Chandler for their helpful comments, as well as Jasper Moiseiwitch for his assistance on the statistical tables.

Notes

1. The Crimean "Republic" is thus the only province with a political, as opposed to purely administrative, status within Ukraine. See Roman Solchanyk, "The Crimean Imbroglio: Kiev and Simferopol," *RFE/RL Research Report*, Vol. 1, No. 33 (1992), pp. 13-16.

2. Peter J. Potichnyj, "The Referendum and Presidential Elections in Ukraine," *Canadian Slavonic Papers*, Vol. 33, No. 2 (1991), pp. 123-38.

3. Belarus also has an identity problem, but no regional cleavages, since all regions of Belarus are Russified.

4. It should be emphasized that the most nationally-conscious Ukrainians, the Western Ukrainians, tend to belong to the Uniate (Greek Catholic) Church.

5. Children could choose their nationality only in the case of mixed marriages. See Victor Zaslavsky and Yuri Luryi, "The Passport System in the USSR," *Soviet Union*, Vol. 6, No. 2 (1979), pp. 137-53.

6. On Ukrainian state-building, see Andrea Chandler, "The Military and Border Control Institutions in Ukrainian Statebuilding 1991-1993: The Question of Coercive Power as a National Priority," paper presented at the Annual Meeting of the Canadian Association of Slavists, June 5, 1993.

7. The CPU, until August 1991, and then the presidential apparatus, since December 1991, have arrogated to themselves the legally unclear power to issue decrees.

8. A roll-call vote is taken when 1/3 of the deputies present at a given session call for one.

9. There is thus no Ukrainian or Russian version of the stenographic reports, only a single version, as bilingual as the debates (although all the titles, names and headings are in Ukrainian).

10. If no candidate received a majority in the first round, a run-off was organized between the top two candidates in a second round. Only a plurality of votes is required in the second round for a candidate to be declared the winner. In the first round, a candidate with a majority of valid votes is not elected if s/he

falls short of a majority when the spoiled votes are counted. A 50 percent participation requirement applies for both rounds. Unlike the all-union elections of 1989, there were no deputies "elected" through lists furnished by so-called "public organizations," i.e. institutions largely under the control of Communist Party bosses. All deputies won an electoral race.

11. Peter J. Potichnyj, "Elections in Ukraine, 1990," in Zvi Gitelman, ed., *The Politics of Nationality and the Erosion of the USSR* (New York, 1992); and "The March 1990 Elections in Ukraine," in Bohdan Krawchenko, ed., *Ukrainian Past, Ukrainian Present* (New York, 1992), pp. 123–33

12. In the 1989 Soviet elections, three dozen highly-ranked party officials in Russia and Ukraine had been defeated despite the fact that they ran unopposed. According to the electoral rules, even a single candidate on the ballot needed a majority of all votes cast, *including* spoiled votes; and in these Soviet cases, a majority of voters *did* spoil their vote.

13. Outside of Crimea, only in a few industrial cities such as Donets'k and Luhans'k do *ethnic* Russians actually have a majority.

14. The data on mother tongue come from censuses, when people were asked to volunteer their "mother tongue" (*rodnoi yazyk*). This is why we emphasize the verb "claim." No official definition of mother tongue was provided by census takers. See Brian D. Silver, "The Ethnic and Language Dimensions in Russian and Soviet Censuses," in Ralph S. Clem, ed., *Research Guide to the Russian and Soviet Censuses* (Ithaca, NY, 1986), pp. 70-97.

15. Preliminary results from a survey conducted by Duke University's East-West Center in the city of Kharkiv in January 1992 show that the indicator mother tongue underestimates the level of Russification, in terms of actual language use at home.

16. The stenographic reports were published as *Persha sesiia Verkhovnoi Rady Ukrains'koi RSR, 12-oho sklykannia*, Bulletins 1-92 (May 15-August 3, 1990); *Druha sesiia*, Bulletins 1-68 (October 1-December 26, 1990); *Tretia sesiia*, Bulletins 1-89 (February 1-July 5, 1991); *Pozacherhova sesiia*, Bulletins 1-2 (August 24, 1991); and *Chetverta sesiia* (September 3, 1991-January 4, 1992). The August 24 session was an extraordinary session following the failed putsch, when the deputies unexpectedly declared independence.

17. Twenty-three back-benchers (5.1 percent) never uttered a word, and could not be included in the database, and an additional ten deputies did not speak sufficiently to have their main language of discourse ascertained.

18. The twenty-six deputies that we coded as using two languages shifted from Russian to Ukrainian, back and forth, throughout the period under study. The expectation by nationalists was that Russified Ukrainians would stop speaking Russian at one point and systematically use Ukrainian.

19. Not all deputies from the agrarian bloc are actually based in the countryside, since many functionaries of the State Agro-Industrial Committee (Gosagroprom) actually reside in cities, usually in Kiev. The representation of ethnic Russians per occupation was the following: They constituted 22 percent of party officials, 12 percent of state officials, 18 percent of agrarian officials, 25 percent of industrial managers, 52 percent of security officials, 28 percent of

workers, 35 percent of those working in liberal professions, 27 percent of the technical intelligentsia, and 5 percent of the humanist intelligentsia.

20. "Narodna Rada v parlamenti Ukrainy," *Literaturna Ukraina* (June 14, 1990).

21. CPU First Secretary Volodymyr Ivashko was first elected Chairman of Parliament in June 1990, over the opposition of the *Narodna Rada*, but he unexpectedly resigned a few weeks later, when offered the post of CPSU Deputy General Secretary by Gorbachev. Kravchuk then became Chairman in July.

22. The deputy was Stepan Khmara, a former dissident imprisoned under Brezhnev. He was charged for having assaulted a police officer in a Kiev underpass on October Revolution Day, in what was most likely a crude set-up.

23. The roll calls omitted dealt with the discussion over the articles of the July 1990 Declaration of Sovereignty, the debate over the first draft of the constitution, in May 1991, and the debates over the post of Presidency, in June 1991.

24. Deputies present in parliament and registered for the session, but failing to vote, were put down as "NH" (*ne holosuvav*, i.e. did not vote). They were counted as absents.

25. Crimea was not included in the score for the South (1.82) just quoted above.

26. Three of these defectors became causes célèbres: Oleksandr Kotsiuba, a Kiev lawyer who voted for the arrest of Khmara; Valentin Terekhov, a Russian writer from Crimea involved in the Crimean drive for independence; and Al'bert Korneev, a Russian from the Donbas who voted against Ukraine's Declaration of Independence, and whose candidacy for the Supreme Court, in early 1993, was blocked by the *Narodna Rada*.

27. The figure should actually be somewhat higher, since many, if not all, of the nine deputies registered as unemployed by the authorities are intellectuals.

28. The figure for language spoken in parliament is slightly lower than ethnic background (127 vs 129), because the language of a few deputies could not be ascertained.

29. Dominique Arel, "The Parliamentary Blocs in the Ukrainian Supreme Soviet: Who and What Do They Represent?," *Journal of Soviet Nationalities*, Vol. 1, No. 4 (Winter 1990-1991), pp. 120-123.

30. A first campaign was held in the fall of 1990, a second one in the fall of 1992, and a third one in the spring of 1993. As this article was going into press, it seemed inevitable that early elections would finally be held in late winter 1993/early spring 1994.

31. Taras Kuzio and Andrew Wilson, *Ukraine: Perestroika to Independence* (New York, 1993); Bohdan Krawchenko, "Ukraine: The Politics of Independence," in Ian Bremmer and Ray Taras, eds., *Nations and Politics in the Soviet Successor States* (Cambridge, UK, 1993), pp. 75-98.

32. See speeches of deputies Zaiets' (Moscow), Chervonii (Rivne), Chornovil (L'viv), and Piskun (Sumy), in *Druha sesiia*, Bulletin 19 (October 23, 1990), pp. 31-41. Nationalists are opposed to any change in the unitary nature of the state, even by democratic and parliamentary means, whereas Russophones are not averse to such changes.

33. Dominique Arel, "Federalism and the Language Factor in Ukraine," Paper delivered at the Annual Meeting of the American Association for the Advancement of Slavic Studies (AAASS), Phoenix, Arizona, November 1992.

34. The list was published in *Demokratychnyi vybir—Informatsiinyi biulleten'* (Kiev), No. 11 (1991).

35. The official roster of deputies at that moment was 449. A majority of all existing deputies (225), not of deputies present in the chamber, was required for a vote to pass.

7

Transitional Institutions and Parliamentary Alignments in Russia, 1990–1993

Thomas F. Remington, Steven S. Smith,
D. Roderick Kiewiet, and Moshe Haspel

The Russian Federation has taken an important step in the transition away from institutions dominated by the Communist Party of the old Soviet Union—the dissolution of the hybrid national legislature that was created in the Gorbachev era. To some observers, this was an essential and inevitable step in the process of democratization. Like the death of the dinosaurs and the rise of mammals, the extinction of the legislative institutions that were created by amendments to the communist-era constitution has widely been considered necessary before democratic institutions had a chance to survive. In our view, that conventional wisdom greatly oversimplifies the 1990-1993 transitional period in Russian political institutions.

We have one primary and one secondary purpose in writing this chapter. Our primary purpose is to provide an introduction to the politics of the 1990-1993 period that ended with the dissolution of the Russian Supreme Soviet and Congress of People's Deputies. We argue that the transitional legislative institutions contributed to the process of political and economic reform, but eventually became obstacles to the adoption of ever more radical reform. In doing so, we examine the evolution of factions and blocs in the Congress and map the evolving voting alignments in the 2nd-9th Congresses (November, 1990, to March, 1993). We are led to the conclusion that three developments—the crystallization of party-like blocs, emergence of a separation-of-powers system, and the domination of the legislative and executive

159

institutions by different blocs—created a deadlock that could be broken only by extra-constitutional means.

The secondary purpose is to demonstrate a productive use of the roll-call record of the Russian parliament. We show how the dimensionality and alignments of voting in the Congress of People's Deputies have shifted as the issues and institutions evolved during the transitional period. We demonstrate the remarkable 28-month shift from a consensus political alignment to one that is sharply polarized and finally to one that is overwhelmingly conservative. We find that splits among democrats after the attempted coup against Gorbachev have undermined liberal party formation.

We have benefitted from the analyses of others, such as Sobyanin and Smyth (Sobyanin and Yur'ev 1991; Smyth 1990). Smyth relates a left-right rating, based upon 24 votes in the first Congress, to deputies' social backgrounds and the urban/rural characteristics of their districts. Sobyanin and his colleagues rate deputies on a left-right scale for several Congresses and examined differences among factional and regional groups. They also examine political "drift" from one ideological position to another. But we need to move beyond hand-picked votes and the construction of simple one-dimensional democrat-communist ratings of the Smyth and Sobyanin studies. In this paper, we characterize voting alignments in the full dimensionality found in deputies' voting and identify important consequences of the two-tiered system.

Before examining the transitional Congresses in detail, we begin with essential background on Russian legislative institutions and the nature of voting practices.

The Institutional Setting

The deputies who make up the Congress were elected in national elections in 1990. Simultaneous with the elections of the RSFSR deputies in March of 1990, there were also elections to city and regional councils (soviets). There is by now a small literature on the 1990 elections. Systematic analysis of the relationship between elections and voting alignments is seriously hindered by the absence of exit-poll data, comprehensive lists of candidates running, and reliable economic performance data at the sub-central level. Consequently, beyond crude surrogate measures, such as the size of the administrative center of electoral districts, we have no data enabling us to link the characteristics of districts with the voting behavior of deputies. Moreover, no single scheme for analyzing the deputies in terms of social background and status is accepted, given the debate 'over the nature of the distribution of status and power in the old regime. Assumptions about the nature of social stratification in Russia strongly influence the explanatory constructs used to classify deputies and thus explain their voting behavior. Simple social categories such as "middle class," "nomenklatura," and "intelligentsia" are too crude to capture more than certain elementary truths.

Information about the institutional features of the elections and the newly designed legislature, on the other hand, is available, and goes far to help explain subsequent patterns of deputy behavior. We single out six points in particular.

1. To a large extent, the elections were competitive. V. I. Kazakov, chair of the Central Electoral Commission, reported to the deputies assembled for the first time following the elections, that 6705 candidates had run for the 1068 seats. Thirty-three districts had only a single candidate running; 300 had over 4, and 24 had over 20. The high threshold for victory—at least a majority on the first ballot—combined with the large number of candidates running meant that on the first round, only 11 percent of seats were filled. The second round succeeded in filling nearly all remaining seats. A good deal of circumstantial evidence exists to indicate that the competitiveness of the elections varied widely across regions. In some, especially in rural areas, members of the old governing elite manipulated the process to ensure victory for their candidates even when an opposing candidate was running.

2. All elections were held under a single-member district, winner-take-all election law based on the traditional electoral system used throughout the Soviet Union. In order to ensure ample representation for Russia's ethnic-national territories (ranked in three status categories from "autonomous republics" at the top through "autonomous provinces" and "autonomous circuits"), special national territorial electoral districts (NTIOs) were formed. Eighty-four deputies from these and an equal number from non-ethnic national-territorial districts were elected, along with 900 deputies from regular territorial districts. This detail is important since all of the members of the "Council of Nationalities," the chamber of the Supreme Soviet designed to represent the interests of national territories, were to be named from among the 168 deputies from NTIOs. This meant that in practice, the Council of Nationalities had from the start a conservative political orientation in comparison to the Council of the Republic, which had a larger representation from the large industrial cities in which democratic candidates had succeeded in winning races.

3. Parties as such played little role in the elections. This statement

must be qualified in two ways. First, the overwhelming majority of candidates and victors were members of the Communist Party of the Soviet Union (CPSU), and second, loose political coalitions formed on the right and the left that allowed candidates to affiliate with an ideological movement. Nevertheless, parties did not select candidates or fund their campaigns. Members of the CPSU could be found on both the left and the right; the party itself lacked a coherent ideological position after the radical and dramatic changes in the country's political life associated with Gorbachev. Therefore, though 86 percent of the winners were party members, party membership as such at the time of election had relatively little effect on deputy voting behavior once deputies were elected. (Note, for example, that more than half of Democratic Russia's deputies elected in Moscow were CPSU members. This is not surprising, given the close association between party membership and holding of elite positions in society.) After the elections, the broad ideological coalitions of the left and right broke down into smaller political groups and factions in the Congress as well as in lower-level soviets in Moscow, Leningrad and other cities.

4. The deputies were elected to a peculiar bifurcated legislature that separated a large, occasionally-meeting Congress from a much smaller full-time parliament. The structure was patterned on that created for the union legislature and remained in force until Yeltsin abolished the system in September 1993. The Congress was assigned power to adopt and amend the country's constitution while the inner parliament, which was given the traditional name Supreme Soviet, was empowered to adopt laws and other acts.

5. The new system preserved the older constitutional principle of soviet (conciliar) power. Under this model, the supreme soviet of the country, like those of the constituent ethnic republics nested within it, was said to exercise the totality of state power in itself and to delegate it to executive organs. Presidential and separation of powers models, although enjoying widespread support among the country's elite and elements of which were also found in the state structure, contradicted soviet power. Yet the soviet model lacked a mechanism for determining the leadership and composition of the cabinet, since no party or coalition of parliamentary fractions commanded a majority.

6. Finally, the new system continued to invest wide powers in an inner body called the presidium, comprising the chairman and deputy chairs of the Supreme Soviet and the chairs of its committees. Wielding substantial power over all aspects of the legislative process, the right to adopt certain kinds of decrees, and responsibility for the day-to-day management of the Supreme Soviet, the presidium

enabled an ambitious chairman to develop a significant power base independent of the executive branch.

The Supreme Soviet, rather than the parent Congress of People's Deputies, was the full-time legislative institution. The Congress was designed to meet intermittently to decide matters of constitutional significance: amendments to the existing constitution, principles governing the drafting of a new constitution, election of a chairman of the Supreme Soviet to coordinate the entire legislative process, election of judges to the Constitutional Court, and various resolutions on one or another topic of current concern. The Congress could also instruct the Supreme Soviet to develop legislation, and require it to present its work to the Congress for final approval.

The constitutional principles governing the post-communist Russian state remained profoundly contentious issues, most of all the problem of legislative-executive relations. While they were overshadowed to some degree by the issue of Russian sovereignty within the declining union, they grew acute in early 1991 and reached a crisis point in 1992 as Yeltsin exercised his presidential powers to appoint a government committed to a painful economic adjustment program. Consequently, the flow of events over 1990-1993, which the Congresses' sessions punctuated at occasional intervals, was dominated by two fundamental issues, Russia's independence of the union, and the struggle between Congress and president for sovereign power over the Russian state.

Polarized Alignments in the Early Congresses

The evolution of voting alignments and its connection to party development within the Congress must be seen in the context of the changing issues and political environment confronting the membership. The Congress conducted nine sessions over the 1990-93 period (see Table 7.1). In this paper, we briefly review these and detail the structure of voting alignments in the eight Congresses—the 2nd through the 9th—for which we have the appropriate data.

The First Congress

When the first Congress of the RSFSR convened in May 1990, 94 percent of the deputies had never been RSFSR-level deputies before. Only 5.3 percent of them were women, 5.6 percent were workers, and 6 were peasants, demonstrating the demise of the principle of "social representation" that formerly governed selection of candidates for

TABLE 7.1   Dates of the Russian Congresses:

1st:	16 May – 22 June 1990
2nd:	27 November – 15 December 1990
3rd:	28 March – 5 April 1991
4th:	21 May – 25 May 1991
5th:	10 – 17 July, 28 October – 4 November 1991
6th:	6 – 21 April 1992
7th:	1 – 14 December 1992
8th:	10 – 13 March 1993
9th:	26 – 29 March 1993

soviet deputies. Candidates embracing the broad insurgency against communist rule had won notable and widely publicized victories in Moscow, Leningrad, and Sverdlovsk. Members of the intelligentsia fared well: of 1025 deputies elected by late April 1990, 135 were from high-skill level, non-administrative occupations. The Democratic Russia coalition seized the initiative and held two preparatory meetings to form a bloc at the first Congress; approximately 200 deputies attended these meetings, but polls of elected deputies indicated that as many as 350 of those elected supported the Demrossiia position.

At the Congress, the democratic movement won a key victory when Boris Yeltsin was elected chairman of the Supreme Soviet; at that time, Russia conformed to the traditional USSR model in which the chairmanship of the Supreme Soviet was equivalent to a head of state—as chairman of the parliament, he controlled the staff, budget and resources of the legislature, and oversaw its agenda-setting Presidium. From this key position, Yeltsin and the democrats took advantage of the momentum of their electoral victories and their relatively high degree of organization to win passage of the decree on power, which claimed full sovereignty for the Russian state (an act falling short of declaring independence of the union but in fact delivering a heavy blow to union level authority). The democrats lost, however, in other efforts: controlling the election of deputies to the Supreme Soviet and naming members to the Constitutional Commission which was charged with drafting a new constitution to replace the old, Brezhnev-era document.

An analysis conducted at the time confirmed the existence of two voting blocs of roughly equal strength at the first Congress: a group of deputies identifying themselves with the democratic cause, and another identified with defense of the old, communist order. Approximately 20 percent of the deputies were in the middle

(Sobyanin and Yur'ev 1991:5). Voting patterns confirmed a high degree of consistency in voting by these two groups. Legislative success went to those who could capture the middle ground: the rules provided that passage of a law required an absolute majority of elected deputies (not of deputies present and voting). Consequently the threshold of victory was high, requiring each side to compromise in order to win passage of a favored act. (The threshold for passage of constitutional amendments was still higher, at two thirds of all deputies.)

Survey data confirm the impression that Sobyanin's data give of a basically bimodal distribution of ideological positions among deputies. A poll of the deputies conducted in June 1990 reveals that identical proportions—37 percent each—regarded the October Revolution as a great progressive event in the history of mankind and a tragedy leading to the downfall of the country. Asked for political self-identifications based on political parties familiar in the context of European politics, 41 percent of those polled identified themselves with the communist party; 36 percent with social-democratic positions; and 23 percent with other parties (Urnov 1991).

Generally, then, one can conclude that there was a rough balance between left and right: each side was strong enough to deny the other a legislative majority unless a motion was softened to appeal to moderates. However, the democrats had won an important advantage in their access to the organizational resources of the chairmanship and the presidium. This they used by seeking to stack membership of committees slightly in favor of the democratic side. Buttressed, moreover, by his assumption of the chief executive position in Russia, Yeltsin announced that Russia would undertake a program of radical economic transition similar to the "shock therapy" that Poland had launched; by putting his full support behind the so-called "500 Days" program, Yeltsin threatened to embarrass and undermine Gorbachev by taking a more radical economic stance and effectively forcing Gorbachev's hand. Yeltsin also took the opportunity to nominate and win approval of Ruslan Khasbulatov as his first deputy chairman, to run the parliament's day-to-day operations. No doubt he has often since regretted his choice.

The 2nd-4th Congresses

By the time the second Congress convened in late November 1990, the political situation in the country had changed appreciably. After initially agreeing to work with Yeltsin on a common program of radical economic transition, Gorbachev had broken with him and was allying himself with the most hard-line elements of the union power structure. The Congresses of the union deputies and the Russian Congress overlapped; it was during the union Congress that Eduard Shevardnadze dramatically resigned as foreign minister, warning of looming dictatorship. The hardline conservative forces entrenched in union structures such as the ministries, KGB, Interior Ministry, CPSU and military, were on the offensive, while democratic forces were in some disarray, taking the political blame for the failure of the newly elected soviet structures at local and national levels to reverse deteriorating economic conditions. The democratic forces themselves had fragmented into competing factions and proto-parties.

At the Russian Congress, the conservatives took advantage of the anti-democratic backlash to win passage of measures such as a resolution favorable to Iraq in the Persian Gulf crisis, to water down a constitutional amendment recognizing the right to private ownership of land, and to defeat a motion giving Yeltsin a free hand to choose deputy chairmen of the Supreme Soviet. To a large extent, the same left-right ideological dimension characterized the second Congress as had characterized the first, but with a shift of support toward the conservative end of the spectrum.

Pressing their advantage, the conservatives attempted to remove Yeltsin. They demanded the convening of a third, extraordinary Congress to hear a report from Yeltsin. Before the Congress met, however, a national referendum was held which affected the balance of forces. Gorbachev initiated the union-wide referendum to prove public support for preservation of the union, although the final wording of the question on the union was so convoluted that it could have been taken as evidence of support for virtually any position. Using his power in the Presidium of the Russian Supreme Soviet, however, Yeltsin won the Presidium's approval for adding a point to the referendum for the Russian Republic, on support for the concept of a popularly-elected presidency in Russia. March 17, 1991, then, produced a hollow victory for Gorbachev, in that 3/4 of the voters declared their support for some sort of reformed union, but 70 percent of voters in Russia declared their support for institution of a presidency.

Thus, the vigorous counter-attack by conservative forces worked to Yeltsin's advantage to some extent since Yeltsin, as in the summer of 1990, linked himself to the popular cause of Russian sovereignty—the "strong state" ideal. Yeltsin and the democrats allied themselves with popular dissatisfaction with Gorbachev, taking up the cause of the coal miners who launched another series of strikes in March 1991, and demanding Gorbachev's ouster. Moreover, the heavy-handed economic measures taken by Gorbachev's Prime Minister, Pavlov, and Gorbachev's furious efforts to preserve the union swung some moderate and conservative deputies back to Yeltsin's side as the defender of Russia's sovereignty. The swing in political advantage back to Yeltsin and the democratic forces became apparent in the tense, extraordinary Third Congress.

The Congress was convened at the initiative of the communist forces. Their demand that Yeltsin report to the Congress was understood as an effort to remove him as chairman. Popular discontent mounted as miners' strikes spread and previously peaceful Belorussia began to erupt in general strikes. Apparently attempting to intimidate the Yeltsin forces, Gorbachev ordered tanks and armored vehicles to ring the Kremlin on March 28, the day the Third Congress opened. Yeltsin won over elements of the communist opposition at the Congress, however, notably including Alexander Rutskoi, an army officer who led a pro-Yeltsin breakaway faction called "communists for democracy" and who later became Yeltsin's Vice-President. Yeltsin won important votes at the Congress, perhaps most importantly the constitutional amendments needed to define the powers of the president. The Yeltsin forces' success in creating a strong presidency can be interpreted not only as a victory for the democratic wing, but also as an issue on which moderates and conservatives joined with them to resist interference by the union government in Russia's sovereignty.

Blocked by Yeltsin and tied to hard-line Union-level power structures that had less and less need of him, Gorbachev now had to seek an accommodation with the leaders of Russia and the other republics. This led to the "Novo-Ogarevo" negotiations on a new union treaty (named for the villa outside Moscow where the talks were held). These negotiations resulted in a framework agreement that would have created a weak federation, thus giving Russia a powerful role in the economic and security arrangements of the prospective new union. The 4th Congress, held after the Novo-Ogarevo agreement was initialed, discussed the office of presidency and the law governing the impending presidential election; a crucial victory by Yeltsin was the Congress's approval of a motion to hold the elections sooner, in June, rather than later—which would have allowed opposition candidates more time to campaign. The campaign began as soon as the Congress adjourned.

Bipolarity in the First Four Congresses

Observers rightly emphasize the bimodal distribution of opinion among Russian deputies. To see this, but without assuming unidimensionality, we have conducted a factor analysis of roll-call voting in the 2nd-9th Congresses. Factors and factor scores were based upon a principal-components analysis of the contested roll-call votes to the Congress or set of Congresses indicated. A non-orthogonal rotation was applied in factor analyses to produce factors that are not necessary uncorrelated with each other. Contested votes were those in which at least 25 percent of the voting deputies voted for the minority position. Those not voting either "yes" or "no"—i.e. abstaining, or simply not voting—are coded as having cast a vote exactly between "yes" and "no," or .5.

A word about voting in the Congress is in order. Most votes in the Russian Congress were conducted by the use of an electronic system that allowed votes to be tabulated instantly. The system provided a permanent record of roll-call votes. Roll calls were, however, not the only way deputies voted in the Congresses. Deputies could decide to hold a secret vote, in which case the rules specified that no record is to be kept, or a regular vote, in which case records were not normally preserved beyond the end of the day's session and were not published. By a vote of at least one fifth of the members, however, deputies could decide to treat a particular vote as a roll call, in which case the official bulletin recorded how each deputy voted. The data employed in this paper come originally from the secretariat of the Presidium, which maintained the electronic records of roll-call votes.

Table 7.2 reports every factor that explains more than five percent of the variance in voting behavior for Congresses 2-6. The table indicates that a single dimension dominates voting in the 2nd through 4th Congresses. A roll-call vote in the 2nd Congress on a motion to

TABLE 7.2   Dimensions in Voting, 2nd-6th Congresses

Congress	Description	Percent of Variance Explained	Correlation with 1st Overall Factor (left/right)	Correlation with Overall Sobyanin Score
2	Left/right	18.2	.87	-.86
3	Left/right	52.0	.87	-.88
4	Left/right	42.4	.71	-.85
5	Pres. power	23.8	.09	-.39
5	Left/right	10.4	-.55	.68
5	Vert. power	6.3	-.04	-.14
5	Uncertain	5.7	-.54	.61
6	soc. welfare?	15.3	-.01	.02
6	Yeltsin	14.4	.42	.84

Source: Calculations from the roll-call votes of the Russian Congress of People's Deputies.

eliminate the term "socialist" from the name of the state was correlated at 0.75 with this dimension; a vote on prohibiting private ownership of land was correlated at 0.81 with it. In the third Congress, a series of votes about the institution of a state presidency for Russia produced correlations on the order of 0.83 with this factor, while motions in the fourth Congress about the future president's powers and rights yielded correlations with this factor of 0.7-0.8 magnitude. The dominant dimension for each of these Congresses is highly correlated with the first dimension drawn from an analysis of the voting record for all five Congresses combined.

We are aided in interpreting the dimension emerging in the 2nd-4th Congresses by what amounts to an interest-group rating produced by Alexander Sobyanin and his associates. Sobyanin selected sets of roll-call votes in each Congress as bellwether indicators of deputies' support for positions of the democratic reformers—similar to the practices of the Americans for Democratic Action and other groups in the United States. In this case, Sobyanin chose issues designed to separate the democrats from the communist conservatives for each Congress. We recalculated a "Sobyanin score" for each deputy for four Congresses for which Sobyanin has provided analysis, as well as an overall Sobyanin score for those Congresses.

Deputies' Sobyanin scores are highly correlated with the factor emerging in the 2nd-4th Congresses—Pearson r absolute values of 0.93, 0.91, and 0.89, respectively, for the three Congresses. As Table 7.2 shows, an overall Sobyanin score is strongly related to the dimension for the 2nd-4th Congresses. These patterns lend credence to the interpretation that conflict in the 2nd-4th Congresses had a strongly left-right orientation.

Figure 7.1 shows the distribution of scores along the left-right dimension of the 2nd-4th Congresses. The scores reported in the figure represent a factor score for the combined votes of the 2nd-4th Congresses. The figure confirms that the left-right dimension underpinned highly polarized blocs of deputies on the left and right. The distribution of scores indicates that the left wing was at least as cohesive as the right wing during this period. It appeared that policy preferences provided a strong foundation for the development of a left-wing and a right-wing parliamentary party.

In these early congresses, the importance of the two-tiered system was transparent. Deputies who had been elected to the Supreme Soviet were, on the whole, substantially more liberal than other deputies. In the 3rd Congress, for example, Supreme Soviet members exhibited a mean left-right factor score of -0.18 and a median of -0.55. In contrast, other deputies had a mean of 0.06 and a median of 0.14.

The differences in median positions indicate a wide difference in majority views within the two groups. Yeltsin's forces were clearly more advantaged in the Supreme Soviet than in the Congress.

Political Upheaval in the 5th and 6th Congresses

The single dimension and polarized alignment of the early Congresses were the product of the 1990 elections and the political dynamics of the struggle of a movement identifying itself with democratic and market ideals against the traditional communist system. Conditions changed by the 5th Congress. Yeltsin's convincing victory in June—58 percent of the popular vote against five other candidates—strengthened his political position, but also now gave his opponents a new focus of opposition—legislative control of the executive branch.

The 5th Congress

New voting alignments emerged in the 5th Congress. The most important factor was very weakly related to the left-right dimension, leaving what was left of a left-right dimension to explain only 10.4 percent of the variance. This pattern is explained by the splitting of both the left and right into parts favoring a strong central executive and those opposing one. The presidential power dimension accounted for more variance in voting behavior than any other dimension in the 5th Congress. Correlations with the Sobyanin rating, a good indicator of support for Yeltsin's positions, suggest substantial fragmentation among Yeltsin's supporters and opponents across the various issues.

As Figure 7.2 illustrates, this new dimension exhibited a very different distribution of preferences than the polarized left-right dimension that had dominated parliamentary politics to that point. Even what remained of the left-right dimension had lost its sharply polarized alignment, as Figure 7.3 shows. The firm foundation for parliamentary parties emerging in earlier Congresses seemed to evaporate.

Yeltsin exacerbated his problem in the 5th Congress by failing to tend to his political base and threatening, shortly after the Congress ended, to dissolve the Congress. Without a party or coalition organizationally dependent on his success, neither he nor the government he appointed could draw upon a significant base of support in the Congress since both the policies and powers of the government drew active opposition. His weakness in the Congress became apparent when he failed to win approval for Ruslan Khasbulatov to succeed him as chairman of the Supreme Soviet. As Sobyanin shows, Khasbulatov was opposed by a large body of the democrats, particularly those working closely with him as full-time members of committees, and by most of the conservatives. The Congress adjourned after a week with an agreement to convene again in the fall.

The failed coup of August intervened and again fundamentally changed the political environment. In the aftermath of the coup, Yeltsin's power and popular support were reaffirmed while Gorbachev's power—and, perhaps more importantly, the power of all the union power structures— suffered irreparable damage. Yeltsin took over more and more governing power in Russia at the expense of the union government, refusing to finance the union government and making any future union agreement dependent on Russia's consent. By the time the Congress reconvened in late October, Yeltsin was demanding additional powers to enact radical economic reform.

Yeltsin's position in the legislative branch was weakened by the departure of friendly deputies to key positions on the president's staff. An important case in point is Sergei Shakhrai, who had headed the crucial committee on legislation. Ten days before the 5th Congress reconvened, Shakhrai, who had earlier been appointed a "state counselor" under Yeltsin, resigned his post as committee chairman when the Supreme Soviet refused to put off elections of local governments. His departure weakened the democrats' position within the Supreme Soviet. In all, over 100 deputies eventually took positions in the executive branch; those who held full-time positions in the Supreme Soviet had to give them up to do so.

Nonetheless, Yeltsin won significant victories at the second session of the 5th Congress, the last time he was to do so. He asked for special powers to enact economic reform measures by decree, and received them; he won consent to put off elections of local heads of government until December 1, 1992, a move previously blocked by the Supreme Soviet; he won approval of constitutional amendments giving him the right to suspend the acts of lower authorities in Russia if he found that they violated the constitution and to suspend legal acts of the union if they violated Russian sovereignty; and he gained approval of his program for radical economic transformation. Shortly after the Congress adjourned, Yeltsin issued new decrees banning the activity of the communist party and nationalizing its property. A few days later Yeltsin assumed the position of prime minister himself, named a new cabinet dominated by young economists committed to rapid economic liberalization, and issued a package of decrees that launched his program of radical "shock therapy."

The 6th Congress

Yeltsin's vigorous use of his presidential powers to carry out a painful program of price liberalization, spending cuts, tax hikes and financial austerity immediately provoked opposition among deputies. Khasbulatov followed the trend by attacking Yeltsin's ministers as "inexperienced boys" and "worms." Yeltsin publicly stated that Russia needed a presidential republic since a parliamentary republic under current crisis conditions would amount to "suicide." These fundamental differences over the distribution of power seemed to be coming to a head as the 6th Congress convened.

From the very start of the 6th Congress, the balance of power seemed to have shifted against Yeltsin. Conservatives managed to get several items directed against the Gaidar government placed on the formal agenda of the Congress, contrary to the wishes of Yeltsin's supporters. Later, deputies debated a constitutional amendment giving the parliament the right to oversee the government, in effect taking back some of the powers granted to Yeltsin the previous December. The deputies refused at first to pass a resolution endorsing Yeltsin's economic program, instead passing an anti-reform measure lowering taxes and raising social spending, provoking the government under first deputy prime minister Gaidar to submit its resignation. Yeltsin then reached an agreement with Khasbulatov's deputy, Sergei Filatov, under which the Congress would adopt a new and modified declaration authorizing the government to continue its program but making needed modifications, and the government would resume office.

Yeltsin had managed to extract a partial victory but the position of his supporters in the Congress was demonstrably weakened. Not only could he not claim the two-thirds support that would be needed for the adoption of a new constitution abolishing the Congress altogether, but he no longer could count on winning passage of legislative measures except at the expense of costly concessions. He exacerbated relations with the deputies further by remarking after the Congress that it would be a good idea to dissolve the Congress and hold new elections. The weakening of his support base in the Congress through the defection of many former supporters, the loss of key supporters to the executive branch, the increasing power of Khasbulatov to steer Congress and parliament into opposition with Yeltsin, and the deepening economic deterioration in the country made further confrontation inevitable when the seventh Congress convened in December 1992.

The 6th Congress revealed a new set of alignment patterns in which two principal factors each explained a modest proportion of the variance. One factor was essentially uncorrelated with any major dimension of earlier Congresses, while the second dimension listed in Table 7.2 was moderately correlated (.42) with the general left-right dimension and somewhat more strongly (.57) with what appears to be the left-right dimension of the 5th Congress. Evidently by the 6th Congress the left-right and executive power dimensions had been supplanted by one pro-Yeltsin/anti-Yeltsin dimension that reflected now mutually-reinforcing views on reform and executive power. And even that dimension did not account for much of the variance in the now fluid lines of division among deputies.

The distribution of scores of the Yeltsin dimension, shown in Figure 7.4, could hardly be more different than the polarized distribution of the left-right dimensions in the early Congresses. It is a basically flat distribution over a wide range of scores, punctuated with a few spikes that reflect cohesive subgroups at various points along the spectrum of support for Yeltsin. The firm foundation for two parties found in the early Congresses had disintegrated by the end of the 6th Congress.

The other dimension in the 6th Congress appears to reflect the growing salience of a new social welfare dimension. This factor is related to votes on tax deductions for investment by industry, pay raises for workers outside of large industries, and the social rights of citizens, such as the rights to health care, education, a minimum wage, and a job. These issues arose in reaction to the tough economic liberalism of the Gaidar government, and reflect an effort to protect industry and citizens from the effects of shock therapy. But the correlations between many of these votes and the underlying factor are only moderately strong, which indicates that the voting alignments represented by this factor are far from identical across these related issues.

The great advantage of the two-tiered system of a Supreme Soviet and Congress had diminished for Yeltsin by the 6th Congress. On the Pro-Yeltsin/Anti-Yeltsin dimension, some advantage remained— Supreme Soviet members had a median of -0.29 and non-members exhibited a median of 0.06. The advantage, in terms of the standard of deviation, was about half as great as in the 2nd-4th Congresses on the left-right spectrum. And, of course, the Yeltsin dimension accounted for a much smaller proportion of variance in voting behavior than the once-dominant left-right dimension.

Yeltsin had clearly failed to link the cause of economic and political reform to presidential power as he had wished. The left-right alignment that dominated the early Congresses had faded in importance and produced an alignment of deputies that married some democrats with the conservatives in opposition to Yeltsin. And the advantage Yeltsin and his close allies gained from the two-tiered legislative system was evaporating. By the end of the 6th Congress, concrete action on the problem of resolving the constitutional distribution of power between legislative and executive branches had been deferred.

Institutional Deadlock in the 7th-9th Congresses

The 6th Congress did not resolve the deepening antagonism between President Yeltsin and his critics in the parliament. The compromises that were reached over the issue of the parliament's control over the executive and over the government's economic policies were short-lived. The Congress instructed the Supreme Soviet and the president to work out a law on government which was to reconcile separation of powers with legislative oversight of the executive branch. Compromise proved impossible, however. The plan Yeltsin submitted to the Supreme Soviet on structuring of ministries and Supreme Soviet oversight of the hiring and firing of cabinet ministers was blocked by parliament. The Congress's proposals on these subjects were unacceptable to Yeltsin.

The dispute over the law on government centered on the Gaidar reforms. Although it was somewhat relaxed after the first quarter of 1992, Gaidar's program of "shock therapy" continued for the entire year without bringing the Russian economy the promised signs of recovery. Inflation did not level off after the early "big bang" of price liberalization. Support for Yeltsin in parliament fell as some deputies grew disillusioned with the reform programs.

Some deputies saw an opportunity to seize political advantage. In September, shortly after Gaidar submitted his economic report to the Supreme Soviet, the Supreme Soviet set a December date for a new Congress over Yeltsin's objections; Yeltsin hoped to delay the Congress until spring, when the economy might have begun to turn around. Meantime Yeltsin and parliament remained at loggerheads over both policy issues and basic constitutional powers. Yeltsin named Gaidar "acting" prime minister but recognized that the Congress would almost certainly refuse to confirm him as prime minister. Yeltsin pressed for a popular referendum on a new constitution with strong presidential power.

The balance of power within the parliament shifted toward the anti-Yeltsin wing for several reasons. Nearly 200 deputies changed their political positions from the democratic wing to the communist wing. A number of democratically-oriented deputies became inactive in parliament as they were pushed or pulled into the executive branch. Some of the democrats were pushed out as Khasbulatov steadily centralized power in his own hands. Other democrats were pulled out by Yeltsin, who recruited deputies to become regional representatives or chiefs of administration, or to join the central presidential staff.

These two trends—deepening confrontation between the president and the parliament, and the expansion of the anti-Yeltsin bloc among deputies, were clearly seen in the last three Congresses, the 7th, 8th, and 9th. The polarization was reflected in the reemergence of a highly polarized alignment on a single dominant dimension in the 7th Congress (data not shown) that had been seen in the 2nd-4th Congresses. Votes relating to the constitutional struggle between parliament and president were highly correlated with this factor. For example, the vote loading most highly on this factor concerned a motion to grant the Supreme Soviet the right to confirm key cabinet positions. Other votes with high scores on the same factor include a proposal to judge the constitutionality of Yeltsin's acts as a basis for impeachment, on holding a vote of confidence in government, on institution of a referendum (.72), and on Yeltsin's proposal for land reform (.71). Thus, it is possible to interpret the dimension as pro- or anti-Yeltsin as well as left-right. The two issues—support for Yeltsin and support for radical reform—had become indistinguishable in the positions of the deputies.

The 7th Congress ended in a compromise brokered by the head of the constitutional court, Valerii Zorkin, which called for a popular referendum to decide basic principles of a future constitution. Unable to win support for Gaidar's nomination as prime minister, Yeltsin proposed and won approval of Victor Chernomyrdin instead, who was considered a state-oriented centrist and advocate of the directors' interests. Chernomyrdin vowed to stay the course of reform, however, and Yeltsin succeeded in making new ministerial appointments before the law requiring Supreme Soviet confirmation came into effect. Yeltsin secured approval for his referendum, to be held in April 1993, but the Supreme Soviet was to approve the questions.

The compromise of the 7th Congress broke down when the two sides could not agree on the wording of questions to be submitted to the populace. Parliament demanded cancellation of the referendum, Yeltsin insisted on holding it. In early March, 1993, the 8th Congress repudiated the Zorkin compromise on the referendum and the compromise on the powers of government, prompting Yeltsin to walk out and vow to hold the referendum in spite of the Congress's decision. Yeltsin then appeared on television to announce that he was assuming special powers.

Although he soon retracted his decision and issued a weaker decree, the deputies met for their 9th Congress for the purpose of removing Yeltsin from office. The impeachment motion failed by a narrow margin, and the Congress instead agreed to a national referendum on four questions: confidence in Yeltsin, support for his economic policy, and agreement to hold early parliamentary and presidential elections. Yeltsin's positions gained a majority of those voting on the first two issues, and around two-thirds of the voters called for early parliamentary elections. About half of the voters supported the proposition calling for new presidential elections. Thus, by the end of April, Yeltsin had demonstrated substantial popular support for his position in his struggle with the parliament. Not surprisingly, the left-right cleavage continued in the 8th and 9th congresses. The dimensions accounted for 35.7 percent of the variance in the 8th and 33.0 percent in the 9th, with no other dimensions explaining more than 5.1 percent. The dominant dimensions in the 7th-9th Congresses are strongly correlated with each other. Figure 7.5 shows the distribution of deputies on the dominant dimension that emerges from an analysis of the roll-call votes for the last three Congresses combined. The distribution shows continuing polarization and the withering of left-wing forces.

The pattern in Figure 7.5 suggests that the bloc on the right virtually constituted a parliamentary party, headed by Khasbulatov and supported by Rutskoi. It was opposed by an opposition bloc lodged in the executive branch. Each bloc sought to use its institution's powers to block the initiatives of the other bloc and institution. Because of the vast gulf between the two blocs, a partisan crisis became an institutional crisis that could not readily be solved by constitutional means.

The intensity of the confrontation between the institutions did not diminish following the 9th Congress. Yeltsin's success in the April referendum had the effect of making the parliamentary leadership reluctant to hold another Congress soon. In any case, Yeltsin acted to preempt the possibility of another impeachment attempt. On September 21, 1993, he declared the Congress and Supreme Soviet dissolved, stripped all deputies of their powers and privileges, and called for new elections in December, 1993, to elect a new parliament under the term of a new constitutional draft. Twelve days later, a violent uprising by armed groups led by Khasbulatov and Rutskoi was forcibly suppressed by military and security units. Khasbulatov, Rutskoi and other leaders of the insurrection were arrested and charged with inciting to riot. The legislative institutions created in 1990 had collapsed.

Conclusion

The polarization of political elites after the disintegration of the Soviet Union and the CPSU may have been inevitable but the demise of the transitional legislative institutions was not. In our view, the dissolution of the legislative institutions was the product of several interrelated developments—the crystallization of party-like blocs, emergence of a separation-of-powers system, and the domination of the legislative and executive institutions by different blocs—as well as the enduring popularity of Yeltsin and his cause. This combination of developments was contingent on decisions made by a variety of leaders under conditions of great uncertainty. There was little inevitable about them.

Underlying the change in institutional arrangements during the 1990-1993 period was a dramatic change in the alignment of forces within the Congress. Bipolarity characterized voting patterns in the first four and last three Congresses, with an intervening period of turbulence in the underlying dimensions of political conflict. The intervening period coincided with dramatic institutional, policy, and personnel changes: the creation of a new presidency, the collapse of the Soviet state, the introduction of radical economic reforms, and the selection of a new parliamentary speaker. Once these changes were absorbed by members of the parliament, voting alignments settled into a lasting left-right, or pro- and anti-Yeltsin cleavage that was dominated by the right-wing, anti-Yeltsin bloc or parliamentary party.

The parliamentary party sought to exercise the constitutional powers of their institution to retract the powers that had been delegated to the new president and to restore the older model of soviet government. Its failure appears to be due to continuing public support for reform, the personal popularity of Yeltsin, and the reserve of institutional strength that Yeltsin was able to build in his two years in the presidency. The parliamentary party's intransigence in the face of Yeltsin's strength resulted in the demise of both the parliamentary party and the legislative institutions in which it was lodged.

References

Smyth, Regina A. 1990. "Ideological vs. Regional Cleavages: Do the Radicals Control the RSFSR Parliament?" *Journal of Soviet Nationalities* 1:3 (Fall) 112–157.

Sobyanin, Alexander and D. Yur'ev. 1991. "S"ezd narodnykh deputatov RSFSR v zerkale poimennykh golosovanii: rasstanovka sil i dinamika razvitiia politicheskogo protivostoianiia." Moscow.

Urnov, M. I. 1991. "Osvobozhdaias' ot avtoritarizma," *Polis* 1:122–135.

FIGURE 7.1 2nd–4th Congresses Dimension

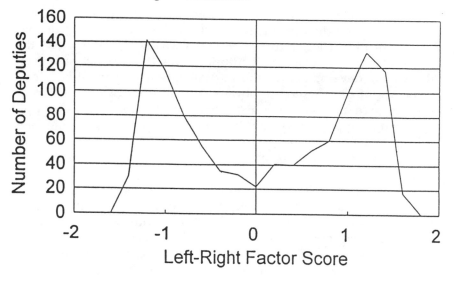

FIGURE 7.2 5th Congress, 1st Dimension

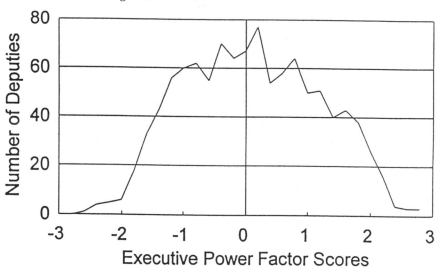

FIGURE 7.3 5th Congress, 2nd Factor

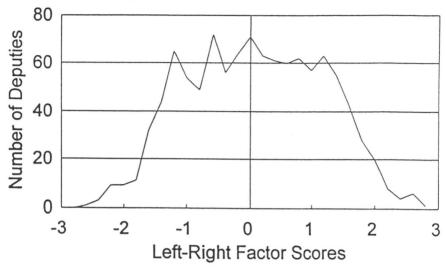

FIGURE 7.4 6th Congress, 2nd Dimension

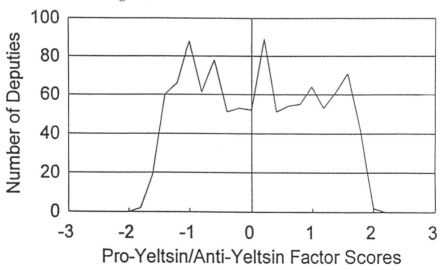

FIGURE 7.5 7th–9th Congresses Dimension

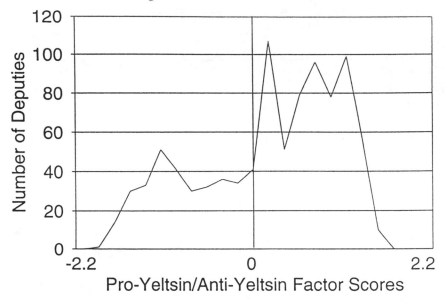

8

Political Cleavages Among the Russian Deputies

Alexander Sobyanin

Editor's Note

We are fortunate in being able to offer a perspective on Russian parliamentary development by a uniquely qualified observer, Alexander Sobyanin, a physicist and political scientist living in Moscow. Following his comments on the state of affairs among Russia's deputies after the Ninth Congress in March and before the April 1993 referendum, we append three reports written by Sobyanin and his associate Edward Gel'man, who, along with O. N. Kaiunov, form a research team called the "Information-Analytical Group." The IAG formed in 1989 during the election of members of the Academy of Sciences as USSR deputies, when they helped overcome the obstacles placed in the way of the election of Andrei Dmitrievich Sakharov as deputy from the Academy of Sciences. Subsequently the Information-Analytical Group provided research support to the Interregional Group of Deputies, which was the first organized, independent and democratic opposition group in the Soviet Union since the revolution. The Information-Analytic Group gathered comprehensive data on the backgrounds and voting patterns of the deputies, which enabled democratically-oriented deputies to develop more effective legislative strategies. In turn the IAG helped the Interregional Group organize the coalition of democratic deputies running under the "Democratic Russia" banner in the republican and local 1990 elections.

After the 1990 elections, the IAG developed a data base on the new Russian deputy corps and the pattern of support for and opposition to democratic reform. While Boris Yeltsin was chairman of the Russian Supreme Soviet, the IAG's reports were used by the parliamentary leadership, and they continued to be used by democratic factions and committees of the Supreme Soviet. The group's analyses of regional patterns of electoral behavior were used by the Yeltsin campaign organization in the June 1991 presidential elections and in the April 1993 referendum on support for the president. In addition, they are widely cited by the Russian press.

Although the reports of the IAG are written in support of democratic reform, they are widely respected by politicians of all shades of opinion for the thoroughness and objectivity of the data analysis. No other research team in Russia has produced such comprehensive analyses of the political behavior of the Russian deputy corps.

The three occasional reports which follow detail the sharp increase in opposition among the Russian deputies toward President Yeltsin's power and policies which characterized the Seventh, Eighth, and Ninth Congresses. In particular they focus on the changing strength of the deputy factions aligned with the democratic, "centrist," and communist-conservative wings. In them, Sobyanin explains the methodology of assigning political ratings or scores to each deputy. In turn, these scores are used to calculate average scores for various factions and segments of the corps of deputies. Sobyanin also analyzes the issues which distinguish the left from right wings of the deputies and provides unique insight into the political dynamics of the congresses.

Alexander Sobyanin and his colleagues have generously allowed us to translate and publish this unique material for the benefit of Western readers. The first two reports were translated by Professor Eugene Huskey of Stetson University, whose consent to allow us to reproduce them here is gratefully acknowledged. Thomas F. Remington translated the third report.

The Current Crisis

Alexander Sobyanin

I would like to begin by saying that I am happy to be in the United States and to be at this conference and to see that there is such a great interest in Russian affairs and sympathy for Russian democracy. As Professor Remington indicated, we regularly conduct observations of the voting behavior of deputies in Russian Congresses. We've done so since the first Congress. What I would like to present today are the results of our observations of the voting at the last three Congresses— the seventh, eight, and ninth—which have led to the very sharp political crisis that Russia is in today.

First, I would like to talk about some peculiar characteristics of the electoral campaign of 1990, some of which are not taken sufficiently into account. In actual fact, the elections of 1990 were not fully democratic. The Communist Party drew conclusions from some of the shocking defeats that it experienced in the elections of 1989 and prepared itself well for the 1990 elections. The party leaders undertook an entire series of measures designed to prevent the same defeat that they had experienced in the 1989 elections, especially at the level of Russia itself. A democratic Russian parliament posed a particularly major threat, because then there would emerge two supreme legislative organs on Russian soil. One was the union-level legislature; the other was the Russian level, the model of which, like that of the new union legislature, resembled very closely the hierarchical structure of the Communist Party itself. No other union republic legislature took this form.

Specifically, the pyramidal and hierarchical structure is similar to that of the CPSU. The Congress of People's Deputies resembles the Congress of the Communist Party, which elected the Central Committee of the Communist Party, and therefore, in that respect, resembles the elected Supreme Soviet. In turn, much as the Central Committee elected a Politburo, so the Supreme Soviet forms a Presidium. Leading the Presidium in the legislature is a chairman. The chairman resembles, in the Communist Party structure, the General Secretary. The Chairman of the Supreme Soviet has a number of deputy chairs who, in turn, resemble the Secretariat of the Communist Party Central Committee. All of this was intended to give the corps of deputies a high degree of manageability and to make them susceptible to guidance and rule from above by the Chairman.

A second measure that was taken was the establishment of two different kinds of electoral districts to elect deputies. One was the nine hundred seats allocated to territorial districts based on population. The other was the one hundred and sixty-eight seats given to national or ethnic-national territorial electoral districts, nearly all of whose members were then immediately elected into the nationalities chamber of the Supreme Soviet. The selection of candidates to run from these one hundred and sixty-eight national-territorial electoral districts was the object of particular care and attention on the part of the Communist Party, and it was intended to insure that at least one of the two chambers of the Supreme Soviet was quite manageable.

A third measure that was undertaken was the creation of a Supreme Soviet that was unusually small in size compared to the size of the Supreme Soviets of other republics. In addition, in the course of the political campaign, measures were taken in order to prevent particularly influential or outstanding candidates from running. In actual fact, as things turned out, such figures were rare in the Russian Parliament. In the communist wing, the only really notable figures were Vorotnikov, Vlasov, and Polozkov, the leader of the Russian Communist Party. All three of these figures played an insignificant role at the union level. Somewhat surprisingly, the democratic wing also did not put forward especially outstanding or prominent candidates, with the exception of Yeltsin.

In fact, the Interregional Group of Deputies, which was the liberal democratic group of deputies in the union legislature, adopted a decision not to run especially strong candidates at the level of the Russian legislature, but instead to concentrate their efforts on elections to the city and local soviets. Thus, for example, Gavriil Popov ran for the Moscow soviet, Anatolii Sobchak ran for the Leningrad soviet, Sergei Stankevich ran for the Moscow soviet, Gennadii Burbulis ran for the Sverdlovsk city soviet, Ilya Zaslavskiy ran for the October city district soviet within Moscow. Thus, of the roughly 250 deputies in the Interregional Group in the Union legislature, only three ended up in the Russian legislature—Yeltsin, Mikhail Bocharov, and Nikolai Travkin. A year later, two additional figures joined them, Galina Starovoitova and Yurii Afanasyev.

The nominating phase of the campaign was conducted under rather strict control by the communist party. Of the approximately 6,000 candidates who ran, only seventy ran on the basis of a fully democratic nominating procedure, that is, through nominating meetings held in the place of residence. The remaining candidates were nominated at meetings of labor collectives, which were conducted under the watchful eye of party committees. Over half of the candidates that were nominated to run were nominated by party committees at the district level, the city level, the regional level or by other organizations and often at the very last minute in the nominating phase, when the party committees already had a clear idea of the balance of forces in the electoral district. Hence there is nothing surprising about the fact that 86 percent of the deputies who were elected were members of the party. 58 percent of the elected deputies represented the middle and upper levels of the administrative echelon.

The democratic forces concentrated their efforts on the election of Yeltsin to the chairmanship of the Supreme Soviet, which succeeded on the third round of voting. However, Yeltsin, once elected, really lacked a team of his own. Of the seven people whom Yeltsin got into the leadership of the Supreme Soviet at that First Congress, six fought for his resignation later at the Third Congress in 1991. Ruslan Khasbulatov was the seventh of those people whom Yeltsin got into the leadership, and he began fighting for Yeltsin's removal by the time of the Sixth Congress. It is striking that Yeltsin's record of mistakes in choosing personnel to be the leaders of the Supreme Soviet was 100 percent.

The democrats never had a majority among the deputies in the Congress. The maximum level of support that the democratic position had was at the Third Congress when they commanded 46 percent of the votes. Consequently, Yeltsin had to conduct a very flexible policy in order to attract to his side a share of deputies holding moderate positions as well as a share of the communists. This is how one can explain his 100 percent error rate in choosing associates in the leadership.

The situation among the Russian deputy corps changed significantly after the election of the president. After Yeltsin was elected president, in June 1991, the democratic wing did not have a leader on whom they could depend. Only about half of the democratic wing supported Khasbulatov. Sergei Filatov might have been supported by a larger number of the democratically-oriented deputies, but, at that point, he chose to align himself with Khasbulatov, and for that he was rewarded with the position of first deputy chairman of the Supreme Soviet. Even so, Khasbulatov was unable to get elected at first to the post of Chairman of the Supreme Soviet. Therefore, in the second part of the Fifth Congress (held two months after the August coup), Khasbulatov allied himself with the communist deputies in order to get elected.

Figure 8.1 graphically depicts the distribution of deputies at each of the congresses according to their political stance.

FIGURE 8.1 Political Structure of the Russian Deputy Corps

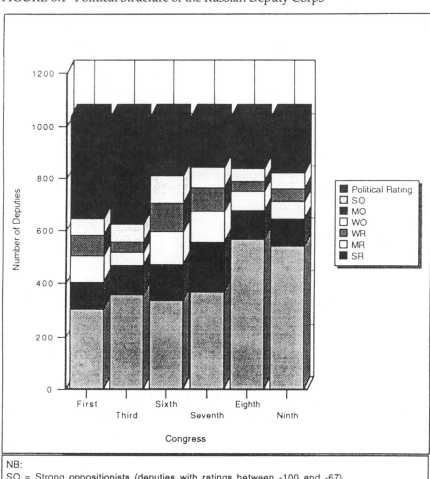

NB:
SO = Strong oppositionists (deputies with ratings between -100 and -67)
MO = Moderate oppositionists (ratings between -66 and -34)
WO = Weak oppositionists (ratings between -33 and 0)
WR = Weak reformers (ratings between 1 and +33)
MR = Moderate reformers (ratings between +34 and +66)
SR = Strong reformers (ratings between +67 and +100)

TABLE 8.1   Distribution of "Deputy-Defectors" by Employment Category (At the Beginning of the Eighth Congress)

Employment	No. People's Deputies	Number of "Deputy-Defectors"			
		VI Congress	VII Congress	VIII Congress	TOTAL
Full-time Deputies in Supreme Soviet	376	26	26	52	104 (28%)
Full-time Deputies in lower-level soviets	46	3	1	1	5 (10%)
Officials in Executive Agencies	203	1	2	9	12 (6%)
Enterprise Directors	279	6	10	15	31 (11%)
Lower-level Management	124	10	11	9	30 (24%)
TOTAL		46	50	86	182

TABLE 8.2   Distribution of "Deputy-Defectors" by Employment Category (At the Time of Election to the Congress)

Employment	No. People's Deputies	Number of "Deputy-Defectors"			
		VI Congress	VII Congress	VIII Congress	TOTAL
Higher-level Management	221	1	1	4	6 (3%)
Middle-level Management	376	11	12	23	46 (12%)
Lower-level Management	211	16	16	33	65 (31%)
Workers & Peasants	51	3	7	8	18 (35%)
"Mental Labor"	174	15	14	18	47 (27%)
TOTAL		46	50	86	182

Through the Seventh Congress, as one can see outlined in the dark element at the bottom of the columns, the most conservative communist deputies remained about constant in numbers, but there began to be a change in the interval between the Fifth and Sixth Congresses. The alignments at the Fifth Congress were somewhat indeterminate. Half of the democratically inclined deputies voted against giving the President additional powers for two reasons. First, they opposed naming as the chiefs of administration at the local level a number of former Communist Party officials. Second, they opposed the deferring of elections of local heads of administration. For their part, about half of the conservative opposition were trying to show their support for the President in the wake of the August coup.

But, at the Sixth Congress, everything returned to its former place. It is characteristic that the number of democratic deputies fell by nearly half in the interval between the Fifth and Sixth Congresses. One reason for this is that a number of deputies felt themselves cut off or removed from power after the establishment of presidentialism. Some were disappointed that they had not been named to high posts in the executive branch. Others were upset at appointments of people they did not like to the posts of local administrative chiefs.

Thus began the predominance of the corporate interest among the deputy corps in preserving full power for the legislative branch and taking back the president's executive and allocative powers. It is in this considerably truncated state that the democratic wing exists today. It is characteristic that, in the midst of the sharp confrontation between Congress and President, a number of the former democrats who had been in the middle and defined themselves as "waverers" only defined themselves as conservatives at the Eighth Congress. The two hundred or so deputies who defected from the democratic wing to go over to the conservative side share some interesting characteristics, which are worth examining more closely.

Almost three-quarters of them, at the moment they were elected, occupied positions in the lower echelons of state and economic administration or they were in non-administrative positions entirely. These were deputies who had a grounds for feeling dissatisfied with their social status. Of that three-quarters, 80 percent work on a full-time basis in the committees and commissions of the Supreme Soviet. These are deputies who have lost their ties with their constituents and do not wish to go back to their regions. A small share of these defectors to the conservative side are directors of enterprises or functionaries in the executive branch. Only about 10 percent of the directors who were deputies went over from a position of supporting the president to opposing him, and this can be explained readily by the difficulty of the present phase of reforms. Thus we could say that most of those who switched over were driven primarily by career motives.

At this last Ninth Congress, contrary to our expectations, there occurred not an increase in the number of opponents to Yeltsin, but rather a certain reduction by about 30 deputies. There is a large group of deputies who are constantly repositioning themselves between the two sides, and who are extremely sensitive to the political approval ratings of various political forces. As soon as the approval ratings of the president began to go back up, a certain share of deputies followed to support him. It is instructive that about 80 percent of these deputies who move back and forth are members of the factions that enter the centrist bloc rather than the factions that are a part of either Russian Unity or the democratically-oriented Parliamentary Coalition for Reform bloc. When Yeltsin was the chairman of the Supreme Soviet, he was constantly having to fight to get 50 percent of the deputies to vote his way. Now he has to fight to get a third of deputies, since a two-thirds vote is required for such important measures as impeachment, and if in the first stage Yeltsin had to fight for approval of the idea of creating a post of president, now he is forced to defend his post by a direct appeal to the general population in order to carry out the long-delayed and long-awaited political reform in Russia. Therefore he insisted on conducting a nationwide popular referendum on confidence in his leadership and his government's policies and on holding early parliamentary and presidential elections. I very much hope he will win the referendum.

Appendix 8.1
Political Positions and Composition of Factions
at the Seventh Congress of People's Deputies

List and Quantitative Composition of the Factions

Currently there are fourteen factions among people's deputies of the Russian Federation. Seven, exactly half, form two broad, inter-factional associations: the Parliamentary Reform Coalition, which brings together most deputies from the Radical Democrat, Democratic Russia, and Consensus for Progress factions, as well as a significant number of deputies from other factions, and the Russian Unity bloc, which unites deputies from the Communists of Russia, Russia, Fatherland, Agrarian Union, as well as a small number of deputies outside these factions.

The seven remaining factions (see Table 8.1.1) are not part of stable, permanently functioning coalitions. While it is true that in the course of the Sixth Congress of People's Deputies [April 1992] three of these seven factions (Change [Smena], Worker's Union, and Industrial Union) announced the creation of the bloc Constructive Forces, this bloc remained inactive, as did another newly-declared coalition, the

TABLE 8.1.1 The Distribution Of Deputies in Factions by Their Support For Radical Political and Economic Reforms at the VII Congress

Factions	Average Rating at Congress	Number of Deputies by Degree of Support					Average Rating in Supreme Soviet	Number of Members of Supreme Soviet by Degree of Support				
		1	2	3	4	Total		1	2	3	4	Total
Factions Supporting Reform												
Radical Democrats	+89	48	2	—	—	50	+88	9	1	—	—	10
Democratic Russia	+82	45	2	2	—	49	+82	9	1	—	—	10
Consensus for Progress	+76	48	2	3	—	53	+85	12	—	—	—	12
Left Center/Cooperation	+24	26	19	7	9	61	+21	9	4	2	3	18
Total		167	25	12	9	213		39	6	2	3	50
Factions with Inconsistent Positions												
Free Russia	+5	18	9	12	17	56	−18	4	4	3	9	20
Motherland	−10	14	9	4	25	52	+7	6	2	1	7	16
Worker's Union	−19	8	6	16	21	51	−39	1	1	7	9	18
Dep. outside Factions	−20	45	29	34	103	211	−21	8	4	3	18	33
Total		85	53	66	166	370		19	11	14	43	87
Factions Opposing Reform												
Sovereignty & Equality	−40	5	1	14	29	49	−43	2	—	8	15	25
Change (New Politics)	−43	5	3	10	35	53	−43	2	2	4	18	26
Industrial Union	−49	4	4	6	38	52	−75	—	—	—	5	5
Fatherland	−67	1	2	4	44	51	−86	—	—	—	10	10
Agrarian Union	−73	4	1	6	119	130	−84	—	—	—	13	13
Russia	−76	2	1	1	51	55	−72	1	—	1	13	15
Communist of Russia	−89	—	—	1	66	67	−90	—	—	1	16	17
Total		21	12	42	382	457		5	2	14	90	111
Congress as a Whole	−20	273	90	120	557	1040						
Supreme Soviet as a Whole							−23	63	19	30	136	248

1=firm support; 2=weak support; 3=weak opposition; 4=firm opposition

Democratic Center, which sought to unite the remaining four factions. The size of thirteen of the fourteen factions registered at the Seventh Congress of People's Deputies [December 1992] is quite small, from forty-nine to sixty-seven deputies. The minimum required for registration as a faction is formally fifty. Only Agrarian Union significantly surpassed the remaining factions in size, with 130 deputies. Of the total of 1040 Congress deputies, 829 (approximately 80%) belonged to factions. Only 211 remained outside of them.

Table 8.1.1 shows the size of factions in the Supreme Soviet [the smaller, standing parliament elected from among Congress deputies] as well as in the Congress itself. Note that the size of factions in the Supreme Soviet is not necessarily proportional to the corresponding factions in the Congress. Thus, factions in the Parliamentary Reform Coalition are represented by only one-fifth of their total membership. The same applies to the Russian Unity bloc. Centrist factions, on the other hand (with the exception of the Industrial Union), are represented by from one-third to one-half of their total membership.

Political Positions of Deputies Based on Analysis of Roll Call Votes

Membership of a deputy in a faction often does not define his political position. The characteristics of the Russian parliament are now such that deputies are not disciplined for failure to attend meetings or to support policies adopted by a majority of the faction. Being elected individually, and not as before by party list, means that deputies are at best responsible to their constituents. Because constituents no longer have the right to recall deputies, one might say that they are responsible only to their conscience.

The platforms of factions are quite vague and are occasionally indistinguishable. Moreover, the actions of factional leaders do not always correspond to the platform of the faction. It is therefore not surprising that right prior to the Seventh Congress many deputies belonged to two or even three factions at once. Only at the Seventh Congress was the practice of joint or multiple membership in factions prohibited (it should be noted that this was done by purely administrative measures and not at the initiative of members of multiple factions).

In view of the above, the only reliable measure for determining the actual political positions of individual deputies and analyzing the political orientation of any of the deputies' groups or factions is roll call analysis, the results of which are discussed briefly below.

Political Ratings [reitingi] and the Actual
Political Divisions Among Deputies at the Seventh Congress

The score of a parliamentarian [on a 100-point system] is the generally recognized method of characterizing his or her political position in roll call analysis. Applied to the Russian parliament, the task of determining political ratings of deputies is greatly facilitated by the polarization of the body into two large and stable groups of deputies, which occupy diametrically opposed positions on literally all questions of political principle. These positions have remained virtually unchanged during the two-and-a-half-year life of the Russian Congress.

Henceforth, we will for simplicity's sake label one of these groups reformist and the other conservative. With these labels, which should not be viewed as having any positive or negative connotations, we refer to distinctions in approach to the implementation of the course of radical political and economic reforms by the new Russian political institutions.

The presence in the Congress of two large and stable groups, which have not changed their basic positions for two and a half years and which account for as many as 60 percent of the deputies, allows us to evaluate objectively and with precision the score of each vote of the Seventh Congress in terms of the differential in the percentage of votes cast FOR a proposal by each of the two groups.

For example, if all of the deputies in the first (reformist) group and none of the second (conservative) group voted for a proposal, then the corresponding differential in voting percentage, that is the *score* of the vote from the perspective of the first group, would be equal to +100. By contrast, if all the deputies in the second group and none of the deputies in the first group voted for the proposal, then the voting score from the perspective of the first group would be equal to -100. If an equal number of deputies from each group cast votes for and against a proposal, then the differential of the division, and hence the voting score (from the perspective of either group), would be equal to 0.

Proceeding in this way, we ranked all 249 roll call votes of the Seventh Congress in descending order based on the ratio of their scores and selected the twenty-five most significant votes from the perspective of the deputies belonging to the reformist group and the twenty-five most significant votes from the perspective of deputies belonging to the conservative group. We further computed the differential of the percentage of votes cast by each deputy *for* their, or the other group's, proposals. It was this differential of deputies' votes, cast for the first and second groups' proposals, that we call the *political rating* of each deputy.

We should note that if in the course of the fifty most significant ("key") votes selected by us a deputy voted only for the first twenty-five proposals, supported by the reformist wing of the Congress, he or she would receive the highest rating (from the standpoint of that wing of the Congress), +100 points (percent). Likewise, if a deputy voted only for the second-most significant proposals, supported by the conservative wing of the Congress, he or she would receive the lowest rating (from the point of view of the reformist wing), -100 points. If a deputy cast votes in equal number for their and the other group's proposals, then he or she would receive a rating of 0 (that is, neutral from the perspective of both wings of the Congress). Naturally, if we reversed the two groups we would change the sign (+ or -) of the deputy's rating, but the raw numerical figure would remain the same. Below, for clarity's sake, we will evaluate the position of deputies only from the perspective of the reformist wing of the Congress (which, in the view of many, is now in power in the country). This approach will not prevent the reader from simply reversing the sign on the ratings to suggest another point of view.

A rough assessment of the balance of forces among deputies can be obtained by dividing the 200-point rating scale into six equal parts and assigning deputies to them on the basis of their political rating. The result is a division of the Congress into six political groups:

1. FR = those deputies, *firmly* supporting reforms (rating from +100 to +67);
2. MR = those deputies, *moderately* supporting reforms (rating from +66 to +34);
3. WR = those deputies, *weakly* supporting reforms (rating from +33 to +1);
4. WO = those deputies in *weak* opposition to reforms (rating from zero to -33);
5. MO = those deputies in *moderate* opposition to reforms (rating from -34 to -66);
6. FO = those deputies in *firm* opposition to reform(rating from -67 to -100).

The two upper and lower groups form, respectively, firm reformist and firm conservative wings of the Congress. The two middle groups may be relegated to the "center" or, as they still say, to the "swamp" of the parliament. Finally, uniting the three upper and three lower groups, we get a division of the Congress into two camps: a camp of deputies supporting reform in some measure and a camp opposing reform in some measure.

TABLE 8.1.2 Number of Deputies in Each Political Group

Political Group	FR	MR	WR	WO	MO	FO
Number of deputies	193	80	90	120	188	369
Percent of total	18%	8%	9%	12%	18%	35%
Share of deputies consistently supporting reform (FO+MO), wavering (WR+WO), and consistently opposing reform (MO+FO)	273 26%		210 20%		557 54%	
Share of deputies in some measure supporting or opposing reform	363 35%			677 65%		

Table 8.1.2 illustrates the number of deputies in each of the actual political groups (revealed by means of the analysis of the fifty key roll call votes described above) and also the number of deputies in various combinations of these groups.

From this table it is evident that at the Seventh Congress, 65 percent, or almost two-thirds, of the deputies were in some measure opposed to reform and to the idea of independent presidential power. Indeed, the consistently conservative wing of the Congress was more than twice as large as the consistently reformist wing, representing an absolute majority (53 percent) of voices at the Congress. Almost the same balance of forces was in place in the Supreme Soviet, which the analysis bears out. Let us now look at the actual political positions and the actual political makeup of the deputies' factions.

The Actual Political Positions and Makeup of Deputies' Factions

The average political ratings of deputies' factions at the Seventh Congress and the distribution of deputies by faction according to the degree of their support of radical political and economic reform is provided in Table 8.1.1, to which we referred at the beginning of the article. From the data in this table it is evident that the most politically homogenous factions are the three comprising the Parliamentary Reform Coalition and the four making up the Russian Unity bloc. However, even in these factions there are deputies whose political position (as expressed in the fifty key roll call votes) diverges diametrically from that of the faction's majority.

In the factions Sovereignty and Equality, Change (New Politics), and Industrial Union the number of deputies not sharing the position of the factions' majority is noticeably higher, though it still does not exceed 15-20 percent of the total. In the four remaining factions (Left Center-Cooperation, Free Russia, Motherland, and Worker's Union) the number of such deputies varies from a quarter to half of the faction! This pattern is particularly evident in Free Russia and Motherland, which, it seems to us, must either disband or fundamentally revamp their membership at the upcoming Congress.

As Table 8.1.1 illustrates, at the Seventh Congress only the factions comprising the Parliamentary Reform Coalition and part of the faction Left Center-Cooperation gave consistent support to the policies of the President and Government.

Evolution of the Political Positions of Deputies' Factions Between Congresses One and Seven

An analysis of roll call votes allows us to follow how the positions of the present membership of factions and the corps of deputies as a whole changed at previous Congresses. The most interesting Congresses in this regard are the First, Third, and Sixth, which were the most prolonged, substantive, and politically divisive.

Table 8.1.3 provides the average political ratings of deputies' factions and also the Congress and Supreme Soviet in toto from the above-mentioned First, Third, Sixth and Seventh Congresses. We see that at the First and Third Congresses the average rating of all deputies was slightly positive, +7 and +4 points, respectively. This means that in the first year and a half of the Congress's work the reformist component of deputies managed to adopt, though with difficulty, significant policies that began the reform process and established new political structures that were essential to this work: the institution of the presidency, the Constitutional Court, and so on.

However, in the period between the Fifth and Sixth Congresses (November 1991-April 1992) the positions of a number of deputies changed sharply, and the Congress adopted a stance in opposition to reform (the average rating of the corps of deputies at the Sixth Congress was -11 points, as is evident from Table 8.1.3). At the same time, this shift did not lead to dramatic consequences, since the consistently conservative deputies did not comprise more than half of the Congress. But at the Seventh Congress, as we saw above, the conservative forces crossed this threshold, and the legislature then entered into irreconcilable conflict with the executive power of the president, which was still oriented toward reform. More detailed analysis would show that at the First Congress 39 percent of the

TABLE 8.1.3 Degree of Support of Radical Political and Economic Reform by Deputies Factions at the First, Third, Sixth and Seventh Congresses (Complete support = 100; Complete opposition = −100)

Factions	Number of Deputies		Degree of support (+) or lack of support (-) of reforms			
	Congress	SS	I Congress May 1990	III Congress March 1991	VI Congress April 1992	VII Congress Dec 1992
Factions Firmly Supporting Reform						
Radical Democrats	50	10	+91	+94	+89	+89
Democratic Russia	49	10	+91	+96	+82	+82
Consensus for Progress	53	12	+89	+89	+78	+76
Total	152	32	+90	+93	+83	+82
Factions Weakly Supporting Reform						
Left Center/Cooperation	61	18	+55	+68	+47	+24
Free Russia	56	20	+43	+71	+33	+ 5
Total	117	38	+49	+70	+40	+15
Factions Shifting from Reformists to Conservatives						
Motherland	52	16	+42	+53	+17	−10
Workers' Union	51	18	+43	+39	− 1	−19
Change (New Politics)	53	26	+42	+29	−29	−43
Total	156	60	+42	+40	− 4	−24

Factions Weakly Opposing Reform						
Sovereignty & Equality	49	25	−39	−34	−29	−40
Industrial Union	52	5	−20	−26	−44	−49
Total	101	30	−29	−30	−37	−45
Factions Firmly Opposing Reform						
Fatherland	51	10	−67	−78	−61	−67
Agrarian Union	130	13	−41	−70	−72	−73
Russia	55	15	−23	−54	−75	−76
Communists of Russia	67	17	−82	−91	−89	−89
Total	303	55	−51	−73	−74	−76
Total Deputies in Factions	829	215	+ 9	+ 5	− 11	−20
Deputies outside of Factions	211	33	− 2	+ 2	− 9	−20
Congress as a Whole	1040	248	+ 7	+ 4	− 11	−20
Supreme Soviet as a Whole	248	248	+18	+12	− 10	−23

deputies belonged to the consistently conservative camp, while 44 percent of deputies belonged to the consistently reformist camp. A year later, at the Third Congress, both camps grew in number, to 45 and 46 percent, respectively. The conservative camp expanded in the main by adding several dozen agrarian deputies and patriotically-inclined deputies from the intelligentsia, who had supported Boris Yeltsin at the First Congress. These deputies entered the factions "Agrarian Union" and "Russia," which led to a noticeable decline in the political rating of these factions at the Third Congress (see Table 8.1.3).

At the Sixth and Seventh Congresses the size of the consistently reformist camp fell from 478 to 273 deputies, that is by 205 persons, half of whom moved into the camp of consistent opposition, and half of whom "became bogged down" in the deputies' "swamp." Table 8.1.2 allows us to identify 188 of these deputies, who reduced their rating by more than fifty points and who, at the same time, significantly influenced the "political face" of the Congress and the Supreme Soviet. This group included representatives of the following factions: Change (twenty-seven deputies); Free Russia (twenty-five deputies); Motherland (nineteen deputies); and Workers' Union (twenty-four deputies). There were significantly fewer such deputies in the factions Left Center-Cooperation (twelve deputies), Industrial Union (nine deputies), Sovereignty and Equality (ten deputies) and Russia (six deputies). The remaining eleven deputies came from six more homogenous factions, which had formed part of the Parliamentary Reform Coalition and the Russian Unity bloc.

We should note that among the 188 deputies, who moved from supporting reform to opposing it, are all or almost all of the deputies declaring their membership in, or sympathy to, the Civic Union. As we shall see below, however, this opposition concerns not so much the economic as the political components of reform, namely presidential power.

Further investigation shows that of the 188 deputies moving from the democratic, reformist camp to the conservative camp, a majority— 109 deputies—work full-time in the legislative branch (104 of this number are members of the Supreme Soviet); fourteen occupy leading posts in the executive, twenty-two are directors of enterprises, three head large trade union organizations and labor collective councils and thirty-four deputies continue to hold the same non-leadership positions or posts in lower management that they had held before their election. Thus, we see that the main source of dissatisfaction in the Congress is not so much rank-and-file deputies as the deputies holding the most "important" and prestigious posts in the legislature.

It is noteworthy that if we exclude these 188 deputies from the legislature, the average rating at all four of the "key" congresses is virtually constant, and the fluctuation of the average rating is reduced severalfold. This shows that the actions of this group of deputies is decisive and fully explains all the unexpected variations in the behavior of the deputies at the last two congresses.

The reader may ask how a relatively small number of deputies, only 18 percent of the total, can cause such a fundamental shift in the position of the Congress as a whole. We gave the empirical answer to this question earlier, when we stated that at the first congresses of the Russian Federation the conservative and reformist camps were finely balanced (with the reformists enjoying only about a 1 percent edge). Naturally, under such conditions the transfer of 18 percent of the deputies from one wing to the other will disturb dramatically the balance of power and, as we have seen, produce a rapid change in the whole system of state power, which can occur because the existing Constitution of the Russian Federation has not set out legal mechanisms that would guarantee an effective separation of powers and prevent the parliament from usurping the power of the other branches. It is precisely this combination of elements that sparked the deep political and economic crisis which the system is presently undergoing.

An Issue-Oriented Analysis of the Positions of Deputies in Factions

An issue-oriented analysis of roll-call voting offers a fuller and more exact account of the positions of deputies in factions and of the factions themselves. At the Seventh Congress conflict developed around the following five basic groups of issues:

1. the agenda of the Congress and various political issues linked with the traditional opposition of the reformist and conservative wings of the Congress;
2. the separation of powers between the President and Congress and the President and the Supreme Soviet;
3. the assessment of the Government's performance and the course of economic reform;
4. the rejection of outmoded, ideologically-inspired articles of the Constitution and articles that strengthened Russia's ties to the old Union;
5. private land ownership.

Table 8.1.4 presents the results of an analysis of the factions' positions on these five issues at the Seventh Congress, based on ninety-

TABLE 8.1.4   Positions of Deputies' Factions on the Main Issues Raised at the Seventh Congress

	Number of Members	R7.1	R7.2	R7.3	R7.4	R7.5	Rating R7
				Issue Ratings			
Factions Not Opposed to Any of the Issues at the Congress							
Radical Democrats	50	+81	+79	+68	+93	+98	+89
Democratic Russia	49	+67	+73	+69	+90	+96	+82
Consensus for Progress	53	+62	+65	+59	+90	+92	+76
Left Center/Cooperation	61	+18	+ 7	+33	+80	+53	+24
Factions Opposed on 1–3 Issues							
Free Russia	56	+7	− 9	+13	+69	+58	+ 5
Motherland	52	− 7	−25	+ 5	+58	+18	−10
Workers' Union	51	−20	−33	− 6	+71	+32	−19
Deputies Outside Factions	211	−18	−27	− 5	+43	+ 6	−20
Factions Opposed on 4–5 Issues							
Sovereignty & Equality	49	−31	−42	−18	+32	−50	−40
Change (New Politics)	53	−36	−53	−27	+33	− 6	−43
Industrial Union	52	−42	−49	−49	+20	−30	−49
Factions Opposed on all Issues of the Congress							
Fatherland	51	−63	−68	−54	−32	−55	−67
Agrarian Union	130	−62	−73	−57	−20	−77	−73
Russia	55	−68	−74	−67	−35	−64	−76
Communists	67	−78	−88	−76	−71	−85	−89
Congress as a whole	1040	−18	−27	−12	+30	− 2	−20
Supreme Soviet as whole	248	−20	−31	−13	+35	− 0	−23

Issue 1   (rating R7.1):   general political questions and agenda
Issue 2   (rating R7.2):   powers of President and Congress/Supreme Soviet
Issue 3   (rating R7.3):   assessment of Government's performance and the course of reforms
Issue 4   (rating R7.4):   deideologization of the Constitution and the place of Russia in USSR/CIS
Issue 5   (rating R7.5):   private ownership of land

eight roll-call votes. From the Table it is evident that the factions that form the Parliamentary Reform Coalition and the Russian Unity bloc occupied diametrically opposed positions on all five issue-areas addressed by the Congress. The number of issues on which other factions disagree with the position of the President and Government varies, from four (Industrial Union and Change), to three (Worker's Union), to two (Motherland), to one (Free Russia), to none (Left Center-Cooperation).

It is noteworthy that even with such a diversity of positions among the centrist factions, all without exception have their lowest rating on the second issue, that is the division of power between the President and the legislature. The next lowest rating relates to the agenda and general political issues, and only in third position do we find opposition to the Government's performance and the course of economic reform. This pattern of opposition to issues by the wavering and centrist factions fully correlates with the ratings of these issues for each of the 188 deputies who moved from the reformist to the conservative camp. On the one hand, this pattern confirms the key role played by these deputies in the shaping of the majority positions in the centrist factions; on the other hand, it illustrates that for them the main issue was not changing the composition of the Government and modifying the course of reform (as many leaders of the factions like to emphasize) but the removal of as many powers as possible from the President.

Summary and Conclusions

First, one of the major conclusions of this short review is that the process of political organization and definition among the deputies is far from complete. In particular, one may expect the emergence at the next Congress of one more reformist faction alongside the three already in existence. This may occur as the result of natural schisms of deputies within the Left Center-Cooperation and Free Russia factions (deputies in each hold similar positions but have very diverse backgrounds). A new reformist faction may also emerge as a result of the seemingly inevitable collapse of the recently-formed Motherland faction, whose deputies come from very diverse backgrounds. Moreover, new factions, whether conservative or reformist, may draw on a reserve of 211 deputies who are currently outside of factions. But whatever further restructuring of political forces occurs among deputies, it is unlikely to lead to the emergence of any new and stable parliamentary coalitions. Indeed the opposite is more likely—the deputies' factions will evolve, at least in the near future, in the direction of a deepening and strengthening of the two existing coalitions, since this more accurately reflects the balance of forces that are now developing in society.

Second, with the huge shift in favor of the conservative camp at the Seventh Congress, one should not expect any concessions or agreements from the conservatives that would preserve an independent presidency. It is sufficient to recall that even the direct appeal of the President to the nation at the Seventh Congress had almost no influence on the firm conservative wing of deputies, only one-seventh of whom voted for the resolution "On Stabilizing the Constitutional Order." Thus, the further development of the conflict between legislative and executive authority seems to us inevitable, and a cancellation or postponement of the referendum, scheduled for April 11, will only deepen this crisis.

Third, and finally, the independent position of deputies who were elected as individuals has made parliament politically ill-organized, unpredictable, and unstable. As a result, it may become a hostage in the hands of a narrow group of deputies, who will readily change their political positions and be guided primarily by institutional, departmental, or personal interests, and not by the interests of the citizens who elected them. This negative experience of the Russian parliament, pregnant with the constant threat of acute and profound political crises, must be considered in preparing for new elections, which may occur in the near future.

Appendix 8.2
Reasons for the Movement of the Corps of Russian Deputies Toward Confrontation With the President and His Reform Course

An analysis of roll call voting at the Seventh and previous Congresses of People's Deputies reveals a category of deputies that bears primary responsibility for the current standoff between the legislative and executive branches. These are deputies who in the first year and a half of the Congress' term firmly supported the President of Russia (formerly the Chairman of the Russian Supreme Soviet) and his reform course, and then crossed over to firm opposition to the President and his policies. This category of "deputy-defectors" consisted of 182 persons at the Eighth Congress, of whom forty-six had deserted the President at the Sixth Congress (April 1992), fifty at the Seventh Congress (December 1992), and eighty-six at the Eighth Congress (March 1993).

The share of deputies firmly supporting the President and his re- form course steadily declined from the Third to the Eighth Congress, as the following figures indicate.

Deputies firmly supporting the President and his reforms:

Third Congress—45 percent
Sixth Congress—40 percent
Seventh Congress—35 percent
Eighth Congress—27 percent

If this trend continues, only 20 percent of the deputies will be supporters of the President at the Ninth Congress, and the number of "deputy-defectors" will rise to 250.

To understand the reasons for this shift of an ever-growing number of deputies from supporters to opponents of the President, we examine the distribution of "deputy-defectors" by large occupation groups, both at present and at the time of election (see Tables 8.2.1 and 8.2.2). These tables indicate that the bulk of "deputy-defectors" work in the Russian Supreme Soviet and are directly interested in shifting responsibilities for policy implementation from the hands of the executive branch. The next largest groups of "deputy-defectors" are enterprise directors and deputies who occupy posts in the lower echelons of management. For enterprise directors, the primary motive for moving into opposition to the President is dissatisfaction with the course of reform (especially as it affects their role as leaders of labor collectives); for deputies from lower-level positions, an important, and perhaps the main, motive lies in their personal dissatisfaction with their social status, which is heightened by the prospect of an early loss of their deputy's mandate.

In this regard, Table 8.2.1 illustrates that the largest percentage of "deputy-defectors" come from those who at the time of their election were in lower social and professional groups.

At the same time, the deputies drawn from the higher echelons of power in the old regime did not change their sharply negative attitude toward reforms (R3=-73, R8=-73, share of defectors=3 percent), and those from the middle echelons only shifted from weak to moderate opposition (R3=-14, R8=-50, share of defectors=12%). It follows from this that these last two groups of deputies may not be regarded as a fundamental source of political destabilization (though of course they do contain deputies who are among the most irreconcilable opponents of the President and his policies).

The distribution of deputy-defectors by factions is especially noteworthy. From Table 8.2.2 it is evident that the largest share of "deputy-defectors" is concentrated in the intermediate, or so-called

TABLE 8.2.1   Defection by Deputy Background

Deputy Backgrounds:	Rating at Third Congress	Rating at Eighth Congress	Percentage of Defectors
Lower management	+51	−17	31%
Workers and peasants	+40	−37	35%
"Mental labor"	+70	+12	27%

TABLE 8.2.2 Distribution of "Deputy-Defectors" by Faction at the Sixth, Seventh and Eighth Congresses

		Number of "Deputy-Defectors"		
Factions	*No. of People's Deputies*	*Sixth Congress*	*Seventh Congress*	*Eighth Congress*
Factions firmly supporting reform				
Radical Democrats	50	—	—	—
Democratic Russia	48	—	—	1
Consensus for Progress	53	—	—	3
Total	151	—	—	4
Factions weakly supporting reform				
Left Center-Cooperation	61	—	4	11
Free Russia	54	3	12	26
Motherland	55	3	12	27
Workers' Union	52	4	9	21
Change	53	8	14	20
Total	274	18	51	105
Factions opposing reform at all Congresses				
Sovereignty & Equality	49	2	5	7
Industrial Union	51	4	5	8
Total	100	6	10	15
Factions sharply opposing reform at all Congresses				
Russia	54	4	4	4
Fatherland	51	2	2	2
Agrarian Union	129	1	2	4
Communists of Russia	67	—	—	-
Total	301	7	8	10
Outside of Factions	207	15	27	48
Congress as a whole	1033	46	96	182

"centrist," factions: Motherland, twenty-seven deputies; Free Russia, twenty-six deputies; Worker's Union, twenty-one deputies; Change, twenty deputies; and Left Center/Cooperation, eleven deputies.

There are significantly fewer "deputy-defectors" in the Industrial Union (eight deputies) and Sovereignty and Equality (seven deputies), factions which have been in moderate opposition to reform at all the Congresses. In the remaining seven factions, which represent the core of the Parliamentary Reform Coalition and the Russian Unity bloc, defectors are almost completely absent. It is tempting to speculate that these intermediate factions, as well as deputies outside of organized factions (see Table 8.2.3), will provide the additional fifty-seventy defectors expected at the Ninth Congress of People's Deputies.

In conclusion we offer, with a short commentary, a list of regions with the largest number of defectors:

1. City of Moscow—seventeen deputies (28 percent of delegation);
2. Sverdlovsk region (Urals)—ten deputies (33 percent of delegation);
3. Rostov region—ten deputies (36 percent of delegation);
4. Tatarstan—ten deputies (42 percent of delegation);
5. Chechen-Ingushetia—seven deputies (70 percent of delegation);
6. Nizhegorod region—7 deputies (26 percent of delegation);
7. Bashkortostan (Urals)- six deputies (22 percent of delegation);
8. Moscow region—six deputies (12 percent of delegation);
9. Voronezh region—five deputies (28 percent of delegation);
10. Cheliabinsk region (Urals)- four deputies (17 percent of delegation);
11. Orenburg region (Urals)- four deputies (33 percent of delegation);
12. Udmurtia (Urals)- four deputies (31 percent of delegation);
13. Krasnodar krai—four deputies (14 percent of delegation);
14. Volgograd region—four deputies (22 percent of delegation);
15. Irkutsk region—four deputies (22 percent of delegation);
16. Mordvinia—three deputies (30 percent of delegation);
17. Marii El—three deputies (43 percent of delegation);
18. Samara region—three deputies (14 percent of delegation);
19. Ulianov region—three deputies (33 percent of delegation).

Especially striking is the large number of "deputy-defectors" in delegations from the Urals (twenty-eight deputies), Volga (thirty-three), Northern Caucasus (twenty-one deputies), and Central regions (twenty-three deputies), and the almost complete absence of such defectors from the delegations of the Far East, Siberia and the Northwest, Central Black Earth, and Volga-Viatka regions. In our view, this pattern is explained by the special difficulties posed by reform in the industrial regions of the Urals and the Central and Volga regions, and in some areas, such as Tatarstan, the Northern Caucasus, and surrounding regions, by the onset of intractable interethnic problems. Obviously, these are the regions that demand the attention of the President and the Government.

Finally, during the last three years only *eight* deputies have moved from opposition to support for the President. These deputies, six of whom occupy positions in agencies of the executive branch, appear to be temporary and unreliable allies.

Appendix 8.3
The Political Positions and Membership
of Deputy Factions at the Eighth and Ninth Congresses

A Short Characterization of the Eighth and Ninth Congresses

The extraordinary Eighth and Ninth Congresses of People's Deputies of the Russian Federation took place, respectively, 10-13 and 26-29 March, 1993, and represented the logical continuation of the Seventh Congress held the previous December.

The Eighth Congress was convened with a single goal—to nullify the constitutional agreement with the President reached at the Seventh Congress, which had envisioned the holding of an All-Russian referendum on April 11 on the basic principles of a new constitutional order for the Russian Federation. Having succeeded in cancelling the agreement, the deputies, not without reason, feared that the vote on the alternative formulations of basic constitutional principles proposed by the President and the Supreme Soviet might turn into a something of a vote of confidence in the President and the corps of deputies; it might therefore assume, in fact, precisely that form which the President had insisted on in his appeal to the nation from the tribune of the Seventh Congress on December 10. At the same time, the course taken by the deputies for cancelling the agreement necessarily meant a further deepening of the conflict between executive and legislative branches of power and the pursuit of it to that extreme point beyond which followed either the early removal of the President from office (or even the very elimination of the institution of presidential power itself, as in fact occurred in Mordovia), or the early dissolution of the deputy corps.

The course of events at the Eighth Congress did not leave the President the slightest hope for a mutually acceptable resolution of the conflict. Over the four days of work of the Eighth Congress (from the 10th to the 13th of March), the deputies rejected all compromise initiatives of the President, nullified the agreement reached at the Seventh Congress, put into effect the Constitutional amendments adopted at the Seventh Congress that reduced presidential power, and ended the Congress by reallocating the funds appropriated by the Supreme Soviet for the referendum to the construction of housing for military servicemen. After that the deputies intent on forcing the resignation of the President needed only wait for the inevitable reaction of the President and to use it as a pretext to carry out a rapid final attack.

The pretext was not long in coming. It was the televised appeal of the President of March 20, in which, along with other measures to resolve the acute political and constitutional crisis, the President promised to publish an ukase on introducing a special regime of government for a period up until a nationwide referendum or poll of the citizens could be held on the question of confidence in the President and the Congress of People's Deputies. The Constitutional Court, meeting the same night in an emergency session, evaluated this portion of the President's appeal as a substantial violation of the Russian Constitution, which, in accordance with the constitutional amendment adopted at the Seventh Congress, could serve as a sufficient juridical basis for posing the question of the President's impeachment.

The extraordinary Ninth Congress, convened on March 26 (just five days after the President's televised speech), concentrated its attention on discussion of three draft resolutions: on the Appeal of the President, on the referendum, and on the media of mass information. However, the central event of the Ninth Congress became, undoubtedly, the secret vote on March 28 on removing the President from office, which logically culminated the entire preceding political period beginning with the Sixth Congress.

The means of introducing the question of impeachment onto the agenda of the Congress, cleverly coupled with the vote on removing R. I. Khasbulatov from the post of Chairman of the Supreme Soviet, was undoubtedly the tactical masterpiece of the opposition. However, in the strategic perspective, the impeachment vote (which failed only by 72 votes) turned out to be the beginning of the opposition's full political defeat. Again, as had happened two years before, at the Third Congress, the President's "Kutuzov" tactics prevailed: that is, he retreated up until what seemed the final possible limit, and then suddenly emerged victorious.

It is curious that the opposition sensed its defeat even before the vote on impeachment, when it saw on the electronic board the results of a series of "secret" electronic votes on the procedure of the vote of impeachment. The very fact that in not one of these procedural votes was the opposition able to collect the required two-thirds of the votes of the deputies of the Congress, forced it to reject its initial scenario, and, contrary to the decision it had just taken, to begin to press all its supporters to vote for Khasbulatov.

The Distribution of Forces in the Deputy Corps: The Eighth and Ninth Congresses

Analysis of the roll-call votes leads to the conclusion that at the Eighth Congress the flight of a substantial part of the deputies from the democratic to the opposition camp, which had begun at the Fifth and Sixth Congresses, continued and even, as subsequent events showed, reached a culminating point.

If we characterize the position of each deputy on the dimension of "support/ non-support of reform" as his political rating, calculated on the basis of a series of crucial roll-call votes and expressed as a score between +100 (for full support of reform) to -100 (for full non-support of reform), then between the Third and Eighth Congresses, some 182 deputies went over from the democratic camp (ratings higher than +33) into the opposition camp (ratings lower than -33). Of these: forty-six shifted to opposition to the President and the reform course as early as at the Sixth Congress (April 1992); fifty shifted at the Seventh Congress (December 1992); and eighty-six at the Eighth Congress (March 1933).

Correspondingly, the share of deputies who firmly supported the President and his course fell from the Third to the Eighth Congress in the following way: At the Third Congress, 45 percent of the deputy corps firmly supported the President and the course of reforms; at the Sixth Congress, 40 percent did so; at the Seventh Congress, 26 percent did so; while at the Eighth Congress, only 23 percent did so. (See Table 8.3.1.)

As a result, at the Eighth Congress the President had only 242 sure supporters among the deputy corps (those with ratings above +33),

TABLE 8.3.1 The Distribution of Political Forces in the Corps of People's Deputies of the Russian Federation at the 8th Congress

Political Group	FR	MR	SR	SO	MO	PO
Number of deputies	193	49	41	74	108	568
Percentage of all deputies	18	5	4	7	1 0	56
Absolute number		242		115		676
As a percentage of all deputies		23%		11%		66%
Absolute number			283		750	
As a percentage of all deputies			27%		73%	

FR = Firm Reformers (rating from +67 to +100)
MR = Moderate Reformers (ratings from +34 to +67)
SR = Soft Reformers (ratings from +1 to +33)
SO = Soft Oppositionists (ratings from -33 to 0)
MO = Moderate Oppositionists (ratings from -67 to -33)
FO = Firm Oppositionists (ratings from -100 to -67)

while the number of firm oppositionists (ratings lower than -33) rose to 676 people and, thus, the opposition had only to win over to its side thirteen more deputies in order to be able to introduce any amendments it needed into the Constitution and to impeach the president.

It is possible that it was this very favorable balance of forces for the opposition that prompted it not to seek any compromises with the President at the Eighth Congress but rather to seek a decisive fight with him at the Ninth Congress.

The attentive reader might wonder how it was that the opposition camp could expand by 122 deputies between the Seventh and Eighth Congresses while the number of the reformist wing of the Congress fell over the same period only by twenty-seven deputies.

The answer to the question consists in the fact that the basic expansion of the opposition wing of the deputy corps at the Eighth Congress occurred not through a decrease in the size of the reformist wing, but through a sharp (by ninety-five people!) reduction in the size of the deputy "swamp."

In this connection it is curious to note that at the Ninth Congress (immediately after the unsuccessful attempt by the opposition to impeach the President), the opposition camp trembled and forty deputies changed their positions; some (thirteen deputies) went back over to the firmly reformist wing, while some twenty-seven switched to the unstable "swamp." At the same time within the reformist wing itself only nine deputies continued their drift toward the opposition camp at the Ninth Congress. Four of these entered the group of the firm opposition while five got stuck in the swamp. Finally, twenty deputies returned from the swamp to the reformist wing at the Ninth Congress, and only three went over from the swamp to the opposition. As a result, at the Ninth Congress, the number of the reformist wing of the deputy corps rose by twenty-nine while the size of the opposition camp fell by thirty-three deputies.

In this way, according to our calculations, at the Ninth Congress for the first time after the Third Congress, the evolution of the deputy corps in the direction of the opposition to reforms not only halted, but even was somewhat reversed with the weakening of the opposition.

In conclusion to this point we would make a small but important comment on the results of the vote on impeachment. In this vote, as previously noted, the opposition fell seventy-two votes short of adopting the decision.

Meantime, according to our estimates, the opposition could have gotten fifty-nine more votes. The solution to this contradiction lies in the fact that in the vote on impeachment some 109 deputies failed to take part (evidently they were absent), half of whom, as our figures show, would have voted to impeach. Thus only the insufficient turnout for the vote prevented the opposition from achieving still another impressive result of voting on the question of removing B. Yeltsin from the office of President.

The Positions of the Deputy Factions at the Eighth and Ninth Congresses

In Table 8.3.2 we indicate the "temperatures" (the mean political ratings) of the deputy factions at the Eighth and Ninth Congresses, and in Table 8.3.3 are indicated the political composition of the factions at the Eighth Congress. We will enumerate below the political positions at the Ninth Congress, and note the rather small number of factions in which the corresponding shifts occurred.

Comparing the data in Tables 8.3.2-8.3.4 with the data for the Seventh Congress (see Appendix 8.2), it is apparent that at the Eighth Congress some seven intermediate factions (calling themselves "centrist") sharply increased the level of their opposition to reforms, while among the three factions of the "Parliamentary Coalition of Reforms" and the four factions of the bloc "Russian Unity" the political positions and membership scarcely changed.

In part, at the Eighth Congress, almost 100 percent support for the President and the reforms was demonstrated, as at previous Congresses, by the factions "Radical Democrats" (100 percent), "Democratic Russia" (98 percent), and "Agreement for the Sake of Progress" (92 percent).

In the factions "Left Center—Cooperation" the President was supported at the Eighth Congress by thirty-one deputies out of sixty-one, or 51 percent of the composition of the faction, and in the faction "Free Russia," by twenty-one deputies of fifty-four, or about 40 percent of the membership. In the remaining nine factions fewer than 10 percent of the deputies supported the President, and in the factions of the bloc "Russian Unity," only seven deputies out of 301, or hardly more than 2 percent.

We would note, finally, that among the deputies outside factions, the President was supported by only thirty-nine deputies of 207, or about 20%; this was fewer by a considerable amount than among deputies in factions, of whom 244 of 826, or about 30 percent, supported him.

At the Ninth Congress, in four factions of the bloc "Russian Unity" the President had the same seven backers that he had at the Eighth

TABLE 8.3.2 Level of Support by Deputy Fractions for Independent Presidential Power and for the Course of Radical Political and Economic Reforms at the 3rd, 6th, 8th and 9th Congresses (Full support = +100; Full Opposition = -100)

| | Number of Deputies | Level of Support (+) or Opposition (-) to Reform | | | | |
| | | | Congress | | | |
		3rd	6th	7th	8th	9th
Fractions strongly supporting President and reform:						
Radical Democrats	50	+94	+89	+89	+91	+90
Democratic Russia	48	+96	+83	+84	+86	+84
Agreement for the Sake of Progress	53	+85	+78	+76	+71	+78
Fractions weakly supporting the President and reform:						
Left Center/ Cooperation	61	+67	+45	+22	+10	+17
Fractions moving from support for reforms to opposition:						
Free Russia	54	+70	+32	+6	−21	−12
Motherland	55	+56	+17	−11	−45	−30
Workers' Union	52	+39	0	−21	−51	−34
Smena (New Politics)	52	+28	−30	−45	−60	−42
Fractions opposing the President and reform:						
Sovereignty and Equality	49	−36	−29	−40	−64	−62
Industrial Union	51	−26	−42	−48	−65	−64
Fractions strongly opposing reform:						
Russia	54	−53	−77	−78	−84	−86
Fatherland	51	−78	−61	−69	−85	−85
Agrarian Union	129	−69	−72	−73	−89	−87
Communists of Russia	67	−91	−89	−88	−95	−93
Total deputies in fractions	826	+5	−11	−21	−35	−30
Deputies outside fractions	207	+2	−10	−21	−43	−36
Congress as a whole	1033	+4	−11	−21	−37	−32
Sup. Soviet as whole	247	+12	−10	−23	−44	−36

Congress, while in the three factions of the "Parliamentary Coalition for Reform" he had eight opponents, that is, one more.

In the factions "Free Russia," "Sovereignty and Equality," and "Industrial Union," the relationship of the number of supporters and opponents of the President did not change. And in the remaining four intermediate factions the number of supporters of the President rose: In

TABLE 8.3.3 Distribution of the Number of Deputies in Deputy Fractions by Level of Support for Independent Presidential Power and the Course of Radical Reforms at Extraordinary 8th Congress (10-13 March 1993): All deputies

	Average Rating at Congress	*Number of Deputies by Level of Support*				
		1	*2*	*3*	*4*	*Total*
	Fractions supporting President and reform:					
Radical Democrats	+91	49	1	—	—	50
Democratic Russia	+86	47	—	—	1	48
Agreement for the Sake of Progress	+71	44	5	1	3	53
Left Center/ Cooperation	+10	26	5	13	17	61
Total		166	11	14	21	212
	Fractions opposing the President and reforms:					
Free Russia	−21	18	3	3	30	54
Motherland	−45	10	3	3	39	55
Workers' Union	−51	5	4	7	36	52
Smena (New Politics)	−60	4	3	4	41	52
Sovereignty and Equality	−64	3	2	5	39	49
Industrial Union	−65	3	2	3	43	51
Total		43	17	25	228	313
	Fractions strongly opposing President and reform:					
Russia	−84	—	1	1	52	54
Fatherland	−85	2	—	—	49	51
Agrarian Union	−89	2	2	2	123	219
Communists of Russia	−95	—	—	—	67	67
Total		4	3	3	291	301
Deputies outside fractions	−43	29	10	32	136	207
Congress as a whole	−37	242	41	74	676	1033

1 = strong support
2 = inconsistent support
3 = inconsistent opposition
4 = strong opposition

the faction "Left Center—Cooperation," by nine deputies (from thirty-one to forty); in the faction "Motherland" by seven deputies (from thirteen to twenty); in the faction "Workers' Union," by five deputies, from nine to fourteen; in the faction "Smena," by three deputies (from seven to ten); and among deputies standing outside factions, the number of the President's supporters rose by six deputies, from thirty-nine to forty-five.

In this way, at the Ninth Congress the deputies of the intermediate factions and the deputies outside factions once again showed their ability to track the political trends of the moment closely.

TABLE 8.3.4 Distribution of the Number of Deputies in Deputy Fractions by Level of Support for Independent Presidential Power and the Course of Radical Reforms at the Extraordinary 8th Congress (10-13 March 1993): Members of the Supreme Soviet

	Avg. Rating in Sup. Soviet	Number of Deputies by Level of Support				
		1	2	3	4	Total
	Fractions supporting President and reform:					
Radical Democrats	+84	9	1	—	—	10
Democratic Russia	+85	10	—	—	—	10
Agreement for the Sake of Progress	+89	12	—	—	—	12
Left Center / Cooperation	+14	8	—	4	5	17
Total		39	1	4	5	49
	Fractions opposing the President and reforms:					
Free Russia	−52	4	—	1	13	18
Motherland	−49	3	1	1	12	17
Workers' Union	−70	—	1	4	14	19
Smena (New Politics)	−62	2	—	2	22	26
Sovereignty and Equality	−77	—	1	2	22	25
Industrial Union	−77	—	—	1	4	5
Total		9	3	11	83	110
	Fractions strongly opposing President and reform:					
Russia	−82	—	—	—	15	15
Fatherland	−91	—	—	—	10	10
Agrarian Union	−95	—	—	—	13	13
Communists of Russia	−98	—	—	—	17	17
Total		—	—	—	55	55
Deputies outside fractions	−58	1	3	3	26	33
Supreme Soviet as a whole	−44	49	7	18	173	247

1 = strong support
2 = inconsistent support
3 = inconsistent opposition
4 = strong opposition

The "Deputy-Defectors"

In our earlier writings we have employed the term so-called "deputy-defectors" to refer to those deputies who originally (at the 1st to 4th Congresses) had a rating of over +10 (i.e. supported the reform course), but at later Congresses lowered their rating by more than fifty points and thus changed the sign of their rating and went over from support for reform to opposition.

At the Seventh Congress there were 188 such deputies, and at the Eighth their number rose by 61 and reached 249. Moreover, in three democratic factions, Radical Democrats, Democratic Russia, and Agreement for the Sake of Progress, the number of defectors rose by only one person and reached five deputies. (At the Ninth Congress they once again fell to four.) In four factions of the bloc Russian Unity the number of defectors did not change at all and at the last 3 Congresses it remained at thirteen. All the remaining defectors (231 deputies) were distributed among the intermediate factions and among the deputies outside factions, as follows: Left Center-Cooperation, twenty-four at the Eighth Congress and fifteen at the Ninth Congress; Free Russia, thirty and twenty-seven; Motherland, thirty-two and twenty-six; Workers' Union, thirty-one and twenty-four; Smena, twenty-seven and twenty-four; Sovereignty and Equality, twelve and twelve; Industrial Union, twelve and eleven; deputies outside factions, sixty-three and fifty-four. As for "reverse defectors," those shifting from the opposition to the democratic camp, at the Seventh Congress in the whole deputy corps there were twenty-nine, at the Eighth Congress twenty, and at the Ninth Congress twelve.

The distribution of the defecting deputies (those moving from the democratic to opposition camps) by occupation is very telling:

Supreme Soviet	140
Soviets of other levels	6
Executive branch	21
State enterprise directors	43
Lower level administration	32
Workers and peasants	8

Thus at the Eighth, as at the Seventh, Congress the chief role in the deputy corps was played by deputy-defectors; moreover, a majority of them (over 60 percent) were deputies who worked on a permanent basis in the Supreme Soviet and were members of the intermediate factions.

Some Conclusions

First, the unsuccessful effort of March 28 by the parliamentarians to impeach the President, together with the results of the referendum of April 25 which confirmed confidence in the President by a majority of those voting, brought to a close a year of constantly rising resistance from among the deputy corps and other power structures inherited from the past, both to the institution of the presidency itself, as well as to the course of democratic political and economic transformations associated with the person of the first President of Russia.

After March 28 and April 25, one could say with certainty that the institution of the presidency created two years ago had survived and would play henceforth a decisive role in all political processes.

Second, the votes at the Ninth Congress permit us to predict confidently that at the next Congress, the number of supporters of the president's line in the deputy corps will rise substantially. In particular, representatives of the intermediate factions will predominate among the President's newly acquired supporters. Nonetheless, even a shift to the President's side of *all* deputies of the centrist factions would by no means guarantee the adoption by the Congress of a new Constitution. Moreover, the Congress, in all likelihood, will not adopt any of the current alternative draft constitutions and their combinations, because all these drafts and combinations almost inevitably will be blocked either by the opposition or the reformist wings of the Congress, or by both together.

Third, the events of the last two Congresses and the referendum showed that for now there is no true political "center" either in society or in the corps of people's deputies. More precisely, the emergence of such a center is hampered by the absence in society and at the Congress of an authoritative and strong right-liberal wing. The absence of this flank has forced the unstable, essentially centrist, reform line of the President and Government (including the former Gaidar government) to seem radical. As a result, either oppositionists begin to masquerade as centrists, or reformist forces claim the center; or, most often, the role of center is simply played by those groupings, factions, and individual deputies who readily change their political positions in accordance with the political weather. Unfortunately, even new elections are unlikely to change this situation.

9

Conclusion: Partisan Competition and Democratic Stability

Thomas F. Remington

The chapters in this book have discussed several of the first generation of elected parliaments of Eastern Europe and the Soviet Union and its successor states following the demise of communist party rule. We have seen how short-lived some of them have been: neither the Czechoslovak nor the USSR federal legislatures could stop the dissolution of their countries as unified political entities, and we called attention to the gathering force of the confrontation between the communist majority in the Russian parliament and a president intent upon pursuing the policy that he believed the population had elected him to follow. The attitudes and backgrounds of these first-wave deputies reveal them to be a transient and diverse cohort, drawn partly from the established communist elite and partly from the intelligentsia and the professions—neither group possessing the skills and outlooks that would suit them as professional politicians.

In the first chapter we regarded these parliaments as bridges between communist rule and the successor regimes, both democratic and authoritarian. We asked what it was that contributed to the stabilization of democratic parliamentary institutions and we compared the countries of the region with respect to the consolidation of structural arrangements. In this final chapter we will seek patterns in the support that populations in the region have given to various families of political forces in the elections that have been held since the founding elections of 1989 and 1990.

One of the most striking of the political trends in those countries of Eastern Europe and the former USSR which have held multiple parliamentary elections since 1989-90 is the volatility of the electorate. Not only have electoral and constitutional arrangements changed significantly, so also have national voting patterns. The single most marked trend has been the collapse of the national fronts and umbrella parties which led the first wave of democratization as they splintered into various competing successor parties. In addition, in some countries a conservative reaction to the initial period of nationalist and democratic hopes has set in, benefitting former communists and neo-centrists. In others, anti-communist democrats have strengthened their positions. Often it is difficult to tell whether it is the change in the identities and capacities of the parties or change in the voters' preferences that is more important in producing the large shifts in voting outcomes in the countries which have held more than one national parliamentary election over the period from 1989-90 to 1992-93.

In Lithuania, Sajudis's share of the popular vote fell to 21% in the 1992 elections after having swept the 1990 races, when it won 99 out of 136 district contests. The major winners were the renamed communists, led by the former communist leader of Lithuania, who won 43% of the party-list votes. The Estonian and Latvian popular fronts had done nearly as well in 1990 as Sajudis, each winning around 2/3 of the districts. In 1992, however, the Estonian popular front fell to 15% (while the coalition of communist successor parties took 17), and in Latvia's June 1993 elections, Latvia's Way, a loose collection of notables, won the largest share of the popular vote, with nearly one third, while the popular front won only 2.6% and thus failed to clear the 4% threshold for parliamentary representation.

In Poland, Solidarity's sweep of 1989, when candidates running under its banner took all but one of the contested parliamentary seats, was not repeated in 1991. Solidarity divided into rival factions and none of its successors took more than 12% of the popular vote. By the time of the 1993 elections, a marked backlash was apparent. Both the Democratic Left Alliance and the Polish Peasant Party, which were the successors to the former ruling communist party and its fellow-traveling peasant party allies, nearly doubled their shares of the popular vote: the former from 11.9 to 20.4% and the latter from 8.7 to 15.4%. Moreover, they nearly tripled their share of seats in parliament, together gaining a substantial outright majority of seats.

In Romania, the National Salvation Front and its principal offshoot, the Democratic National Salvation Front, together took only 38% of the popular vote in the 1992 parliamentary elections, whereas the NSF had won two thirds (albeit under less than fully free conditions) in the 1990 races. Here the beneficiaries of the changed alignments were three small parties which merged to form a new union, called Democratic Convention of Romania, which took 20% of the vote. In Czechoslovakia, the two major intelligentsia-led opposition movements, Civic Forum in the Czech lands, and Public against Violence, in Slovakia, joined forces and created an electoral alliance which took half of the popular vote and 56% of the seats in the Federal Assembly in the 1990 elections. By 1992, however, two changes had occurred, as David Olson points out in his chapter: the broad popular movements, Civic Forum and Public against Violence, had broken apart into successor parties; and in each republic, political life came to center on the interests of the republic at the expense of the federation. As Olson shows, this was in part a consequence of the constitutional rules that rewarded parties for appealing for votes in the separate republics rather than for seeking support in both. In the June 1992 elections, therefore, the principal successor parties of the original democratic movements each took only one third of the vote in each of the republics for each of the two chambers of the Federal Assembly.

In East Germany, by contrast, the share of the vote won by the major contenders remained much the same between the first and second elections: but in this case, the time lag was only March to December (1990) and the rapid pace of unification overshadowed other issues. The ruling West German CDU, moreover, opted to give the East German population significant initial advantages in the unification process, such as granting GDR's citizens the chance to exchange their currency for the Federal Republic's mark at extremely favorable rates.[1]

The Hungarian case is interesting to compare to the others where popular fronts dominated the initial round of elections. The impending races of spring 1994 will shed light on the question of whether changes in the party system or changes in voter outlooks are the more powerful factor in producing different outcomes. Hungary entered the transition with a more highly articulated system of opposition parties than did most other countries in the region. The Hungarian Democratic Forum did not cast the long shadow over politics that Civic Forum, Sajudis, or Solidarity did in their countries. For one thing, the communists had a well established reformist wing that proposed a smooth, stable crossing to the market. For another, many of the strongly market-liberal, anti-communist political activists had gone into two other prominent

---

1. The unexpectedly severe economic hardships that both sides in this rapid unification have experienced since 1990 have led to a good deal of latter-day recrimination against the Kohl government for making false promises to the citizens on both sides of the border about how relatively easy unification would be. But it should not be forgotten that the alternative to a generous, and inflationary, economic and political union was the chance of heavy and destabilizing emigration from east to west.

opposition parties, the Free Democrats, and the Alliance of Young Democrats. Moreover, the structure of the electoral law (which mixed PR and single-district majoritarianism, but lacked West Germany's PR-oriented rule that the party list vote ultimately determines the shares of seats that each party will receive) rewarded moderately strong parties while reducing the opportunities that small parties had of entering parliament. The 1990 elections therefore produced an outcome that allowed a governing coalition to form under HDF leadership while giving the opposition ample opportunities to hold positions of influence in parliament. As Gerhard Loewenberg's chapter shows, committee chairmanships and deputy chairmanships were distributed both to governing and opposition parties in rough equivalence to their strength in parliament. On the other hand, the elections dealt all the leftist and socialist parties a significant defeat: the reform-minded communists, renamed Socialists, had won only 11% of the votes in the first round, and the Social Democrats and hard-line communists only about 3.5% each. The spring 1994 elections will let us judge the strength of the backlash effect if party identities remain roughly the same, and voters react to the hardships of economic transition by giving the socialists or other opposition parties an electoral rebound.

The most stunning example of anti-democratic backlash was the December 12, 1993, parliamentary election in Russia, held under a new electoral law that President Yeltsin put into effect by decree. The law reserved half the seats in the lower house of the new parliament for deputies elected from party lists in a single Russia-wide electoral district (subject to a 5% threshold). The other half of the seats of the new State Duma were to be filled by plurality vote in single-member districts. The large number of seats set aside for proportional representation turned out to benefit the extremist Liberal Democratic Party of Vladimir Zhirinovsky, which received 23% of the party list vote, while the party associated with Yeltsin and the reform policies of the government, Russia's Choice, received only 15.4% of the party list vote. Even though the contests in single-member districts, few of which were won by LDP candidates, offset these results to some degree, Zhirinovsky's success shocked observers in Russia and abroad. His deliberately belligerent, demagogic rhetoric, focusing on Russian grievances against neighboring countries and offering quick, simple solutions to the problems of crime, corruption, and economic decline, won far wider support than anyone anticipated, while Zhirinovsky's skillful use of television impressed on voters a clear, personal image which the PR mechanism converted into a sizable bloc of votes in the new parliament.

Zhirinovsky had run for president in 1991 and received around 6 million votes, or around 7.8% of the votes cast. His 1993 showing doubled his vote in absolute terms even though overall turnout fell from 75% to 53%. The surge for Zhirinovsky reflects a notable characteristic of electoral volatility in Russia: instead of turning primarily to parties with roots in the former communist regime, as voters did in Lithuania and Poland, Russian voters dissatisfied with the regime's performance turned even more strongly to a "third force" that appeared to offer an alternative both to the old regime and to the somewhat discredited democrats. Moreover, the geographic distribution of the Zhirinovsky vote was instructive: his party was most successful in southern Russian regions that have seen the largest inflow of refugees from neighboring republics, where crime and social tensions are relatively high, and which are closer to the sites of wars in the Transcaucasian and Central Asian regions. The rapid and profound social changes occurring since the first wave of democratic elections, in 1990, therefore strongly altered the pattern of electoral behavior in Russia.

Are there commonalities in the development of the new party systems of the region? Herbert Kitschelt has proposed a scheme which places political parties of the post-communist systems in a simple two-dimensional policy space (1992). His framework is able to account for much of the variation across countries in party systems, and may be useful in predicting shifts in the identities and political positions of parties in the future. It posits two axes of political cleavages: an economic or market/anti-market dimension, and a political, or liberal/authoritarian dimension, termed "libertarian-cosmopolitan." (It actually subsumes two more abstract issues, which, broadly speaking, correspond to freedom versus order and individual versus group rights.) He proposes an interesting explanation for the contrast between the political alignments found in Western, market-oriented societies and those found in East Central Europe. Where the predominant social structure is capitalist, the political liberals, or left, react against it by calling for social-democratic solutions; in turn, he claims, the economic liberals are politically authoritarian. Where the former status quo was communist, the political liberals, or left, advocate moving to a free-market economy. As a result, he believes that the economic left, the socialists and social-democrats, have nowhere to go for votes but to embrace populist and nationalist positions that are implicitly authoritarian, and to construct clientelistic political machines that provide selective benefits to segments of the population that are threatened by market-oriented change. As parties search for electoral bases, they will position themselves along this principal axis near the points where the largest number of voters are to be found. Therefore the less modern societies, which are characterized by larger peasant populations and lower aggregate educational attainment levels, are likely to give majorities to parties offering to protect market losers through authoritarian and collectivist solutions. Often, as Kitschelt observes, such parties are successors of the former communist rulers; they have considerable skill in running clientelistic political machines and frequently seek out the vulnerable, impoverished, collectivized peasantry as their natural ally.

A more recent and comprehensive framework offers a somewhat more complex classification (Evans and Whitefield 1993). Observing that in certain countries of the region, politics may lack *any* class, ethnic or ideological bases around which parties may mobilize support, Evans and Whitefield point out that voters may exhibit high levels of volatility as they rally behind one or another valence issue or charismatic leader. In such cases, the weakness of intermediate social associations and the difficulty of economic transition promote a politics of mass protest, based on ressentiment and personality. Other types of party systems, in turn, may resemble the class-based systems of Western Europe, and still others may revolve around ethnic divisions that make the definition of the national community problematic.

The former communist world offers a series of test cases for assessing the debate in the literature on Western political parties over whether previously "frozen" socio-political cleavages are now being transformed by the rise of a "new politics" or whether, following a functional theory of parties, parties themselves are facing an irreversible decline in importance of contemporary democratic politics because they have lost much of their capacity to link the electorate to policy makers (Dalton, Flanagan and Beck 1984:454). A variety of possibilities are conceivable. First is that the new post-communist party systems will come to approximate those of Western democracies, recapitulating the mobilization along socio-economic, religious and other divisions which have traditionally provided the foci for party development. Another is that new cleavages, such as the militant ethnic exclusivism of the Western new right parties, will dominate politics in the region as class and regional identities prove too weak to nourish party organizations. Still another, following the logic of the functionalist theory of parties, is that the emergence to democratic government in the post-communist world will "jump over" the era of political party linkages between elites and electorates, and that the elaborate educational and mass media systems built up under communist rule will keep political party organizations relatively weak and encourage issue-based and other forms of articulation quickly to compete with them for followings and influence.

Kitschelt hypothesizes that socio-economic and political-ideological cleavages will be the dominant forces shaping the party systems of Eastern Europe, but that the communist experience will leave a significant imprint that will distinguish the post-communist party systems from those of Western Europe. He also emphasizes that the present period is one in which citizens and elites are still figuring out their own interests and how best to pursue them (1992: 9). Since structures are fluid, political activists are uncertain how to use any given set of arrangements to their advantage, and are unsure what set of structures may serve them best. But with time, as the initial populist fervor of the early plebiscitary elections recedes, a spectrum of parties is likely to take shape that more or less reflects the distribution of voter preferences and the relative strength of major social segments. In turn, the stabilization of a competitive party system is likely to contribute to the consolidation of the rules of electoral competition and representative government (Coppedge 1993).

Assuming, then, that time tends to move the relationship between the party system and the structure of political cleavages and alignments of the population closer toward equilibrium, we should expect that the shape of the party system at any given point will be a joint function of the structure of opinion among the electorate and the current set of constitutional arrangements: the same underlying distribution of interests among the voters might support a multi-party system if district magnitude is large and thresholds to representation are low, and a two- or three-party system if not. By the same token, if countries in the region prosper economically, enjoy peace at home and abroad, and expand the modern sector of society, then the size of the economically and politically liberal part of the electorate should grow at the expense of the authoritarian/statist parties' base of support. The equilibrium assumption implies that political elites will look for support by mobilizing voters around causes that appeal to large parts of the population and not persevere in quixotic crusades for hopeless causes. If we have a sound understanding of the structure of social cleavages, including the advantages and disadvantages various segments of the population face in coping with the new post-communist environment, we should be in a good position to predict the rough outlines of the structure of the party system that will eventually emerge. So long as the populace is free of deep and polarizing cleavages, a competitive party system is surely a necessary condition for the stabilization of democratic politics through representative government.

But is it a sufficient condition? One might suggest an alternative sequence. A competitive party system may include "semi-responsible" or "irresponsible" parties, to use Giovanni Sartori's terminology (1976:131-145). They have little stake in the continuation of the present parliamentary system because they have little or no chance of gaining a place in government, and are inclined to seek support by opposing the system. Where do they seek votes? If they calculate that they cannot win a place in a governing coalition no matter what they do, they may choose not to broaden their electoral base by appealing to a *wider* spectrum of popular interests. Instead they may seek to "outbid" rival parties by appealing *more intensively* to a particular segment of the population (Sartori 1976:139-140; Horowitz 1985:333-364). Typically they turn up the rhetorical heat, denounce moderation and demand resolve, promise that once the political kingdom has been stormed and won, and the people's enemies (including the movement's own moderates, who are denounced as sell-outs) have been defeated, the cause of justice will triumph. Although their irresponsibility disqualifies them from consideration as governing partners, both politicians and voters may be attracted to them for strategic reasons (Levi and Hechter 1985). On the other side of the divide, opposing parties feel greater pressure to defend their own constituency's vital interests and to demonstrate their fidelity to it. The intensity of the conflict escalates. Competition between parties for the support of deeply opposed constituencies replaces competition between parties for support from among the larger electorate. Ideologically absolutizing, politically irresponsible competition of this kind in settings of polarized pluralism is destabilizing because parties promise anything knowing they will not be obliged to make good on their promises or held to account for them. Political stability is undermined while extremist parties gain strength (Horowitz 1985:348; Sartori 1976:140). The political center is weakened as the median positions of politicians on either flank move outward from it.

This type of system-disequilibrating party competition is particularly likely to occur in ethnically divided societies, as Donald Horowitz has shown. Here politicians, if not given an incentive to seek votes from members of other ethnic groups in society, concentrate their efforts on promising collective benefits for their own groups, whether material or symbolic. Some material values are simultaneously symbolic, such as exclusive language rights, territorial secession, independence, or reclamation of irredenta. Some of the objects of struggle, such as the right to use a national flag and other representations of group identity, are purely symbolic. But, whether material or symbolic, such values are "exclusive" collective goods, in

Mancur Olson's terms, because they cannot be enjoyed jointly by two competing groups (Olson 1971:38). Moreover, because of the peculiar emotional intensity of ethnic identification, it becomes extremely dangerous for elites to open themselves to charges by their rivals that they are not keeping faith with their people. This primordial dimension helps explain the difficulty that politicians have in mobilizing voters across alternative identities, such as class, when polarizing competition over ethnic politics is escalating.

The politics of outbidding may help to explain how the problems of ethnic-national identity, historically so important in the politics of Eastern Europe and the Soviet Union, have overwhelmed the capacity of the weak democratic institutions of the transition to contain them in a number of countries of the region. It is not necessary to invent fanciful theories of a peculiar communist psyche to explain the resurgence of ethnic nationalism in the post-communist states, any more than theories of the effects of infant swaddling could seriously be invoked to explain Russian communism.[2] Certainly the prevalence of ethnic nationalist politics in the transitions from communism distinguish the Soviet and East European region from the countries of Latin America and southern Europe, where writers on transitions to democracy invariably worry about how to keep the military out of politics. It is telling that not in a single one of the twenty-seven or so countries to have emerged from the breakup of the Soviet sphere has there been a military coup. But all three ethno-federal states in the region, the USSR, Czechoslovakia, and Yugoslavia, have dissolved. Civil war over ethnic-territorial conflicts rages in several of their successor states, including Bosnia-Herzegovina, Moldova, Azerbaijan, and Georgia. War and civil war threaten in several other countries over minority rights and irredenta.

The disintegration of the three ethno-federations has also led to the sudden disenfranchisement of whole populations, which suggests that more destabilizing political conflict is likely to occur in the future unless rampant nationalism is curbed. In the Latvian elections of 1993, a quarter of the voting-age population, mostly Russians, was not

---

2. A recent article on the recent explosion of ethnic nationalism in Romania and other post-communist states offers a variety of explanations of the phenomenon, including theories of a post-communist "self" and structural theories of the political economy of the transition (Verdery 1993). But the author does not attempt to measure or weigh these explanations against one another, or to compare Eastern Europe with post-colonial Asian and African countries in this respect, or even to analyze how recent nationalism in Eastern Europe might differ from the pre-communist varieties in the same territories.

allowed to vote, although they had voted in 1990 when Latvia was still part of the Soviet Union. In Estonia's 1992 elections, over one third of the population—again, nearly all Russians—was disenfranchised. Citizenship in both republics was automatically conferred on individuals who had been citizens before 1940 and their descendants, but for those who had settled there since the war citizenship was made difficult if not impossible. Very rapidly, over 1991-92, nationalist politics in these two states had turned from an anti-USSR movement to an anti-Russian movement (Lieven 1993:302-315). One reason for the failure of the popular fronts in the 1992-93 elections was that a sizable part of the previous electorate, much of which had supported the more universalistic popular fronts in their drive for independence, had been deprived of political rights. Lithuania, too, changed its citizenship requirements toward more restrictive ethnic criteria: initially it allowed all permanent residents to receive citizenship, but later restricted citizenship rights to those who had resided in the republic for ten years and satisfied a language requirement.

Competing claims to exclusive rights by ethnic groups breed extremism. Only under fortunate, and perhaps unusual, circumstances does time favor a more inclusive, territorially-based, and universalistic definition of citizenship over a more ethnically-based conception.[3] Indeed, the resurgence of nativism in Western Europe links the "new right" to a pre-industrial, primordial past as established parties are unable to respond effectively (Minkenberg 1992). As David Olson's chapter shows, through the process of outbidding for support within the two national republics, political entrepreneurs appealing to the ethnic cause rendered the further existence of Czechoslovakia impossible. Similarly, by increasing the salience of purely ethnic claims over other, cross-cutting issues, politicians may provoke counter-drives for territorial integrity and ethnic rights on the part of the dominant ethnic nationality of the country, and opposing demands for territorial secession by minority ethnic regions. This is the case, for instance, in the Georgia-Abkhaz conflict, where the Georgian authorities responded to the independence declaration of the Abkhaz parliament by revoking the constitutional status of Abkhazia as an autonomous republic. In the Azerbaijan-Karabakh conflict, Armenian demands for political rights in Nagorno-Karabakh escalated to demands by the parliament in Karabakh for secession from Azerbaijan

---

3. Juan Linz shows that in the Basque country and Catalonia, somewhat less exclusive, ethnic notions of national citizenship have gained currency (Linz 1985:203-253).

and incorporation into Armenia, which was followed by massacres of Armenians in Azerbaijan and open warfare between Armenians and Azerbaijani. In the Moldova-Transdnestr conflict, the predominantly Russian population of the eastern bank of the Dnestr River declared independence of Moldova in reaction to Moldovan independence.[4] Dominique Arel's chapter in this volume uses an ingenious method to identify a political cleavage among deputies to the Ukrainian parliament that may become more intense with time if the issues which trigger it—mandatory language use and regional autonomy, for instance—are sufficiently salient to inspire leaders to build followings around them.

The dynamics of democratization create incentives that reward nationalist extremism in other former members of the bloc as well, not only in the former communist ethno-federations. The region continues to cope with the burden of a long history of ethnic-national injustice and violence. Both World Wars I and II resulted in profound territorial and demographic changes that still powerfully influence post-communist politics, when many historical grievances and long-dormant issues offer themselves to enterprising political elites. Anti-semitism, as in the radical nationalism of Istvan Csurka in Hungary, crops up perennially in the region even in the absence of Jews.[5] Virtually every country in the region—including the new successor states of the former ethno-federations—has a significant ethnic minority population.[6] These include the Hungarian minorities in Romania, Slovakia, and the former Yugoslavia; the Turkish minority in Bulgaria; the Czechs in Slovakia and Slovaks in the Czech Republic; the 25 million Russians living outside the Russian Republic; the Uzbeks in Tadjikistan and Tadjiks in Uzbekistan; and many others. Most of these risk either forced assimilation or forced exclusion, and some face both. Problems over the demarcation of borders and irredentist claims have hardly begun to reveal their potential for

---

4. Helpful background sources on the ethnic-national conflicts in the former Soviet Union include Suny (1990), Nahaylo and Swoboda (1990), Denber (1992) and Bremmer and Taras (1993).

5. But note that the Csurka faction within the Hungarian Democratic Forum was defeated and Csurka split off to form his own party.

6. The two countries that are more or less ethnically homogeneous, as a result of the Holocaust, expulsions, and forcible border changes, are Poland and Hungary. Poland is 95% ethnically Polish and religiously Roman Catholic. Hungary is 90% Magyar; its principal ethnic minority, the Gypsies, constitute about 3% of the population. On the background of ethnic national conflict in Eastern Europe, see Brzezinski (1989/90), Deak (1990), Schöpflin (1990) and Banac (1990).

escalating, destabilizing political conflict. The Russian Supreme Soviet's declaration in July 1993 that Sevastopol', where the Black Sea Fleet of the former USSR has its home port, is Russian rather than Ukrainian, raised the intensity of the conflict over defining and defending Russia's national interests between Yeltsin and the communist-nationalist opposition coalition. Zhirinovsky played deftly on resentments over Russia's apparent decline as a state and feelings of national injury at the hands of outside powers. Issues that have low salience in public opinion at one point in time may become valence issues connected to major political battles when they are used to provoke a crisis (Dalton, Flanagan and Beck 1984:458). The volatility of public opinion, especially in the inchoate period of the early transition from communism, means that a situation of polarization can be generated by political elites through the outbidding process. The ensuing political crisis may then bring about the system's collapse. Ambitious political entrepreneurs often find themselves unable to restrain the movements they mobilize. As we know, in weak states, those who rise to prominence on waves of revolutionary and ultranationalist passion are often devoured by them as power passes to successively more radical rivals or gives way to warlordism once civil order breaks down entirely.

Other cleavages besides national ones are available to turn the political arena into a state of polarized pluralism, with similarly destabilizing outcomes. Gorbachev succeeded remarkably for six years in balancing his conservative and radical-democratic flanks until the center proved untenable and he was expendable. Partly this was due to the opportunity for ethnic-national mobilization that liberalization gave to republican elites, and partly it was due to the widening gap between the conservative old order and the surge of anti-communist, democratic populism. The dynamics of liberalization in the Gorbachev period created an opportunity structure in which republican elites built political followings by demanding greater autonomy and power for their republics which provoked a counter-action by the hard-line forces of the center, and ultimately rendered preservation of a federal or confederal union impossible. The phenomenon of "nomenklatura privatization" testifies to the high stakes raised by competition for ownership and control of the communist state's vast legacy of property—farms and forests, productive assets, housing, raw materials, car parks, office space, television, publishing houses and newspapers, police files and historical archives. So immense an inheritance can foster an intense struggle for power which may not successfully be contained by the rules of parliamentary opposition. The relatively short and peaceful nature of the initial phase of transition presages a more difficult and protracted period of economic reordering thereafter, as Laszlo Bruszt and David Stark suggest (Bruszt and Stark 1991:245).

Since it is a revolution in reverse, the transition to a market economy ought to provoke furious opposition on the part of the old administrative classes that are losing their privileged control over state property. Where it does not, we may suspect that the economic transition has not occurred, or that it has been quietly diverted into a process of "privatization without the market" where old elites acquire new property rights in a highly monopolized economy. Where we do see vehement opposition to reform, as in Russia, each of the two opposing camps have fought for power in that branch of government in which it is stronger in order to gain control over economic policy. As Alexander Sobyanin's contribution to this book shows, the communist-nationalist alliance captured the national legislature and defended the traditional power of the soviets to control the executive branch, while Yeltsin and his supporters staked their hopes on a powerful and independent presidency enjoying the support of the populace as expressed through referenda. Parliamentary deputies and their support base became, as many commentators observed, a parliamentary "party" opposed to the presidential "party": the branches of power became mechanisms of partisan competition between two, intensely opposed, political coalitions (Rodin 1993). As parliament moved under the near-total control of the communist-nationalist alliance, the political center point in the congress shifted farther and farther out to the communist end of the spectrum, as evidenced by the overwhelming majority favoring Yeltsin's impeachment at the Ninth Congress.[7] Yeltsin, in response, sought to ignore the elected parliament as much as possible and attempted to find a way to adopt a new constitution that bypasses the congress's jealously guarded exclusive right to make constitutional changes. The contest over basic policy thus moved away from the parliamentary arena itself and turned into a crisis over the basic rules of the political system, which ended in a violent confrontation following Yeltsin's dissolution of parliament. Similar power struggles between president and parliament have appeared in Moldova, Georgia, Tadjikistan and other newly independent states.

It is scarcely surprising, therefore, that the emerging political

---

7. The rules required a two thirds majority of *all* current deputies for a motion to remove the president from office (an action termed impeachment). 617 deputies voted for removal, which was 72 short of the requirement. Since 109 deputies did not vote, the motion could conceivably have carried.

parties in the new countries of the post-communist world do not always adhere to the rules of democratic competition. Self-reinforcing processes such as outbidding and conflict escalation have the potential to bring down the constitutional order itself. Moreover, the former East European and Soviet region is particularly vulnerable to destabilizing political battles of these kinds because of the legacy of unresolved ethnic-national disputes over minority rights and inter-state borders, and because of the high stakes of the policy issues facing the new governments.

The danger that democratization opens Pandora's Boxes of political issues which cannot be dealt with through parliamentary means has led some analysts both in the former communist world and in the West to advocate various forms of "strong man" or "Chinese" models of reform, where political order is maintained through authoritarian rule while the process of opening the economy to property relations and market competition is pursued steadily and over a long time. In the ethnically diverse and politically mobilized societies of Eastern Europe and former Soviet states, however, this alternative poses the risk that major organized segments of the society, excluded from the political arena, will respond by turning to destabilizing forms of opposition. In modern, plural societies, successful transitions are more likely to occur under conditions of political democratization, incorporation, and accommodation. These may include guarantees for minority representation and self-government, as have been granted, for instance, to political parties representing ethnic minorities in Poland, Hungary, and Romania for which the ordinary threshold requirements for parliamentary representation are lifted. Polities where traditional class, ideological and religious cleavages do not structure party competition are fertile ground for neo-totalitarian political movements. Those political leaders who are committed to preserving democratic institutions must compete for power by appealing *across* those cleavages that encourage polarizing, winner-take-all political contests, and instead build the broadest possible coalitions of support consistent with democratic stability.

References

Banac, Ivo. 1990. "Political Change and National Diversity." *Daedalus* 119: 141–160.

Bremmer, Ian and Ray Taras, eds. 1993. *Nation and Politics in the Soviet Successor States.* Cambridge: Cambridge University Press.

Bruszt, Laszlo and David Stark. 1991. "Remaking the Political Field in Hungary:

From the Politics of Confrontation to the Politics of Competition," *Journal of International Affairs* 45: 201–45.

Brzezinski, Zbigniew. 1989/90. "Post–Communist Nationalism." *Foreign Affairs* 68: 1–25.

Coppedge, Michael. 1993. "Parties and Society in Mexico and Venezuela: Why Competition Matters," *Comparative Politics* 25: 253–274.

Dalton, Russell J., Scott C. Flanagan and Paul Allen Beck. 1984. "Political Forces and Partisan Change," in Russell J. Dalton, Scott C. Flanagan and Paul Allen Beck, eds. *Electoral Change in Advanced Industrial Democracies: Realignment or Dealignment?* Pp. 451–476. Princeton: Princeton University Press.

Deak, Istvan. 1990. "Uncovering Eastern Europe's Dark History," *Orbis* 34: 51–65.

Denber, Rachel, ed. 1992. *The Soviet Nationality Reader: The Disintegration in Context.* Boulder: Westview.

Evans, Geoffrey and Stephen Whitefield. 1993. "Identifying the Bases of Party Competition in Eastern Europe," *British Journal of Political Science* 23:521-548.

Horowitz, Donald L. 1985. *Ethnic Groups in Conflict.* Berkeley: University of California Press.

Kitschelt, Herbert. 1992. "The Formation of Party Systems in East Central Europe," *Politics and Society* 20: 7-50.

Levi, Margaret and Michael Hechter. 1985. "A Rational Choice Approach to the Rise and Decline of Ethnoregional Political Parties," in Edward A. Tiryakian and Ronald Rogowski, eds. *New Nationalisms of the Developed West: Toward Explanation.* Pp. 128–146. Boston: Allen & Unwin.

Lieven, Anatol. 1993. *The Baltic Revolution: Estonia, Latvia, Lithuania and the Path to Independence.* New Haven: Yale University Press.

Linz, Juan. 1985. "From Primordialism to Nationalism," in Edward A. Tiryakian and Ronald Rogowski, eds. *New Nationalisms of the Developed West: Toward Explanation.* Pp. 203–253. Boston: Allen & Unwin.

Minkenberg, Michael. 1992. "The New Right in Germany: The Transformation of Conservatism and the Extreme Right," *European Journal of Political Research* 22: 55–81.

Nahaylo, Bohdan and Victor Swoboda. 1990. *Soviet Disunion.* New York: Free Press.

Olson, Mancur. 1971. *The Logic of Collective Action: Public Goods and the Theory of Groups.* Cambridge: Harvard University Press.

Rodin, Ivan. 1993. "Sud'ba parlamenta i nyneshnego parlamentarizma v Rossii." *Nezavisimaia gazeta* (28 July), p. 1.

Sartori, Giovanni. 1976. *Parties and Party Systems: A Framework for Analysis.* Vol. 1. Cambridge: Cambridge University Press.

Schöpflin, George. 1990. "The Political Traditions of Eastern Europe." *Daedalus.* 119: 55–90.

Suny, Ronald Grigor. 1990. "Transcaucasia: Cultural Cohesion and Ethnic Revival in a Multinational Society," in Lubomyr Hajda and Mark Beissinger, eds. *The Nationalities Factor in Soviet Politics and Society.* Pp. 228–252. Boulder: Westview.

Verdery, Katherine. 1993. "Nationalism and National Sentiment in Post–socialist Romania." *Slavic Review* 52: 179–203.

About the Contributors

Dominique Arel is currently on the faculty of the Department of Political Science at McGill University in Montreal, Canada. He received his Ph.D. at the University of Illinois at Urbana-Champaign. His research centers on nationality politics and language policy in Ukraine, and he is currently working on a project in conjunction with a University of Chicago research group investigating "Nationality Politics: The Dismemberment of the Soviet Union" (with support from the National Science Foundation).

Timothy J. Colton is the Morris and Anna Feldberg Professor of Government and Russian Studies at Harvard University and Director of the Russian Research Center. He attended the University of Toronto where he received a B.A. (1968) and a M.A. (1970). In 1974 he earned his Ph.D. in Government from Harvard University. Professor Colton taught in the Department of Political Science at the University of Toronto until 1989. His publications include: *Commissars, Commanders, and Civilian Authority: The Structure of Soviet Military Politics*, *The Dilemma of Reform in the Soviet Union*, and *After the Soviet Union: From Empire to Nations*. He has recently completed a book entitled *Moscow: The Government and Politics of the Socialist Metropolis* and is now engaged in studies of legislative and electoral reform in the Soviet Union.

Moshe Haspel is a graduate student in political science at Emory University.

Jerry F. Hough is James B. Duke Professor of Political Science and Director of the Center on East-West Trade, Investment, and Communications at Duke University, and Senior Fellow at the Brookings Institution in Washington, D.C. He has recently completed a book on the political transition in Russia, which will be published by the Brookings Institution. Currently, together with Timothy Colton, he is conducting a nation-wide opinion survey of Russian voters.

D. Roderick Kiewiet is Professor of Political Science and Dean of Students at the California Institute of Technology. He has received several academic awards, including the Gladys M. Kammerer Award of the American Political Science Association (shared with

Matthew D. McCubbins) for the best book on U.S. national policy, for their book *The Logic of Delegation: Congressional Parties and the Appropriations Process* (1991). He is also the author of *Macroeconomics and Micropolitics: The Electoral Effects of Economic Issues* (1983) and of numerous articles on the American Congress.

Gerhard Loewenberg is Professor of Political Science at the University of Iowa. He is author of *Parliament in the German Political System* (1967), co-author of *Comparing Legislatures* (1979), co-editor of *Handbook of Legislative Research* (1985) and Managing Editor of the *Legislative Studies Quarterly*. He is currently serving as co-chair of an international project to assist the newly democratic parliaments of Central and Eastern Europe in the development of their organizations and procedures.

David M. Olson is Professor of Political Science at the University of North Carolina at Greensboro. His research interests include comparative parliaments, the democratization process of Central Europe, and representation in federal systems. Recent publications include: *Legislatures in the Policy Process: The Dilemmas of Economic Policy* (1991, edited with Michael Mezey); *Representation and Policy Formation in Federal Systems: Canada and the United States* (1993, edited with C.E.S. Franks); and "Compartmentalized Competition: The Managed Transitional Election System of Poland," *Journal of Politics* (May, 1993).

Thomas F. Remington is Professor of Political Science at Emory University. Among his publications are *Politics and the Soviet System* (1989); *The Truth of Authority: Ideology and Communication in the Soviet Union* (1988); *Building Socialism in Bolshevik Russia: Ideology and Industrial Organization, 1917-1921* (1984); and, with Frederick C. Barghoorn, *Politics in the USSR* (1986). He has published numerous books and articles dealing with Soviet and post-Soviet politics. His most recent research focuses on the new Russian legislative branch.

Steven S. Smith is a professor of political science at the University of Minnesota and a former senior fellow at the Brookings Institution, with which he maintains an affiliation. He received his Ph.D. from the University of Minnesota. He has authored and co-authored *Committees In Congress* (1984, 1990), *Managing Uncertainty in the House of Representatives* (1988), and *Call to Order* (1989). In addition to his work on Russian legislative politics, he is currently writing a book on Senate party leadership, a textbook on Congressional politics, and articles on the role of Congressional party leaders in foreign policy.

Alexander Sobyanin is a physicist by education, having graduated from Moscow State University in 1966 and received the doctorate in physics in 1975. He has published over 100 articles and books on the theory of superconductivity and superfluidity and phase transition theory, and is Senior Research Associate of the Lebedev Physics Institute of the Academy of Sciences. He has been engaged in political analysis since 1989 and has published numerous reports and articles on contemporary Russian political affairs. He is a consultant for the Human Rights Committee of the Russian Supreme Soviet and for several democratically-oriented deputy fractions and was a staff specialist for the Constitutional Assembly meeting in Moscow in June and July 1993.

About the Book

This pathbreaking book provides a cross-national exploration of legislative politics in the democratizing societies of Russia, Ukraine, the former Czechoslovakia, and Hungary. Distinguished specialists in legislative politics and area studies set the post-Soviet legislatures in the perspective of democratic and democratizing legislatures elsewhere in the world. Their contributions provide in-depth views of the new legislators' backgrounds, outlooks, parliamentary behavior, and political relations inside the legislature and in the larger political arena.

Index

Accommodation/compromise, 47, 48, 230. *See also* Consensus
Advocacy, 68, 71, 73(n6)
Afanasyev, Yurii, 184
AFD. *See* Alliance of Free Democrats
Age
of Hungarian politicians, 34–35, 35(fig.)
and political ideology in Yaroslavl, 85
of soviet deputies, 57
and Ukrainian politics, 136
Agrarian Union (Russian faction), 189, 191, 198
Agreement for the Sake of Progress (Russian faction), 210, 214
Agriculture
Russian politicians on reforming, 80, 82(Table 4.7), 87
Ukraine and land ownership, 151, 152
Albania, 5, 16
Aliev, Gaidar, 7
Alliance of Free Democrats (AFD; Hungary), 31, 34, 41, 42, 45, 47, 220
Antall, József, 36
Anti-communism, 151. *See also* Communists
Anti-semitism, 227
Armenia, 226–227
Assimilation, 125–126. *See also* Russification
Authoritarianism
and economic reforms, 88, 230
legacies of, 118, 119
and nationalism, 221
Autonomy, Ukrainian regional, 148–149, 149(table), 152, 153, 154, 157(n32). *See also* Sovereignty
Azerbaijan, 7, 225, 226–227

Balance of power. *See* Powers, constitutional
Balkan countries, 4–5. *See also specific Balkan countries*
Baltic republics
elections in, 3, 23(n2), 129
separatism in, 9
See also specific Baltic states
Belarus, 20, 155, 167
Belgium, 118
Belorussia. *See* Belarus
Bicameralism, Czechoslovakian, 100–101, 101(table)
Bocharov, Mikhail, 184
Bosnia-Herzegovina, 225. *See also* Yugoslavia, former
Brazauskas, Algirdas, 7
Bulgaria, 5
Burbulis, Gennadii, 184
Burke, Edmund, 65

Call to Order (Smith), 11–12
Canada, 112, 118
Casework, deputy, 68, 71
Central/Eastern Europe
elections in, 5, 10–11, 217–220. *See also* Elections
electoral law in, 12–16, 13(table), 24(nn 9, 10)
extremism in, 221–230
political parties in, 104, 105. *See also* Political parties
transition in, 29–30, 48–51, 99
See also specific countries
Central region (Ukraine), 139–140
Centrists
and Russian factions, 189, 191, 200–201, 204, 210, 215
in Ukraine, 140, 154
See also Political positions/ideology

237